KEVIN VAN DER STRAETEN

How to Organise Impactful Events

Lannoo Campus

CONTACT US

General feedback: do you have questions about a specific aspect of this book? Do you have a suggestion or would you like to hire me as a speaker? Please send an e-mail to kevin@eventplanner.net.

Errata: although we have made every effort to ensure that the content of this book is as accurate as possible, it is possible that occasional errors may have been made. Have you noticed something that needs correcting? If so, we would appreciate if you could let us know.

Pirating: have you come across illegal copies of our work on the internet? We would be most grateful if you could send us the URL. Please contact us via info@eventplanner.net and provide us with the link to the material in question.

This book was originally published in Dutch as *eventplanner*, LannooCampus, 2025.

D/2025/45/5 – ISBN 978 94 014 3623 6 – NUR 801, 802

Cover design: Keppie & Keppie
Interior layout design: Peer De Maeyer
Typesetting: Wendy De Haes
Translation: Ian Connerty
Author's portrait: Klaas De Buysser
Cover image: Crew Factory – photographer: Rob Willems (BLINK)

© Kevin Van der Straeten & Lannoo Publishers nv, Tielt, 2025.

LannooCampus Publishers is a subsidiary of Lannoo Publishers, the book and multimedia division of Lannoo Publishers nv.

All rights reserved.
No part of this publication may be reproduced and/or made public, by means of printing, photocopying, microfilm or any other means, without the prior written permission of the publisher.

LannooCampus Publishers
Vaartkom 41 box 01.02
3000 Leuven
Belgium
www.lannoocampus.com

P.O. Box 23202
1100 DS Amsterdam
The Netherlands

Contents

Foreword	11
Why organise your event?	15
Why?	15
Events as part of the marketing mix	20
What is an event?	21
Event objectives	22
Types of objectives	22
Formulating objectives	24
Return On Investment	26
ROI model	26
Measuring	28
Creating value	29
Target group	31
Target sub-groups	33
One or more target groups?	33
Profile	34
Number of guests	35
Micro-events	36
I.	
Team, action plan and project management	39
Organisational team	39
Organising yourself – or getting others to do it?	40
Internal team	43
External suppliers / service providers	44
A mix of internal and external?	48
A new tool: AI	48
Action plan or call sheet	51
How detailed does your action plan need to be?	52

Project management for events	54
The 'classic' project approach	54
The 'agile' project approach – Scrum	56
II.	
Event logistics	61
Process thinking	61
Process chains	62
Capacity calculations	66
III.	
Budget	69
Drawing up a budget	69
Functional cost classification	69
Fixed and variable costs	70
Combination of cost assessment methods	71
Ticket price and strategy	72
Business case	73
Cash flow	74
Creative business models	74
Sponsoring	76
Budget checklist	77
IV.	
Date, duration and time	81
Date	81
Target group	81
Unsuitable periods	82
Which days?	82
Competition	83
Duration	86
Time	87

V.
Concept and programme — 89
Programme elements — 89
Theme — 93
Event concepts and visitor experience — 96
- *The hero's journey* — 98
- *Gamification* — 104
- *Creating concepts* — 106

Hybrid & online events — 107
- *Why organise a hybrid or online event?* — 108
- *Format* — 109
- *Interaction* — 110
- *Business model* — 111

VI.
Briefing — 113
Four elements — 113
Company — 113
Event — 114
Supplier — 114
Budget — 116
Event briefing — 116

VII.
Promote your event — 119
Guest list — 119
Invitations — 121
- *Essential information* — 122
- *No-show* — 123
- *Medium* — 125
- *Dress code* — 126

Checklist for the invitation trajectory — 128
Marketing — 130
- *Marketing plan* — 132
- *Media plan* — 133
- *Content marketing* — 135
- *Growth hacking* — 137
- *Website* — 140
- *E-mail marketing* — 143
- *Marketing automation* — 146
- *Google* — 147
- *Analytics* — 149
- *Social media* — 149
- *Press* — 159

VIII.
Printing and branding — 165
Layout and visual identity — 165
Printer — 167
Type of paper — 169
Format — 169
Printing tickets — 170
Visual images — 171
Checklist for printing and printed matter — 172
- *Invitation trajectory* — 172
- *During the event* — 172
- *After the event* — 172

IX.
Venue (location) — 175
Choosing a venue — 175
Checklist for venues — 176
Original locations — 180
- *Tents* — 182
- *Open air* — 183

Capacity, room layout and set-up — 183
- *Meetings and congresses* — 185
- *Festive occasions* — 186

Events abroad — 188
Accessibility — 190

X.
Catering — 193
Which party caterer? — 193
Culinary choices — 198
- *Vegetarian food, allergies and intolerances* — 201

Numbers and averages — 202
- *Drink* — 202
- *Appetisers and hors d'oeuvres* — 204
- *Service* — 204
- *Number of guests* — 205

Healthy and sustainable catering 205

XI.
Transport 209
Own transport 209
  Route description 209
  Parking 210
  Cyclists 213
  Shuttle service 214
Organised transport 215
  Bus 216
  Train 217
  Boat 217
  Taxi 217
  Limousines 218
  Aeroplane or helicopter 218
  Other methods 219

XII.
Entertainment and speakers 221
Function 222
Checklist entertainment 227
Speakers and moderators 230
  Great speakers – and how
  to find them 232
  Types of presentation 233
  Presentation tips 234
  Day chairman/presenter 238

XIII.
Decoration 243
Location as decor 244
Decorative elements 244
  Floral decoration and the use of
  greenery 245
  Themed decoration 250
  Furnishings 250
  Lighting 252

XIV.
Event technology 255
Audio 257
  Sound systems 257
  Microphones 258
  Translation facilities 259
Visual equipment 262
  Projector/beamer 262
  Projection screen 264
  Smart boards 264
  Plasma and LCD screens 265
  Video walls 265
  LED screens 265
Light 266
Podia 267
Special effects 269
  Laser show 270
  Video show 270
  Fireworks 271
  Recent developments 271
(Live) photograph and
video captation 272
  Drones 274
Internet 275
  Capacity? 276
Interactive voice systems 280
Event apps 280
Video conferencing 282

XV.
Security, first aid and hostesses 285
Security and surveillance 285
  Personal security 286
  Security meetings for (public)
  events 290
Crisis communication and
disaster management 291
Crowd and traffic management 294
  Traffic flows 297
Fire security 298
First aid and doctors 299
Safety first 299
Weather monitoring 301
Hosts and hostesses 301
  Registration 304

XVI.
Permits and insurance — 307
Permits — 307
- *Event permits* — 308
- *Copyright, royalties and performance rights* — 308
- *Excess noise* — 308
- *Erection of tents, podia, scaffolding and tribunes* — 309
- *Hours of closing* — 309
- *Serving of alcohol* — 309
- *Food* — 310
- *Fireworks* — 310
- *Drones* — 310

Insurance — 310
- *Civil liability* — 311
- *Material damage* — 312
- *Cancellation* — 313
- *Accidents involving physical injury* — 316
- *Money* — 317
- *Transport* — 317

XVII.
Sustainable events — 319
Sustainable suppliers — 320
Waste — 320
Technology and equipment — 322
Transport and travel — 322
Catering — 323

XVIII.
Production — 325
Production office — 327
Keep calm! — 328

XIV.
Cyber security and privacy — 331
Why is privacy so important? — 331
- *Privacy legislation* — 331

What is cyber security? — 333
- *Cyber threats* — 334

XX.
Evaluation and wind-up — 341
Wind-up — 341
Evaluation — 342
- *Preparations* — 346
- *Event* — 346
- *Wind-up* — 347
- *A thank-you mail* — 347

XXI.
Wedding planner — 349
Wedding planner or master of ceremonies? — 349
Marriage proposal — 350
Start with a mood board — 350
Action plan and planning — 351
Invitations and RSVP — 351
- *Wedding procession* — 352

Printing — 352
Dream venue and catering — 353
Getting ready for the most wonderful day of your life — 355
Ceremony — 355
Reception and evening dinner & dance — 357
- *Seating plan* — 358

XXII.
Follow the trends... — 361
eventplanner.net event software — 361
eventplanner.PRO — 362
eventplanner.net-app — 362
eventplanner.tv and podcast — 363
'Get Inspired' events and eventplanner.live — 363

Reference works and further reading — 364

Acknowledgements — 366

Foreword

When I wrote my first Events book almost 15 years ago, I never imagined that it would reach the top of the 'bestseller' list. Originally, the book was intended to inspire those commissioning and arranging events to organise better ones, but it soon became clear that the book was also popular in the educational world and even with seasoned professionals. In the years following the book's publication, the event industry evolved dramatically and has now grown into a fully-fledged professional field in its own right. I am also proud that with eventplanner.net we have been able to make a contribution to this professionalisation through our books, TV shows, podcasts, websites and event software.

This book, *eventplanner*, that you now have in your hands is the fourth and fully revised version of that original edition. Of course, all the practical aspects of event organisation have been thoroughly updated. At the same time, I will show you how your marketing can achieve even more spectacular results, how you can better ensure the safety of your event, and how you can deal effectively with cyber security and privacy. In addition, I will also tell you everything you need to know about organising a wedding – and all this in addition to the broader knowledge contained in the most widely sold book ever written for event organisers. In short, *eventplanner* is a complete toolbox to turn your event, whatever it might be, into a huge success.

People have been organising events for thousands of years. Think, for example, of the gladiator contests of Ancient Rome, the Olympic Games of Ancient Greece or the sumptuous royal banquets of the Middle Ages. However, it is only during the last decade that event marketing has acquired what might be called 'top sport' status. As an event planner, you are no longer the person who simply arranges the necessary logistics, such as finding and hiring a band, a venue, the catering, and so on. Instead, you are now like a film director, who immerses your guests in a wonderful experience, creating emotions and added value for those attending the event and for the person(s) who commissioned it.

At some time or other, everyone organises an event, whether professionally or privately: an adventurous teambuilding, an inspirational congress, the annual staff dinner, a customer event, a festival, a wedding reception, or even just your child's birthday party. With this book, I will guide you on your way with dozens of practical tips and useful checklists. I will help you to become the hero of your event.

Although the book has strong theoretical and scientific foundations, I have deliberately chosen to write it in an accessible style and with a pragmatic focus, avoiding too much jargon and boring theory. Whoever reads between the lines will discover the necessary depth for themselves.

The book was developed with the cooperation of dozens of professionals from the event industry and educators in event management.

Throughout the book I regularly give links to our website, where you can find additional information and videos. You can use these sources when you want to zoom in more closely on a particular aspect of event organisation.

Do you have any questions after reading *eventplanner*? Or would you like extra tips and examples for the practical sections? Please feel free to mail me via kevin@eventplanner.net.

Kevin Van der Straeten
Founder eventplanner.net

Follow me:
linkedin.com/in/kevinvds
instagram.com/kevinvds
instagram.com/eventplanner_net

Why organise your event?

It is tempting to immediately start with the practical planning of your event. This is only logical; after all, it is the most fun part of the work. Even so, it is smarter to first do all your homework thoroughly. With events, you never get a second chance to put things right. So you need to get everything that matters right first time. You can be sure that Murphy's Law will always be waiting for its chance to strike. This is the unwritten law that states "if something can go wrong, it will go wrong". You can only avoid this by ensuring that your event is properly prepared, right down to the very last detail. If you fail to do this, you run the risk that your event will not give the desired results or will cost you more time and money than was really necessary.

WHY?

The first question you need to ask yourself is 'why' you are organising an event. You might think that you know this. But you may be wrong. What do you really want to achieve with your event? An event is never an end in itself. It is always a means to an end, to something else. In a business context, for example, you probably want to influence your guests, to persuade them to change their behaviour in some way. Your aim might be to give them a positive feeling about your brand, or to make them buy more of your products, or to make them loyal in the long term to those products. And even beneath this motivation lies a deeper 'why'. Consider the case of Apple. It is stating the obvious to say that they want to sell more iPhones. But why do they want to do that? In one of the most widely viewed TED talks, Simon Sinek offers the following explanation for the Apple 'why': *"In everything we do, we believe in challenging the status quo. We believe in thinking differently. The way we challenge the status quo is by making our products beautifully designed, simple to use and user friendly. We just happen to make great computers."* And it is because we all believe in this 'why' that the company is so successful.

www.eventplanner.net/book/why

At eventplanner.net we want to *inspire you to push your boundaries and help you to organise better events with more impact, so that you can continue to grow.* That is our 'why'. We seek to achieve this by sharing knowledge, creating a strong platform and developing state-of-the-art event software for our users. Of course, we also have commercial ambitions, but this is not what gets us out of bed each morning with the same great passion and enthusiasm for what we do. It is only your 'why' that can do this – and it is something that your target group notices.

What's more, it is not just companies that have intrinsic motivation of this kind. As an individual, you also have a personal 'why'. Even when you are organising something like a wedding reception, you still have a story to tell. For example, you might want your family and friends to witness your marriage vows or to share in this important moment in your life. If you have the real 'why' clear in the back of your mind, you will organise a very different event than if you rush straight away into the organisational side of things without thinking things through. Does this all sound a bit far-fetched? Perhaps the following example will convince you.

Events that have a clear 'why' are better and more successful. Do you think that the organisers of Tomorrowland are better than other festival organisers? Not in my opinion. True, they are brilliant at what they do, but in strict organisational terms they are no better than many others. So, what makes the difference? Why is their festival such a massive worldwide hit? The answer is simple: the organisers had a dream to create a festival that would allow people to briefly escape from their daily lives. They wanted to take their guests to a totally different and colourful world, a place where they could forget about all their worries and become part of a single large family of festivalgoers. That is the Tomorrowland 'why' and that is what makes their event so different. Not the DJs. Not the remarkable stages. It is the total package, which perfectly translates the organisers' vision into a concept, so that we now talk automatically about 'People of Tomorrow'. These people are a close-knit community, a tribe of followers and ambassadors that make the event into something much greater than the organisers could ever have dreamed of. The festival is worth talking about because its 'why' is authentic and we all believe in it 100 percent. Or as Simon Sinek has put it: "People don't buy 'what' you do; they buy 'why' you do it."

> **Events that have a clear 'why' are better and more successful.**

Do you find it difficult to identify your 'why' or the 'why' of your company or the person requesting the organisation of an event? If so, read the book

Start with Why by Simon Sinek. It is highly recommended! Would you prefer a shorter summary? Watch my interview on this subject on eventplanner.tv:

▶ www.eventplanner.net/book/tv-why

Perhaps you think that this all makes sense for a festival, but you are only organising a congress, a business event or even a small private party. Surely it doesn't apply in these cases? Yes, it does. The principle is always the same. A strong story ensures that people will want to be part of your event. Just look at the example of TEDx, which also started off as something small, but quickly grew into a phenomenal international concept because of its passion to "share strong ideas with the world".

All too often organisers attempt to copy the 'why' of others, instead of finding a 'why' of their own. They seem to think that imitating a tried and tested concept is a sure-fire way to earn money quickly. Of course, they all fail, time after time. If your 'why' is not authentically yours, you will soon lose all credibility with your target public and the concept will no longer work its magic.

In other words, your 'why' is the basis for telling your story. Storytelling might be widely promoted as the new hip marketing trend, but people have been telling stories as a way of communicating a particular message for centuries. It is a language that allows you to create an experience that makes it possible for your guests to become involved in your event at different levels. And, as an organiser, that is exactly what you need. People stand in queues all night long for the launch of a new iPhone, not because they need a new phone, but because they believe in the story that Apple tells. And it is the same with Starbucks. You can drink a delicious cup of coffee almost everywhere, but Starbucks offers something more: its stores are meeting places that create an experience around coffee, a place where you like to go with your friends. Even the simple writing of your name on their cups has become a kind of 'cult' happening. You need to find a way to tell the story of your event in a similar manner.

Organisers are sellers of emotion.

This will make all the difference between a perfectly orchestrated, but essentially soulless succession of event elements, and an event experience that touches people emotionally, so that they will still talk about it long after it is over.

Jan Vereecke, the organiser of the successful 'Night of the Proms' concerts thinks that organisers must be 'sellers of emotion'. And he is right. Of course, the success of NOTP is based in part on its original mix of classical and pop music, but the event would never have lasted for as many years as it has without the energy and enthusiasm of the orchestra and its conductor. "People come to the Night of the Proms and other concerts to recharge their emotional batteries with positive energy. There needs to be laughter, but there can also be a tear or two. Above all, it has to be a celebration."

Remember, however, that to tell a good story you need more than just a 'why'. You need to have people in your story and you need to have a link with your target audience. The listener, your guest, must be able to recognise himself (or herself) in your story and feel in some way involved in it. I interviewed journalist Tim Verheyden on precisely this subject. He expressed the principle perfectly: "Imagine that you are making a report about a sad subject, like hunger in Africa. You could make a straightforward report about a youngster begging on the street to get enough money for food. But those are circumstances that people in Europe or the USA are not familiar with and cannot relate to. But if I make a story about a youngster begging on the street that also involves a dilemma – for example, 'Should I use the little money I have collected to buy food for myself or for my dying mother?' – this becomes the kind of story that is better known to me and my public, because it is about the hard choices that you sometimes have to make in life." If you want your event to excite people's emotions, you need to make sure that your story touches and moves your target group.

EVENTS AS PART OF THE MARKETING MIX

It is remarkable that events are still sometimes seen as 'stand alone' activities. In reality, an event is just one of the communication tools that marketeers can use to reach their target group. As a company, you use event marketing as an integrated part of your marketing mix. It contributes towards your wider marketing objectives and is the common thread in all the communication that you generate online, offline and live.

Red Bull is a good example of this. The company does not organise events involving extreme sports as an end in itself. For them, these events are contact moments with their target audience that allows them to project their message and, ultimately, sell more energy drinks. And if you read between the lines, you can see that Red Bull has a very clear 'why': "Red Bull gives you wings and wants people to push their boundaries as far as they will go." Their story is perfectly translated into an event concept that has an authentic ring. Many companies would not take the risk of linking their image to extreme and dangerous sports, but in Red Bull's case it perfectly matches their company culture. It says something about who they are. It was this that allowed them, when still a relatively small company, to compete with the soft drink giants like Coca-Cola and Pepsi.

Events are therefore touchpoints or moments of contact in a wider customer journey that give added emotional value to a brand. Together with TV advertising, samplings and other marketing activities, they strengthen your image and build on relationships.

WHAT IS AN EVENT?

I am not a fan of too much boring theory. I like to keep things pragmatic and directly applicable. Even so, a few definitions are necessary to make sure that we are all on the same wavelength.

> **WHAT IS AN EVENT?**
> "An event is an organised activity or live experience with a start and a finish, which is focused on a specific target group to achieve a previously determined objective by changing the perception or the behaviour of the participants."

There are many different kinds of events, such as meetings, congresses, (staff) parties, workshops, open days, product launches, sporting events, team-buildings, trainings, wedding receptions, online events – to name but a few!

Events are the best communication tool for making a unique and personal approach to your target group, in which the 'experience' of your product or brand is central. This gives events a much greater impact on the target group and therefore yields the company significant economic value.

It is important to note that the use of the word 'live' in the above definition does not necessarily imply a physical venue. An event can also take place online or in a hybrid form. You will read more about this later. For now, however, we need to further define what is meant by 'live communication', since this term is being used increasingly in the business world and is often confused with events or event marketing.

> **WHAT IS 'LIVE COMMUNICATION'?**
> "Live communication is every form of marketing through which brands come into direct contact with their target group."

This means that 'live communication' involves channels like social media, brand activations, etc. – but also events. In other words, an event is a form of 'live communication'.

EVENT OBJECTIVES

Objectives are not the same as the 'why' of your event. Your 'why' says something about your deeper motivation or mission. Your objectives are the concrete expression of this mission. If – like eventplanner.net – your mission is to inspire people, the concrete objective of your event might be to attract at least 400 participants, who you will expose to the arguments of three inspirational speakers, in the hope that people will go home with at least one concrete idea that will change their lives. Or, less dramatically, that will be immediately applicable in their jobs.

Whether you are organising a staff party, an international congress or a pop festival, the formulation of clear and (above all) measurable objectives is a wise investment of your valuable time. These objectives form the foundations on which each further stage of your event will be built. They set out the general guidelines for the event and together with your 'why' serve as a source of inspiration for decisions relating to the atmosphere, originality and concrete programme of your planned activity. Clear ideas and practical objectives will help you to convince the managers who need to approve your budgets and in a later stage will also provide a useful basis for briefing suppliers and/or colleagues, so that everyone is pulling in the same direction.

Types of objectives

There are hundreds of possible reasons for organising an event: an anniversary, the opening of a new building, the launching of a new product, the presentation of your annual accounts. Alternatively, you may wish to focus on some less welcome news, such as falling sales figures. But a reason is not an objective! If you want to raise your event to a higher level, you will first need to decide in your own mind exactly what you hope to achieve.

With a business event, it is possible for you to have both internal and external objectives. Reporting bad news can also be an objective. Below you can find a number of examples of the most common objectives:

- **Stimulating sales** (directly or indirectly) is one of the most important objectives for companies.
- **Motivating** a team to reach ambitious targets (teambuilding, etc.). Perhaps you also wish to adjust **general attitudes or the company culture**.
- Introducing a **new product or service** to the market or the press.
- **Thanking** your staff for their years of loyal service (anniversary) or **rewarding** them for exceptional performance.
- **Sharing information** or **imparting knowledge** about a particular subject or field of expertise (congresses, seminars, etc.). In this case, education or training is the objective.
- **Communicating the vision and strategy** of your company or organisation to staff, customers and stakeholders.
- **Building up or strengthening** internal and/or external relations (staff activities, customer open day or partner days). Promoting loyalty and creating goodwill can also be objectives.
- **Improving the image** of your product (charity events, etc.) or the **brand awareness** of your company.

- ✓ **Making unpopular decisions more acceptable**; for example, restructurings. Sometimes an event can also help to improve morale and motivation after a challenging period.
- ✓ **Raising money for a good cause**. This is especially relevant for non-profit organisations.
- ✓ **Celebrating success or showing appreciation**; for example, to recognise important milestones, successes and performances in a company or organisation.
- ✓ ...

You will soon notice that your events are often related to a combination of different objectives. If this is the case, try to choose a single main objective and adjust your approach to the remaining sub-objectives to reflect your most important priority.

Remember not to lose sight of the interests and concerns of the people you invite. What's in it for them? Why should they make time and take the trouble to come to your event? Do they see it as a good opportunity to network or are they just looking for a bit of mindless fun? Take account of these considerations when you are formulating your own event objectives. Remember also, however, that your objective must go further than 'giving all our guests a pleasant evening'!

Formulating objectives

'I want everyone to know that we are launching a new product' is an understandable wish – but it is not a good objective. So, what would be a good objective in these circumstances? Perhaps something like: 'I want a 5% increase in turnover within three months after the event', 'the Net Promoter Score (loyalty) needs to be up by 2% by the end of the month' or maybe even 'I want ten prospects from the guest list to be new customers by the start of next year'. These last examples take account of the five (SMART) building blocks for the setting of a good objective:

- ✓ **Specific**
  Describe what you want to happen in concrete terms. What do you want people to remember about your event? What do you want them to do with this memory? What experience do you want to give them? What practical benefits do you expect this to bring? The more concretely you are able to describe your objectives, the more easily you will be able to plan and act accordingly.

✓ **Measurable**
Make sure that it is possible to measure afterwards whether or not you have achieved the desired results. This allows you to make a proper assessment of your event. Use figures and define them in the correct manner.

✓ **Acceptable**
Are your objectives in keeping with the company culture? Will the management be willing to approve your plans? What is the importance of the event to your business interests? Can you support your arguments with facts and figures? Can you make others enthusiastic for your project? Are you enthusiastic about the project? Whatever you put forward, it must match the commercial objectives, corporate values, desired image and marketing mix of the company.

✓ **Realistic**
Is the objective realistic? Are you sure that you have not overestimated the figures and the percentages? Or are you perhaps not being ambitious enough? Remember to consider the perspective of others; do not look at everything exclusively from your own point of view.

✓ **Time-related**
Make sure that you set deadlines – and that you can keep them. Otherwise, it will be impossible to carry out further monitoring and evaluation. As the old business adage puts it: "If you don't set a deadline, it ain't going to happen." It is possible to measure some of your objectives while the event is still taking place; others will only be capable of assessment months later. So remember to state clearly in your planning not only 'what' you are going to measure, but also 'when' and 'how'.

Well-formulated objectives will help to ensure that you can accurately calculate your ROI (Return On Investment) during the evaluation process. This calculation assesses the benefits of your event in relation to its cost.

KEEP YOUR OBJECTIVES CLEARLY IN FOCUS

The organisation of an event may take place over a period of weeks, months or even years, and may therefore undergo several evolutions during this period. For example, budgets may be reduced as a result of falling sales figures. Moreover, you will often be confronted with pressures of time, so that the full implementation of your plans may become difficult. In short, you are dependent on your partners. In the face of such changing circumstances, it is important to keep your original objectives clearly in focus. This will help you to make the right decisions quickly and efficiently when you are compelled to make adjustments. But do not take this to extreme limits. You must not be blind to changing market circumstances which make your objectives unrealistic. In exceptional cases, you may need to change these objectives in the course of the project's development, but you should only do this if it is absolutely necessary and only after close consultation with all the parties involved.

> Good objectives are **SMART** objectives
> **Specific**
> **Measurable**
> **Acceptable**
> **Realistic**
> **Time-related**

RETURN ON INVESTMENT

If you are organising an event for a company, that company will want to know if their investment in the event is cost-effective. ROI (Return on Investment) is the profit, benefit or return resulting from your event, expressed as a percentage of its total cost. This can be expressed as a mathematical formula:

$$ROI = \frac{(\text{created value} - \text{costs incurred})}{(\text{costs incurred} / 100)}$$

For a commercial company created value can easily be expressed in terms of financial gain. This is less easy for an organisation or association. Even so, it is still possible to calculate the ROI for sponsors or the impact of your event on others. For example, the introduction at a medical congress of a new and cheaper form of treatment for cancer patients will have a positive impact on the expenditure of health care organisations.

ROI model

The ROI methodology, which was first developed from a research model devised by Donald Kirkpatrick and Jack Phillips, has been further refined over the years and in the version now used for events contains a number of different levels that together provide a return.

The highest level (**ROI**, level 5) has already been described above. The next level (**impact**, level 4) indicates your success or otherwise in terms of actual value creation. If the purpose of your event was to increase sales, this impact will be equivalent to the real conversion in terms of sales; in other words, an increase in turnover.

Level 3 deals with objectives relating to **desired behaviour**; the behaviour you want to encourage in order to achieve your desired level of impact. This behaviour might be a simple request for information, such as downloading a brochure, or the greater use of recyclable material for an SRE (socially responsible enterprise) congress. Or perhaps you want your event participants NOT to do something; for example, not to spend money unless absolutely necessary within the framework of a cost-cutting exercise. You have read in an earlier chapter how you can formulate these objectives in a SMART manner.

*You only create value if you are able to **change the patterns of behaviour** amongst the participants.*

Level 2 covers the **learnings** (or educational requirements): what do you need to give your participants to bring about the change in their behaviour that you want to achieve? This might simply mean passing on information or knowledge, but it could also be the teaching of particular skills.

Level 1 is all about **satisfaction**. What is necessary to make your participants feel comfortable or happy? How can you create the right environment to ensure that your learnings have the best possible effect? These elements can range from the self-evident – room, decoration, catering, etc. – to the less immediately obvious – temperature, thematic development of your programme, etc.

Level 0 is where we find your **target group**. This is the lowest level, but does not mean that it is the least important. Far from it! Later in this chapter, I will look more closely at the best way to determine your target group. For now, all you need to remember is that in order to increase the ROI of your event it is crucial to only invite people who are relevant for the higher levels of the pyramid. This might sound obvious, but you would be surprised how often this simple rule is overlooked. Sometimes we invite people simply because we know them and so we think that they ought to be there, even if we are aware in advance that their contribution to the ROI will be negligible.

Before you start using this model, it is therefore very important to evaluate and categorise your different stakeholders (participants, speakers, sponsors, etc.). For each of these target groups you can then formulate objectives for each level of the ROI pyramid, working from the top downwards (levels 5, 4, 3, 2, 1, 0), so that after your event you can measure results on the basis of the formulated objectives, working from the bottom upwards.

Measuring

In order to be able to measure meaningfully, it is important to try and isolate (as far as possible) the effects that you wish to achieve from other environmental influences. For example, make sure that you do not plan your event to coincide with a major advertising campaign. Why? Because this will make it difficult to assess which channel has helped to convince your customers. Of course, in many circumstance your advertisements and your event will complement each other. And in some cases, it may be deliberate strategy to plan them at the same time. This is fine, but it is then probably better to measure the combined ROI of both elements.

Working with a control group is another possibility. This might mean that you deliberately fail to invite part of your target group, so that after the event you can compare the (purchasing) behaviour of the absentees with the behaviour of those who were present.

Creating value

You have formulated an objective and are able to measure it. Great! Unfortunately, however, this does not yet mean that you have actually created value with your event. You only create value if you are able to change the patterns of behaviour amongst the participants. Consequently, you need to ask yourself what changes you want to see – and in whom.

To define the creation of value, I can do no better than to borrow the wise words of Rob Captijn, one of the leading advocates of ROI for events, who unfortunately isn't any longer amongst us. He refers to the story of the supermarkets, which on the basis of various studies and scientific research projects, have learnt how to influence the buying behaviour of their consumers, so that they often end up at the check-out with far more purchases in their shopping trolley than they had originally intended. And what the supermarkets do with the strategic placing of products and special offers, you can also do with your event, by making the best possible use of light, music, decoration, catering, etc. It is not enough simply to book a few entertaining acts on the basis of your own gut feeling – and then trust to luck that this will have the desired effect on your participants. Instead, you have to persuade them through a well-considered strategy, based on a combination of elements, to actually change their behaviour. You want to turn their 'no' into a 'yes'.

Three elements in particular will determine whether or not you are able to bring about this change.

- ✔ **Sense of urgency**. Your target group needs to recognise the urgency of the need for change. Otherwise, there will be no stimulus to persuade them to request more information or make a purchase after the event has taken place.

- **Relevant arguments**. If you have identified your target group correctly and have a good idea of what they think about your objective, it should be possible to develop convincing arguments that will help you to bridge the gap between 'no' and 'yes'. This is the reason why 'storytelling' must be an indispensable part of any (commercial) event. By the careful stage-managing and programming of your events (carefully chosen speakers, acts, content, etc.), you can have a real influence on your participants' patterns of behaviour.

   An event is the only marketing channel that can play on all the senses of your target group at the same time. If you make efficient use of this opportunity, you can communicate with power and conviction. It is not without good reason that 'experiencing' is nowadays central to the organisation of any event.

- **Activation**. All the positive work that you have done during your event will come to nothing unless you have an effective way to activate your target group once the event is over. This means that you need to find a way that makes it easy for them to say 'yes'. You can do this, for example, by requesting the placement of an order online or, alternatively, you can ask for feedback at the end of the event. These are the kinds of action, if properly implemented, which will also make your ROI measurable.

The creation of value does not take place exclusively during the event itself. You need to adopt the same consistent line of approach during both the invitation and follow-up phases. For example, using the right media, design and content for your event website can be vital for setting the right tone. Similarly, during registration on the day of the event you can ask for the additional information you will need later to further refine and focus your story. And afterwards you can spread photos via social media to try and convince the last few remaining doubters.

Focus your efforts on those elements within the target group who you think can most easily be influenced to change. In other words, the ones for whom you need to make the least effort to obtain a positive result. This will produce maximum effect at minimum cost, and with fewest disappointments. It also leaves room in your budget to do a little bit extra for those who are really hard nuts to crack!

Would you like to listen to the ROI story of Rob Captijn? If so, why not take a quick look at the following eventplanner.tv video:

 www.eventplanner.net/book/tv-roi

One of the other good things about ROI is that when you start to think about it you usually organise better events as a result. If you have a clear picture in your mind about the change of behaviour that you want to achieve in your target group, this makes it easier to build up your entire event around that objective. If you know, for example, why your prospects currently do business with one of your competitors and can identify what experience might persuade them to change their minds, you can work in a much more focused way. At the same time, you also know exactly what you need to ask in order to evaluate the event afterwards. All too often, event organisers ask questions like 'How satisfied were you with the catering', whereas it is much more useful to know if a customer is planning to switch from your competitor to one of your products. I interviewed Elling Hamso on precisely this subject:

▶ www.eventplanner.net/book/tv-roi2

TARGET GROUP

You now know what you want to achieve. But do you know **who** you want to achieve it for? Which target group are you trying to reach? Make sure that you find out as much as possible about this target group before you actually begin the planning of the event. Conduct a thorough analysis and try to get a feel for the environment in which this group lives and works. For example, try to establish what the group expects to get out of the event. What are their attitudes towards the event's main theme or subject? What will they consider to be 'appropriate' and – more importantly – what not? Moreover, this mental exercise may help you later on by allowing you to better assess the likely number of guests.

On the basis of your target group, you can classify business events into one of three main categories (or any combination of them):

- ✔ **Business-to-Business** (B2B): when the event is aimed at customers, suppliers and other business relations.
- ✔ **Business-to-Consumer** (B2C): when the target group consists of consumers (private individuals).
- ✔ **Business-to-Personnel** (B2P): when you organise an internal event specifically for the personnel of the company.

Do not forget the other stakeholders. Actors such as the government (local or national), neighbouring local people, the media, action groups or even busi-

ness competitors may not immediately form part of your main target group, but they can all exert considerable influence on the company which has engaged your services. Depending on the type of event you are organising, it is sometimes a nice gesture to invite one or more of these groups to attend.

Target sub-groups

The more detailed your description of the target group can be, the better. If your first definition of the target group is too general, try splitting up the group into smaller sub-groups. Decide which sub-groups you really need to invite and which ones can stay at home.

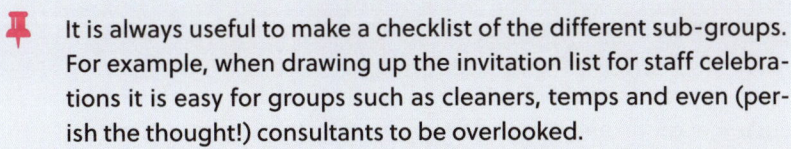
*Do you really want to invite **every-one** who has ever bought one of your products?*

Imagine, for example, that you want to organise an event for your customers. Do you really want to invite everyone who has ever bought one of your products? Of course you don't! It is therefore useful to divide your (too) broad target group into sub-groups such as loyal customers, new customers, customers who bought something from you during the previous year, customer prospects, influencers, etc. Remember to define the sub-groups with equal care. What is a 'loyal customer'? Someone who buys your products weekly? Or monthly? Or annually? And for what amount or volume? This will help you in your search of the customer records and will ensure that everyone involved in the project knows from the start exactly who you are talking about.

> 📌 It is always useful to make a checklist of the different sub-groups. For example, when drawing up the invitation list for staff celebrations it is easy for groups such as cleaners, temps and even (perish the thought!) consultants to be overlooked.

> 📌 Ask yourself whether it is wise to invite some groups – staff and shareholders, customers and prospects, etc. – to the same event. Sub-groups often have different objectives and expectations, which may make them feel uncomfortable in each other's presence.

One or more target groups?

A homogeneous group certainly simplifies the organisation, but this does not mean that the organisation of a single event for different sub-groups should not or cannot be undertaken. Be careful, however, to weigh up the pros and cons. Inviting the partners and children of participants may help to create the right atmosphere for your event, but they may have other – and conflicting – expectations.

Your target group will often be defined by a number of different profiles, which must all be taken into account when putting together the practical aspects of your event programme. A delegation of executives may have different tastes and preferences to a delegation of union representatives – but they may both be attending the same activity.

Once you have finished identifying the different elements within your target group, it is useful to establish the different inter-relationships between them. Do they all get on with each other? Is it useful to allow a number of networking moments, so that the guests can get to know each other (better)?

Profile

On the basis of a number of different parameters, you can learn a lot about your target group. However, this requires you to draw up a number of clear profiles. Who are the people in your target group? What things appeal to them? What are they expecting from your event? What is their attitude towards the main theme of this event? Where can you find your target group? How can you persuade them of the value of your event? More importantly, how can you persuade them to come? The characteristics used to compile your profiles can be based on socio-demographic characteristics (such as ages, level of education, etc.) or communicative characteristics (such as interests, behaviour, use of media, etc.). But be careful when using profiles. Avoid the temptation to put people into neat little boxes – this never works. You can avoid this professional pitfall by drawing up a number of different profiles for your target group and then searching for the common denominators.

SOCIO-DEMOGRAPHIC CHARACTERISTICS:
- Ages (categories)
- Gender
- Nationality
- Culture
- Religion
- Family situation (+ age of the children)
- Social class
- Place of residence (region)
- Profession

- ✓ Function level
- ✓ Education/training level
- ✓ ...

COMMUNICATIVE CHARACTERISTICS:
- ✓ Interests and/or hobbies
- ✓ Media use (how can you reach your target group?)
- ✓ Linguistic ability (language, formulation, jargon, style, etc.)
- ✓ Behaviour (purchase behaviour, frequency of purchase, etc.)
- ✓ ...

> 📌 Never underestimate the influence of cultural traditions and usages. If you are organising an event for an international public, this must be one of your key points for attention. Consider the following good example – or rather, bad example! A major Belgian company wanted to invite its most important international customers to a prestige event. During their stay, the guests from more than fifteen different countries attended a concert at the Night of the Proms in Antwerp. Although the concert was brilliant, the Japanese guests left long before the end. In their culture, it is simply not done to mix classic music and pop in this 'flippant' manner!

In other words, always remember to consider the possible effect of cultural differences. You don't want to offend your target public, however unintentionally! So make sure you watch this eventplanner.tv broadcast:

▶ www.eventplanner.net/book/tv-culture

Number of guests

Now that you have a clear picture of your target group, you can make a first estimate of the number of guests who are likely to attend. This estimate is vitally important, since it will determine both the size of your budget and your choice of venue.

In order to make an estimate that is as realistic as possible, you should follow this simple three-step plan:

1. Calculate the total potential number of the target group you have defined.
2. Make an estimate of the number of positive responses you can reasonably expect from this group. Perhaps you can use figures from similar events in the past to help you with this assessment.
3. Reduce the number of likely positive responses with a 'no-show' percentage (guests who say they will come, but then fail to turn up). For obvious reasons, the no-show percentage for internal or paying events is likely to be lower than for other events. Use an average of 10% for internal events, but remember that the figure for external events can be much higher: in extreme cases, as much as 40-50%. At the other end of the scale, some events are so attractive – for example, a U2 concert or the final of the World Cup – that everyone turns up, or there are even more people than you had expected.

 When you are organising an (external) event for the first time, it is particularly difficult to estimate the number of likely guests with any degree of accuracy. Because this estimate can have a huge impact on your budget, you will need to give this matter your very closest attention. Conduct reliable market research and check the target group figures for other comparable events that have already taken place. These can be useful benchmarks.

Micro-events

Do not become over-focused on the idea that events always need to attract large numbers of participants. There are good reasons why micro-events are becoming increasingly popular. These small-scale gatherings, often targeted at a niche public, prefer to concentrate on the quality rather than the quantity of the interactions, so that more attention can be given to developing deeper relationships. Micro-events usually involve between 10 and 50 participants, which helps to create a more intimate atmosphere. These events can take various forms, such as workshops, trainings, product launches and teambuilding activities. Moreover, mini-events often have less impact on the environment, offer more flexible organisational possibilities and give organisers greater freedom to experiment with unique locations and alternative types of interaction.

Team, action plan and *project management*

Now that your objectives are clear and you have a well-defined target group in mind, you can confidently move on to the next step: the putting together of your team and the drawing up of a detailed action plan. The organisational team is responsible for the event from A to Z. For this reason, a carefully compiled and balanced team is essential.

The various tasks and responsibilities of the team members are further developed in the action plan. This plan will inevitably need to be amended as the preparations progress. Organising an event is a complex process involving many different people. As an organiser, you need to possess the necessary project management skills to ensure that everything runs smoothly.

ORGANISATIONAL TEAM

You can organise certain events on your own, but you will soon realise just how much work this involves. You will find things much easier if you have an organisation team. Working in a team has the advantage that you can count on the creative and conceptual input of other minds, particularly if your team members already have experience in the field. It also means that you have back-up if for any reason you are unable to do something yourself (for example, if you are sick).

 Make sure that you have clear task descriptions for all your team. In this way, everyone will know what is expected of him or her and there is no uncertainty about people's different responsibilities.

Organising yourself – or getting others to do it?

You can either opt to organise an event yourself with the help of your colleagues or you can decide to call in an external events agency to do it for you (known as 'outsourcing'). Both choices have advantages and disadvantages.

ADVANTAGES OF OUTSOURCING

- Events agencies have **wide experience** and are aware of all the most recent trends in the sector. An event might either be so large or so delicate that it outstrips your own ability to organise it. Outsourcing means that you no longer have to bear the responsibility for many of the risks involved. Moreover, it is quite possible that your company simply does not possess the necessary in-house knowledge and creativity to create an event of the required quality and standing.
- Events agencies have an **objective view** of your company and are therefore better able to exploit your strong points and minimise your weak ones. Your own staff are more likely to suffer from selective blindness as far as the latter are concerned! In addition, an agency is an ideal sparring partner and sounding board for the exchange and development of new ideas.
- Events agencies have an **extensive network** in the events sector. They know how to find the right people and the right materials, often at **much better prices**. If you try and do the things for yourself, it is often difficult to see the wood for the trees: there is often a huge difference in price and quality between the different suppliers.
- If you rely on your own staff to organise an event, they are usually required to do this in addition to their normal responsibilities. You must therefore take account of the fact that they will have less time to perform their normal daily duties. Outsourcing means that your **internal resources remain available** for your current projects and core tasks. Working with a (large) events agency also means that there is continuity throughout the preparations phase (for example, in the event of sickness).

 By engaging the services of a professional events agency in good time, you can avoid many costly organisational blunders.

DISADVANTAGES OF OUTSOURCING

- The event agency does **not (yet) know your company**. This means that they do not initially know what is possible and what is not. To begin with, they do not even know your wishes or anything about the style/culture of your organisation. A good briefing is therefore essential. The best idea is

- to try and develop a long-term relationship with the same events agency, so that these disadvantages can quickly be eliminated.
- ✔ Notwithstanding the effective approach of most events agencies, you need to take account of the additional **cost** of outsourcing. On the positive side, this at least means that you clearly know in advance the total price for your full event package. With internally organised events, the hidden costs are often far greater than you first imagined.

Weigh up the pros and cons of outsourcing for each individual event that you are planning to organise. Take due account of the available know-how, the required creativity, the timing, the budget and the risks. In general, it is probably wiser to put complex events in the hands of an experienced events partner. In many cases, the best results are achieved through a combination of your own company-specific knowledge with the expertise of a professional agency.

If you do eventually decide to engage the services of an events agency, it is probably best to do so through a 'pitch'. A pitch is a tendering process between different agencies, in which they must provide you with a clear specification and an estimate based on your detailed briefing. This briefing must contain as a minimum clear information about the objective, target group and provisional budget for the event, as well as details of your selection criteria. Normally, the strongest value-for-money concept will be awarded the contract. When you decide to organise a pitch, there are a number of **guidelines** you should follow:

- ✔ **Never allow more than three events agencies to take part.** This is sufficient to make a relevant choice and avoids unnecessary costs, both for you and for the participating agencies. Always let an agency know how many of its competitors have also been invited to take part in the pitch, so that they can decide for themselves whether or not the risk is worthwhile: taking part in a pitch means a considerable investment of time and resources for the agency concerned. The drawing up of a detailed event proposal can take two to three full days. For more complex pitches, it can even take as long as 1 to 2 weeks for an entire team.
- ✔ Make clear arrangements about possible **financial compensation** that you are prepared to pay for the time and effort involved in making a pitch. This is by no means an 'obligation', but it shows that the project initiator is serious, if he is prepared to pay the out-of-pocket expenses incurred by the participating agencies.
- ✔ Unless other prior arrangements have been made or financial compensation has been agreed, there is a gentleman's agreement that the intellectual rights relating to the **creative concepts** put forward in the propos-

als of the unsuccessful events agencies remain at all times the property of those agencies. It not done to reject an agency, but then run off with its ideas.
- ✔ Inform all the participating agencies with a minimum of delay as soon as you have reached your decision and the **result** of the pitch is known.
- ✔ Stick to the time lines set out in your pitch and make sure that the process is honest and fair. Never ask for the submission of tenders simply to compare prices with a previously determined 'favourite'.

 Depending on the size and complexity of your event, it can sometimes be useful to also recruit, in addition to your event bureau, an independent technical producer who can focus exclusively on the technical aspects of the event. A technical producer has the necessary know-how to deal with the ever more rapidly emerging technical evolutions in the event sector and the logistical challenges that these evolutions present. He can also help to compare the various audio-visual tenders and ensure that the input of your AV suppliers is properly coordinated. Many event bureaus already work regularly with a technical producer or have an in-house expert of their own.

www.eventplanner.net/book/eventagencies

WHAT DO YOU PAY FOR THE SERVICES OF AN EVENT BUREAU?

In contrast to other industries, there is no 'fixed' business model that is applicable to all event bureaus. Most bureaus **combine** elements from different models:

- ✔ **Hourly or daily rate** (also known as 'time and material' or 'T&M'). The bureau charges the client for the number of hours they have spent on consultancy, production, direction, supervision, etc. The hourly rate varies depending on the nature of the task and the level of the event manager involved (senior/junior). This can lead to rates varying from 65 to 185 dollars per hour.
- ✔ Some event bureaus work on a **fixed price** basis. To calculate this total price, they make an estimate of the number of hours involved, increased with a risk margin.
- ✔ **Mark-up** (bureau fee) on the various elements of the event. In this model the event bureau adds a percentage fee to the tenders received from the various suppliers. Percentages varying from between 7.5 and 25% are not

uncommon. The percentage is often reduced in accordance with a sliding scale that takes account of the size of the event budget. For example, 20% for events under 250,000 dollars, 17.5% for events up to 500,000 dollars and 15% for events up to 1 million dollars. A distinction is also usually made between labour-intensive elements to which a higher mark-up is applied (for example, 20% for arranging and coordinating the event speakers) and simpler elements to which a lower rate is applied (for example, 8% for arranging the venue and catering). Most of the event bureaus that make use of this model are transparent about such matters in their tender.

- Many event venues and suppliers give bureau discounts. These discounts are usually retained by the bureau as **commission**. This makes no difference to the client, since they would never have received such discounts in the first place.
- Some organisation bureaus charge a fee for their creative **concept or idea**. This is usually a fixed amount, which can vary significantly from bureau to bureau.
- Sometimes a **variable model**, such as a percentage of the ticket price, can be used when the event bureau shares responsibility for the marketing and promotion of the event.
- ...

At the end of the day, the event bureau needs to pay its people, cover its costs and make a fair profit. By using a combination of the above models, a bureau aims on average to secure a margin of between 20 and 30% on the event. Of course, this is dependent to a large extent on the type of event, the level of the work, the risks and the creativity involved, and the scale and level of the bureau itself.

Internal team

If you decide to organise the event yourself, you need to think very carefully about how you put together your team. Make sure that there is a good balance of knowledge and skills. For this reason, you should not only look for people from different departments (marketing, human resources, finance, safety, etc.), but also with different personalities, ages and interests. Choose people who you think can work well in a group. Also make sure that your team remains manageable (the ideal number is between five and ten people). If the team is too large, it will be difficult to reach decisions quickly and efficiently. Are you organising a very large event for which you need a larger organisational team? Split the team into sub-teams and make each sub-team responsible for a specific part of the event. Yet while you need to keep your team relatively small, remember also that it is important to secure the commitment and involvement of everyone in the company. Agree a central contact point or person where people can ask questions and submit ideas, and give regular feedback and updates about recent developments.

Draw up a list of all your team members, showing their individual tasks and responsibilities. These tasks may include: coordination of the catering, scouting the event location, publicity and communication, etc. Appoint someone to manage the budget and just one single controller with overall responsibility. This controller has the final say and must resolve any differences of opinion which may arise.

The team must also have a clear mandate from the management to take necessary decisions. If, for whatever reason, this is not possible, someone from the management who does have the necessary decision-making authority must be added to the project team.

> Remember to ask yourself whether or not your team members are willing and able to bear the organisational and financial risks involved in your event project. All eyes will be watching them and not everyone can deal with this kind of pressure. Events often require an 'on the spot' approach, which some people find difficult to handle.

> Develop a smart system of communication between your sub-teams, so that people never lose sight of the 'big picture' or become isolated on their own little island of responsibility.

> If you are working with volunteers, you will need to make clear arrangements with them about what they can reasonably be expected to do or not to do. You will also need to adjust your communication style: these people are not paid professionals and so you cannot talk to them as such. Good briefing is also crucial: never let volunteers arrive on the day of an event without knowing in advance what they are supposed to do.

External suppliers / service providers

An incompetent supplier can ruin your entire event. Booking an amateur 'bedroom' DJ for a cheap price might sound appealing, but is it really such a good idea? Make sure you search for and find the right suppliers. Take the necessary time and effort when choosing your partners. Ask for an exploratory meeting to find out exactly what they can and cannot do. And always check the references they provide. To avoid any unpleasant surprises later on, also ask to see their sale and delivery conditions.

How can you be certain that the people who you are engaging are professionals and will not let you down? How do you know that they work with quality materials and fresh products? There are many super-efficient and highly respected companies working in the event industry, but sadly there are also a number of cowboys. Here are some tips that will help you to identify the real event professionals:

- ✓ **Reviews**

    As with hotels, reviews now play a significant role in the choice of event venues and suppliers. Reviews are a useful aid for quickly finding the venue, caterer or sub-contractor that best matches your event.

    > **Reviews play a significant role in the choice of event venues, caterers and suppliers.**

    If, for example, you read in a hotel review that children can play freely, this is not necessarily either a good thing or a bad thing. It depends on whether you are looking for a venue where the atmosphere is calm and relaxing or a venue where the kids don't feel obliged to keep quiet all day.

    In some cases, reviews can raise points for attention and/or improvement that are also relevant for your event. No supplier is ever 100% perfect. Everyone makes mistakes from time to time. The reaction of a supplier to a less than favourable review is often a good indication of whether he has learnt anything from his mistake and has taken the feedback to heart. These are the suppliers that you want to work with.

    You can find thousands of reviews on www.eventplanner.net. Thanks to our secure review platform, you can read the authentic testimonies of other event organisers that will immediately give you an accurate impression of the company concerned.

 After your event, also take the necessary time to write reviews about the venue and suppliers you have used. In this way, you will help other event organisers, give credit where it is due to the venue and suppliers concerned, and will save coins for free eventplanner.PRO membership!

✓ Quality labels
Although there is no overarching quality label for the event industry, there are specific labels for certain categories within the sector, such as hotels, caterers and various local initiatives. The eventplanner.eco label identifies all companies that are committed to the principles of corporate social responsibility. The certificates for compliance with ISO quality norms awarded to event bureaus for their specific processes are also a reliable indication of professionalism.

The business pages for event venues and suppliers on eventplanner.net contain a list of the relevant quality labels awarded to the organisations concerned, so that you have quick and easy access to a summary of each organisation's qualifications.

✓ Professional associations
There are numerous professional associations covering the event industry. Although membership of such an association is no guarantee of quality, most of the associations have a code of good practice and/or a set of entry conditions applicable to their members.

Membership of a selected list of professional associations is also recorded on the relevant business pages on eventplanner.net.

✓ Environmental permits
A fundamental procedure in the organisation of safe events is checking whether or not a venue has all the required permits and complies with the health and safety provisions laid down by the authorities. Think, for example, of regulations applying to the maximum number of people, emergency exists, technical controls, etc.

Checking such matters individually can be very time consuming. The solution is to be found in a document that every event location should possess: its environmental permit.

You can check whether an event venue is fully compliant by searching for the venue in question on eventplanner.net. You can see at a glance whether or not the venue has the necessary environmental permit and when it was uploaded. If you are an eventplanner.PRO member, you can also view the details of the permit.

What if no environmental permit has been uploaded for the venue you are interested in? You can always encourage them to take the necessary action to correct this omission. The venue itself is always responsible for the accuracy of any document it uploads.

✓ Conversations

You can gain much valuable information from an exploratory conversation with a candidate supplier.

Good suppliers lead this conversation and focus on the specific requirements of your event. They know exactly what they need to ask. By contrast, less professional event suppliers often overlook important details or fail to pose essential questions.

You need to be aware of how suppliers react to potentially difficult tasks or specific event requirements. Do they answer 'yes' or 'no' too quickly? Do they think about why you asked particular questions and show that they understand what the necessary solutions will involve?

Do they make notes of all the details you provide them with? No one can remember everything that is said in a conversation and with events every detail counts. For this reason, it is also important to make your own report of each conversation or meeting, which should then be circulated to everyone who was in attendance. In this way, there can be no discussion about what was agreed.

✓ Live test

The best acid test is to monitor your supplier's performance during a live event. Ask if you can view another event in which the supplier is involved and check all the details that are relevant to your own event.

✓ Tenders

Examine the tenders thoroughly. Are they complete? Are there no hidden costs? Take the necessary time to compare all the suppliers and all the tenders and do not be afraid to renegotiate certain conditions, if appropriate. Also make sure that you are comparing like with like. For example, ask all the suppliers to provide details of all the relevant technical specifications when they submit their technical tenders.

Remember that your event supply chain is only as strong as its weakest link. There is no point hiring in a star performer at great expense if your sound system is going to let you down on your big night!

A mix of internal and external?

Even if you decide to organise the event yourself, you can still leave some of the elements to the professionals, if this is appropriate. Catering, security and audio-visual presentations can all be handled separately and consequently are farmed out by most event organisers to specialist firms.

A new tool: AI

The advent of AI has revolutionised many different business sectors and the event industry is one of them. I pondered for quite some time about how I could best deal with AI in this book, bearing in mind that the speed with which the technology is currently changing means that what I write might already be out of date by the time the book is published! For that reason, I do not intend to focus on specific tools, but rather on a general approach.
Generative AI – a technology that is capable of producing new texts, images, music and other media – can help you to work more creatively and more efficiently. This technology is based on neural networks that are 'trained' by using massive data sets that allow AI to identify patterns on which it can build to generate new and original content.

How can AI support the organisation of events? Here are some ideas:

- **Brainstorming**
  Generative AI can be a powerful tool when you want to brainstorm about your event. By providing AI with all the relevant information about your target group and objectives, its software can put forward new and interesting ideas for themes, activities, decoration, etc. This can often provide a fresh angle of approach and help to break through creative blocks. AI can even suggest an original name for your event.

- **Writing texts for invitations and marketing material**
  The writing of invitations, press releases and other marketing material can be a time consuming business. Generative AI can help you by producing professional texts at high speed, which you can then adjust to meet your own requirements. AI can also generate personalised invitations based on the details and known preferences of your guests, as well as creating posts for social media. Last but not least, AI is useful for translating texts into other languages.

- **Virtual assistants**
    AI-driven virtual assistants can be used to question your event participants and process their answers, both before and during the event. For example, AI can offer your guests information about the programme, the venue and the available technical support facilities.

The possibilities offered by AI are increasing daily and we are already using AI on eventplanner.net to make the organisation of events more efficient. That being said, there are also a number of pitfalls involved in the use of AI. Here is a summary of some of them:

- **Quality control**
    AI is (and will remain) a computer model that seeks to predict the next word or pixel. Although this often works impressively well, AI models can still sometimes make errors or generate inappropriate content, especially if the training data is imbalanced or unrepresentative. In AI terminology, these errors are known as 'hallucinations'. So make sure that you always check any AI output you intend to use!

- **Ethics and privacy**
    The use of AI raises a number of ethical and privacy issues. For this reason, it is important to be transparent with your event participants about such matters and to always ensure that you comply with the existing privacy legislation. Never share anyone's personal details with an AI system if you are unaware of how the system will deal with those details. Also make sure that the AI systems you use do not contain any prejudices that may lead to unethical or discriminatory outcomes.

- **Cost and environmental impact**
    The implementation of advanced AI solutions can be expensive, particularly for smaller events. It is important to make a balanced assessment of costs and benefits, as well as taking due account of any impact on the environment. Although AI is rapidly increasing in popularity, it is not necessary to use it for everything. For many tasks, Google is just as good. Moreover, a system like ChatGPT uses 25 times more energy than a search request in Google.

By integrating AI into your event organisation in a correct manner, you can make the best possible use of the advantages it can bring, thereby raising your event to a higher level of efficiency and experience.

ACTION PLAN OR CALL SHEET

An action plan, call sheet or event specification is a chronological list of the activities, agreements and tasks relating to your event. Consequently, it is used to show **who is responsible for what (and where) at each moment of the preparation phase**. A good action plan is essential for good organisation and for the all-important delineation of responsibilities. The action plan will help you to see where problems are likely to arise and where a special approach or specific intervention may be necessary.

 Ensure that a copy of the action plan is included as an annex to all contracts and agreements with all relevant parties (internal staff, suppliers, guest speakers, etc.). Provide these parties with (mobile) contact coordinates and also with back-up coordinates, in case the first contact is not available. A list of other relevant addresses/numbers for weekend services (taxis, doctors, chemists, emergency services, etc.) is likewise useful. Do not forget to include a route plan and a plan of the venue, a copy of the site evacuation plan and a checklist of things they need to bring with them on the day of the event (badges, identity documents, invitations, office material, etc.).

It is a good idea to make a template in five columns for your call sheet:

Date & Time	Activity	Location	Responsible person	Remarks

Make sure that you number the bottom of every page of your call sheet or else staple all the different pages together. The plan will eventually consist of multiple pieces of paper. If you drop them in the heat of the moment, you will be glad that they are all fixed together or that you can at least put them back in the right order!

Although there is nothing wrong with compiling your action plan in Excel, nowadays dedicated event planning software is available that offers a number of extra possibilities. A professional planning tool such as the eventplanner.net software is particularly necessary for larger and more complex events.

For example, a small last-minute change in one part of your planning can also have consequences for several other parts of your event. Good event software immediately maps out these consequences and assesses their impact, whereas it would take several hours to complete the same task using a spreadsheet. With the eventplanner.net app, your entire team will always have access to an up-to-date planning. The tool also makes it possible to print off personalised call sheets quickly and easily, so that everyone has their own individual 'to do' list readily to hand.

www.eventplanner.net/book/eventsoftware

How detailed does your action plan need to be?

Sometimes it is necessary to include all activities for a period of six weeks before the event in your action plan. For other events, preparations may be minimal, so that you can focus all your attention on the event itself.

> In the final sprint towards the big day, there will no doubt be many changes to your call sheet. Make sure that each new version is given a new and sequentially correct number, so that everyone is working to the same plan! If you are using the eventplanner.net software, your entire team will automatically have access to the most recent version of the plan. Go through the changes in each version with the people concerned. This will help to identify possible weak points and will allow you to check that everyone is still aware of their proper responsibilities.

Internal staff need a full copy of the action plan, including all the details. This is not necessary for external suppliers: prepare a shortened version which is confined to a general summary of the event, with specific reference to the matters for which they are directly responsible. This means that you might have to draw up a number of separate action plans: for example, for artists, hostesses, catering personnel, etc. Our event software automatically compiles personalised call sheets. Major events might also require separate action plans for site construction and demolition. If an event is taking place in more than one room or location, it is useful to give each room/location coordinator a sheet which details the aspects relevant to that room/location. However, always include a general summary of the event as a whole, so that everyone has some idea of the true nature of the experience to which they are contributing.

When the practical implementation of your event requires you to work with a large number of different people, many of whom will not know each other, it is useful to hold an operational briefing which runs through the action plan step by step. This makes it easier for people to know who is responsible for what, and also creates a kind of team spirit. In these circumstances, however, it is always important to appoint one person who will direct and coordinate all the different aspects of the day.

If you are planning a show or act as part of your event, you will also need to draw up a technical action plan. This must detail almost on a second-by-second basis every action which needs to take place on, around or behind the stage. The compilation of this kind of action plan is a complex business. In addition to the more obvious matters, it must also include all cues, stage directions, lighting changes, scenery changes, etc.: in short, everything that is necessary to allow the performance to run smoothly. To make things even more complicated, much of this information is 'specialist' and needs to be communicated to many different people (the artists, the director, stage hands, technical staff, etc.). For this reason, it is usually better to draw up this action plan with the director and his technical assistants.

One of the most frequent problems with call sheets is a failure to devote sufficient attention to 'post-event' activities, such as venue clearance and evaluation. As a general rule, everyone is responsible for his or her own part of

the dismantling and clearance of the venue, although as organiser you (or your technical producer) remain responsible for the overall coordination and for the materials involved. If you have made use of furniture, decoration, etc. hired from various suppliers, remember to take account of the fact that they will only collect their property during normal working hours, unless you are prepared to pay an additional charge.

PROJECT MANAGEMENT FOR EVENTS

The organising of an event can quickly become a complex challenge involving many different parties. As overall organiser, you must possess the necessary project management skills to coordinate the activities of all these different people. You need to be able to separate the important matters from the unimportant ones and – above all – you need to keep a clear view of the overall picture in your mind. On this basis, you must set the correct priorities and delegate responsibilities to the right people, when you are not able to do something yourself. In short, you have to adopt a well-considered and structured approach to your task.

In view of the fact that an event is subject to the constraints of time and resources, and also results in a very specific end product, it is not unreasonable to regard its organisation as a project – to which classic project management techniques can therefore be applied.

The 'classic' project approach

Although the classic 'waterfall' method, which involves taking successive steps in a pre-determined order, is nowadays used less frequently for the organisation of events, I still intend to refer to it briefly, so that readers will have a full summary of all the different project methodologies. My personal preference, which is also the preference of the most modern event planners, is now to use the agile approach, to which I will return later on.

In order to effectively manage all the different aspects of the event and its preparation, you can divide up the project and its individual phases into further trajectories, which may or may not run parallel to each other. This might include, for example, a communications trajectory (covering publicity and public relations) or a content trajectory (which focuses on the speakers and/or other entertainment elements).

It is particularly important that you should agree a clear set of **critical success factors** for the project, together with deadlines for their completion. These are the elements that must be dealt with effectively, if your project is to become a success. High on the list of such elements are matters such as choosing the right venue, booking the right artists, getting the budget approved, attracting sufficient advance interest, etc. After each success factor has been dealt with, plan a 'go/no go' moment in which you evaluate your intermediary targets and agree with all relevant parties whether or not the project should still proceed. If one of the critical success factors cannot be realised, it may be necessary (in a worst case scenario) to cancel the event.

For each of these 'milestones', you must draw up a list of related tasks, making clear who in your team is responsible for what – and by what date. This means that you need to make realistic time estimates for the completion of each task.

> Compile proper minutes for every production meeting. Note down the names of those in attendance, list the decisions taken and specify the action required before the following meeting. Also keep a logbook of all the relevant decisions, so that you can avoid unnecessary discussions later on.

> Make sure you get an official 'handshake' from the different stakeholders before the start of each phase or when important decisions need to be taken in the middle of a phase. Formalise this approval in a signed document. In this way you can prevent your boss or the project initiator from calling your decisions into question at a later stage or from trying to change all your carefully-made arrangements at the last minute.

A useful tool for monitoring and adjusting your project planning is a so-called **GANTT diagram**. The vertical axis contains a number of rows which represent the different tasks within the project. The horizontal axis indicates the time necessary for the completion of the project in full. Each task is also allocated a time bar, which shows how much time is necessary for the completion of that particular task. The mutual interdependence of these tasks can be indicated with arrows. For example, this will make clear that your invitations need to be printed before you can actually send them! Software programmes such as Microsoft Project or Omniplan (for Mac users) are also useful instruments for project management and administration.

EXAMPLE OF A GANTT DIAGRAM

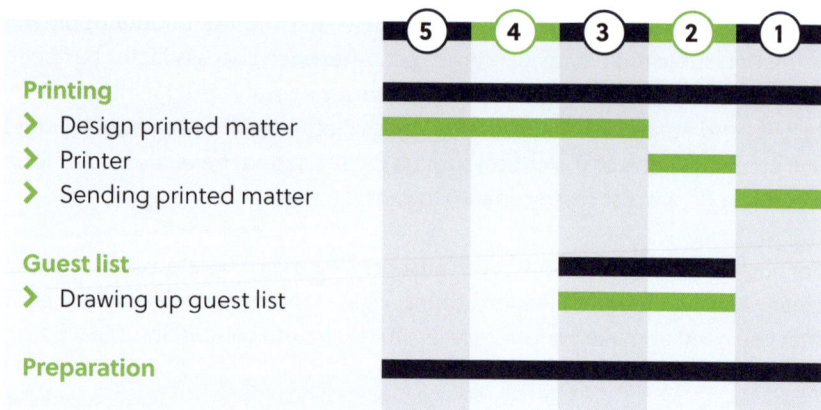

How far in advance do you need to start with the organisation of your project? To a large extent, this will depend on its scale, nature and complexity. The organisation of an international exhibition requires months or even years of planning, whereas the organisation of a teambuilding day or a staff dinner & dance can be completed within a matter of weeks. In an ideal world, you really need at least a year in order to prepare a major event properly. If you shorten your preparation time too drastically, there is a very real risk that the quality of your event will suffer. You may find that the best venues and the best artists are already booked, so that you are forced to settle for 'second-best'. Make a retro-planning to assess exactly when you need to start preparing for the type of event you have in mind. And have the courage to postpone your event, if you conclude that there is no longer sufficient time to prepare it properly. A badly planned event will not meet your objectives and can only do harm to your company's reputation.

The 'agile' project approach – Scrum

The main disadvantage of the classic project approach that makes use of GANTT charts is that there is only one thing of which you can be 100% sure: namely, that the estimates you make in advance will inevitably turn out to be wrong. That is logical, because they are – after all – only estimates. For an event, the level of uncertainty that this creates can be fatal for your planning. You cannot put back the date of your event by a couple of days at the last minute, simply because your faulty estimates mean that you are not ready on time. Moreover, with the classic project approach it is also possible that you will lose a significant amount of time in the early stages of the trajectory by over-focusing on the details that come first in terms of chronology, so that you have too little time for dealing with more important matters later on. An agile approach, of which Scrum is an example, makes use of a completely different methodology that offers major advantages for event organisation.

Agile has been a widely accepted project approach for many years in the tech industry, assisting companies in Silicon Valley like Facebook and Google to roll out high-quality projects at almost lightning speed – which should sound like music to the ears of every event planner!

With an agile approach, you divide up your event project into smaller and more manageable parts. You work with a scrum team, which for reasons of efficiency should be kept to a maximum of 10 people. You also appoint a scrum master, whose task is to keep things moving forward and to supervise progress.

You start by drawing up a list of all the different tasks involved in your event. In our eventplanner.net software we work with a Kanban board on which the tasks are categorised in three columns: 'to do', 'in progress' and 'done'. This gives a good overview of what everyone is doing at any given moment and also the status of each task.

The team gives each task a certain level of priority. During the project, tasks can be added, adjusted or scrapped, depending on the changing nature of your event's requirements. It is important that each task is clearly and adequately defined. Phrases like 'find a venue' are too broad and are better sub-divided into elements like 'draw up a venue short list', 'visit locations', 'negotiate price', and so on. This also makes it possible to allocate each of the sub-tasks to a different person. Our event software can fill in your Kanban board with a template of the standard tasks that are most common for the type of event that you are organising, so that you do not need to start from scratch. Alternatively, you can upload a task list from a previous event for your new event. The software also carries over all the details and procedural rules of the previous call sheet and adjusts them to take account of the new event date. This is an ideal way to build on the knowledge you have gained from your past events.

Once you have correctly compiled your task list, the real work can start. Delegate the different tasks to specific members of the team, starting with the tasks that you have assessed as having the highest level of priority.

Monitor the progress being made on a daily basis. With this in mind, each day should begin with a 'stand-up' in which each team member gives an account of what they did yesterday, what they are going to do today and where they have encountered problems, if any. In this way, it is possible to lend immediate assistance to anyone who is failing to make progress as quickly as desired. These meetings are held standing, so that they can be kept as short (maximum 10 minutes) and as efficient as possible.

The main advantage of the agile approach is that you can continually make adjustments to your action plan, which allows you to respond flexibly to market conditions, whilst also making possible the rapid identification of mistakes and problems, which can then be addressed by the whole team. This very direct way of collaboration and the sharing of challenges has a powerful positive effect on the 'yes we can' mentality of all the team members. In other words, with this method you achieve better results with the same team over the same period of time. Better, because priority is constantly given to the things that are truly important.

The disadvantage of this agility is that it crucially demands a greater level of involvement and commitment from the client, whilst at the same time providing less clarity in advance about what the end result will actually look like. To make this work, you need to trust the process and the team. In this context, having an experienced team leader (if you can find one) is a major bonus.

www.eventplanner.net/book/eventsoftware

 Learning to work with our eventplanner.net event software is not difficult, but it is important that you become thoroughly familiar with its full range of possibilities and the impact of the different settings. With this in mind, we have made a free training video that offers a step-by-step explanation of how the system works. You can find this video by clicking on the link below.

www.eventplanner.net/book/academy

Event logistics

One of the most underestimated (and often overlooked) aspects of event management is the logistical side of things. It is not only important to ask *what* needs to be done; it is just as vital to ask *how* it can be done.

PROCESS THINKING

Processes are the basis for any company that provides goods or services. There are buying processes, production processes, payment processes, etc. In terms of event management, these processes might be related to admission fees, parking and ticket sales.

All processes can be shown schematically with the help of an input-transformation-output model. You can apply this model to large-scale processes, such as the organisation of an event in its entirety, but also to small and very detailed processes, such as the noting of someone's registration at an entrance desk.

Logistics is also a process. Moreover, it is a process with a number of easily recognisable sub-processes, such as transport, traffic flow, facilities, crowd management, food and beverages, etc. Nevertheless, the sub-processes do not give the necessary insights that will allow you to work in a concrete and structured manner. Consequently, we need to zoom in on even smaller sub-divisions.

Consider, for example, the sub-process 'transport'. This can be further divided into cars, public transport, bikes, kiss & ride, etc. The visitors who travel to your event by car can also be similarly divided into processes for arrival, parking and departure. But it doesn't stop there: the process 'parking' can also be split into processes for searching for a parking place, parking in the place once found, and then leaving your car to go to the event venue. You can continue this sub-division until the function of the process is explicit. This is the only way to be sure that the process can actually do what you want it to do. If you look at these matters in sufficient detail, the key questions will soon emerge: for example: **how** exactly should people park?

Once you have identified and mapped out all the different processes, it is important to check that they are properly synchronised with each other. Perhaps the actual act of parking presents no problems, but what if there is a huge tail-back of traffic at the entrance to the car park, because the access gateway is too narrow?

Process chains

For an event, it is the capacity of the different processes that determines how many visitors can be accommodated or assisted in a particular period. This is known as the service capacity.

Let's look again at the arrival process for people coming to your event by car. When dealing with large quantities of traffic, the capacity of the approach roads is the all-important factor. But what other criteria might affect this capacity? The approach roads might be wide or narrow, long or short, lit or unlit, with traffic lights and roundabouts or without... In a chain of processes, it is the process with the smallest capacity that determines the maximum flow through that chain as a whole (Goldratt, 1992). The following diagram shows this schematically.

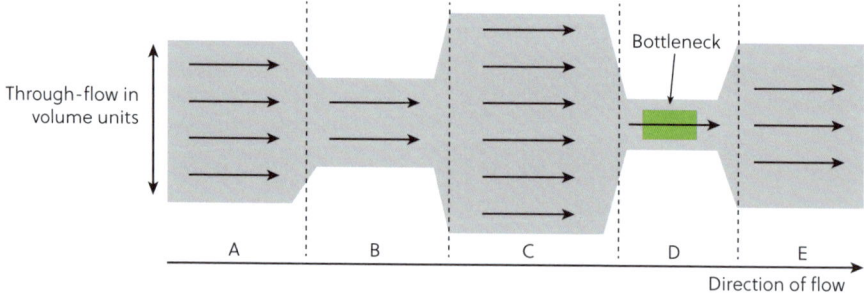

The bottleneck in your process therefore determines the maximum through-flow per unit of time for the process in its entirety. Of course, identifying this problem is one thing; actually doing something about it is another. Because there is yet another problem. The flow of visitors and their distribution over the duration of the event is usually uneven – and therefore uncertain. This is almost always the case with 'open' events, when it is not known in advance who will arrive and at what time. This means that there is a risk that at some point the throughflow of arriving visitors will be (temporarily) greater than the available capacity of the bottleneck, which may result in a traffic-jam. Avoiding such jams (and any other forms of waiting) is essential if you want to achieve the required level of service and safety for your event. It can also be important for your budget. If you are planning to sell beer during the interval in a concert, but long queues form because the tapping of the beer is too slow, you will actually sell much less than you were hoping – so that income from this part of your budget might be significantly reduced.

*Avoiding queues is essential for your **event experience**. But it is also important from a security perspective and for your budget.*

By studying all the different processes involved in your event, you should be able to avoid queues altogether. A useful tool in this respect is the onion skin model. The processes developed for the visitor form a chain and can be roughly divided into four different sections, which are folded around the core (the event) in a manner not dissimilar to the skin of an onion.

1. The first layer is formed by the processes that have an influence on the choices the visitor will make about how he travels to and from the event.
2. The second layer is the guidance layer. The method of transport has been chosen. The visitor must now be guided/directed to the place where he can park his car.
3. The third layer involves the process designed to get the visitor from the parking area to the event venue.
4. The fourth layer – the core – focuses on the processes that will allow the visitor to enjoy the reason for his visit: a performance, an attraction, VIP treatment, catering, etc.

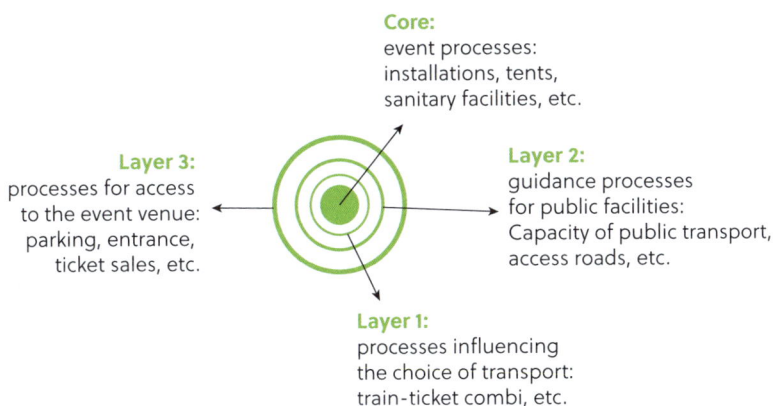

Core:
event processes:
installations, tents,
sanitary facilities, etc.

Layer 3:
processes for access
to the event venue:
parking, entrance,
ticket sales, etc.

Layer 2:
guidance processes
for public facilities:
Capacity of public transport,
access roads, etc.

Layer 1:
processes influencing
the choice of transport:
train-ticket combi, etc.

CAPACITY CALCULATIONS

To calculate the capacity of your processes, so that you can avoid queues and long periods of waiting for your visitors, you need to collect as many details as possible. This is the only way to make an accurate assessment.

Let us return to our example of an interval during a concert or play. In this situation, all the visitors leave the performance area at the same time, causing a log-jam at the bar and the toilets. Calculating the waiting time at a log-jam moment is not difficult. Let us assume that a visit to the ladies toilet takes an average of 2.5 minutes. Let us also assume that there are five toilets, that the interval lasts for 15 minutes and that there are 60 women bursting for a pee. The first five ladies do not need to wait. The next five need to wait 2.5 minutes. The next five after that another 2.5 minutes, and so on. After 5 minutes, 10 ladies have relieved themselves; after 10 minutes the number has risen to 20. But this means that not all the ladies will be able to use the toilet before the interval is over (15 minutes). As organiser, you therefore have two options: you must either increase the number of toilets or the length of the interval. In this instance, the capacity calculation for the ladies toilet is based on an average visit time of 2.5 minutes. In reality, of course, this can either be longer or shorter.

To assess whether you have any potential capacity problems, you will therefore need to collect details – and plenty of them. In the above example, you need to know the average length of time of a ladies' toilet visit. But you may also need to make time assessments for processes such as parking, ordering at the bar or using automatic payment machines. In view of the large number of different processes involved in the organisation of an event, there is no one single method you can use to collect all the data you need. Nevertheless, you must do all you can to be as comprehensive as possible.

Budget

Drawing up a budget is a continuous, on-going process. It is best to start with a global approximation of costs. Do this before you ask for price tenders. This will allow you to check whether or not you are approaching your project realistically. Gradually adjust your initial rough estimate as and when more accurate information becomes available; in particular, when price tenders are received and approved.

Is your budget too high? If so, check each individual budgetary post to see where cheaper alternatives may be available or where particular items can be deleted. Never remove anything from the budget that will reduce the overall quality and/or safety of your event. As an alternative, consider sponsoring by outside third parties: this is a useful way to increase your available financial resources. A partnership with another company that has the same target groups is another possible solution, which may allow you to share costs.

 Never accept verbal prices; always get everything on paper! Make sure that there is a clear description of what is included in the price and what is not. This will help you to avoid unpleasant budgetary surprises.

DRAWING UP A BUDGET

There are different systems that you can use as a basis for drawing up an event budget. Each has its own different avenue of approach and its own specific advantages and disadvantages. In other words, there is no single standard method or template.

Functional cost classification

Opting for a functional classification of your event costs means that you will build up your budget on the basis of your main categories of expenditure, such as catering, venue, audio-visual services, etc. You totalise the costs for all the activities in each category. The total of all the individual categories is then the total amount of your budget. You should only use this method of classification for relatively small events; it will not be sufficient to ensure the proper financial management of larger, more complex projects.

(+) This method gives you a good overview of the relevant balance of cost between the different categories of activity. This means that a functional classification allows you to draw up a well-balanced budget. Are the costs for catering too low in comparison with the costs for technical support? By checking the figures against your previously defined objectives, you can see whether your estimate is realistic, optimistic or pessimistic. If there is no other alternative, it will also make it easier to see where you need to make changes to your event programme in order to make the budget balance.

(-) The interaction of different categories on each other is often overlooked, which can result in an increase in unforeseen costs at a later stage. For example, if you decide to invite more guests, it is not only the budget for catering that needs to be increased; you will also need to increase the budgets for communication (more invitations), location (a bigger venue) and safety (increased insurance, extra security agents).

Fixed and variable costs

As the name implies, with this system you make a distinction in your budget between the fixed costs and the variable costs for your event. Fixed costs are not dependent upon the number of invitees, and cover matters such as entertainment, guest speakers and audio-visual equipment. Variable costs increase or increase in accordance with the number of guests. The most obvious variable cost is catering, but matters such as programme books, promotional handouts, etc. should not be overlooked.

(!) Some fixed costs are only fixed up to a certain limit. For example, the hire charge for your event location is in theory a fixed cost, but as soon as the number of guests exceeds the capacity of the hall it will be necessary to seek a new, bigger and more expensive venue. In other words, a fixed cost can sometimes become a variable cost.

(+) The division between fixed and variable costs is a useful and often necessary instrument for assessing the maximum number of guests allowable in relation to the available budget.

(-) It is more difficult to follow the budget provisions for the individual categories of activity.

Calculation and extrapolation of costs per programme element

With this method, you make a summary of the costs for each section of your event programme. For example, if you are planning an all-day event, you might have separate budgets for teambuilding in the afternoon and dinner in the evening. As far as overarching costs are concerned, such as invitations or website management, an agreed coefficient is applied to the total costs per programme element.

(+) You have a very clear view of the budget for each element/activity of your event.

(-) The use of a coefficient for overarching costs is often arbitrary and inaccurate.

Combination of cost assessment methods

Of course, you can always opt for a combination of cost assessment methods. For example, you can use a functional classification method to draw up a separate budget for each programme element, whilst at the same time calculating separate subtotals for the location, catering, etc. for your evening dinner. Various other permutations of this kind are also possible.

> 📌 Always build a buffer into your budget by allowing an additional 10% of the total budget for 'unforeseen expenditure'.

> 📌 Are you organising a commercial event with an admission charge? If so, base your budget on the average sales price of the tickets (taking account of discounted rates, free tickets, tickets for PR purposes, etc). Do not base your calculations on the advertised admission fee: this will lead you to overestimate your likely income.

www.eventplanner.net/book/eventsoftware

TICKET PRICE AND STRATEGY

If you are organising a pay-to-enter event, the ticket price is an important part of your business case. However, setting the ticket price and devising the right sales strategy for your event can both be challenging tasks.

To set the ticket price at the right level, you need to take account of your costs, but also what a visitor is likely to be willing to pay for your event. This event must provide value for the visitor. That value might be in the form of entertainment (if the event is a concert) or knowledge (if the event is a congress). You need to put a price on this value, whilst at the same time bearing in mind the prices charged by your competitors. What do they offer the visitor and how much do they ask for it? Is your price higher? If so, do your visitors get more perceived value for their money?

The way you price your tickets and the strategy you use for selling them can have a significant impact on the number of visitors you attract. Fortunately, there are a number of techniques that you can use to sell more tickets:

- ✓ **Offer an 'early bird' option**
  By creating a feeling of urgency, linked to the possibility of saving money, you can encourage people to buy their tickets more quickly. An 'early bird' option can help to convince doubters to buy their tickets sooner rather than later, providing you with liquid cash that you can put to good use during this initial phase of the event process.

- ✓ **Set clever pricing options**
  Let's imagine that you want to sell tickets priced at $ 200. In order to properly contextualise your prices (which will make them seem more attractive), you need to offer three purchase options for different amounts. The first option is a straightforward entry ticket, priced at $ 170. The second option is an entry ticket plus a cocktail dinner, priced at $ 200. For the third option priced at $ 250, the participants get an additional 'meet-and-greet' with the speakers/artists. These prices are, of course, fictional, but the basic principle remains the same: by offering three options, you allow potential participants to see exactly what they are getting for their money. Research has shown that in such circumstances people most frequently choose the second of the three options: not too expensive, but not too cheap. The benchmarks of the higher and lower price make this middle price feel 'right'.

✓ **Give discounts to different target groups**
Discounts can be a powerful selling tool – so don't forget to use them! People like saving money, especially if you indicate clearly just how much they will save. The exception is when you are organising an event that you want to be 'exclusive'. In this case, discounts have the effect of 'cheapening' the image of the event. In other cases, it is wise to draw up different profiles for your target group and set the level of discount accordingly. If, for example, you are organising an academic event, set different prices for professors, students and the representative of other educational institutions. In this way, you make the event affordable for a larger group of people, so that you can attract more participants. Make sure, however, that you keep your full margin for the target group that can easily afford to pay the full ticket price.

BUSINESS CASE

As well as making an assessment of your costs, you also need to make an estimate of your potential income or return. For a public event or a congress, this means sales from tickets and catering (food and drink), as well as any sponsoring you have been able to obtain. If you are organising a business event, your return can take a number of different forms, as we saw in the section on ROI. If, for example, you organise an event for your personnel, you may hope for a return in the form of improved team spirit, so that your productivity increases and the level of sickness absence decreases. These are elements that you can also quantify in a business case analysis.

By setting all your costs against all your different forms of income, you can see how many participants you need to attract before you reach break-even (the point where costs = income). If you expect more participants, you can calculate your profit. If you expect fewer participants, you have advance warning about your potential loss.

Enter all the figures into your event software, so that you can make simulations for what might happen if, say, you sell 10% fewer tickets than anticipated. This will mean a reduced level of income, but some of your variable costs may also decrease. In this way, you can work out your best-case and worst-case scenarios.

Cash flow

In addition to your overall budget, also draw up a plan to monitor incoming receipts and outgoing payments. This cash flow plan must show accurately when money is likely to be coming in and also when you need to pay it out again (advances to suppliers, final settlements, etc.). It is important that the balance of your cash flow should remain positive at all times, so that you can meet your payment commitments without going overdrawn at the bank. If this is not possible, the visualisation of the cash flow will help you to identify potential problems in advance, allowing you to renegotiate terms of payment with your suppliers or arrange a temporary short-term loan. Bear in mind that for many events the costs often need to be incurred significantly in advance, long before your income from ticket sales starts to come in.

Creative business models

If you are organising an event for your own company, you will probably be paying all the bills yourself. If you are organising a festival, you will no doubt be selling tickets. Nevertheless, there are several other business models that can be used for events. Hopefully, the following examples will give you some ideas about the best way to fill out your budget.

- **Crowdfunding**
  Crowdfunding is a low-threshold financing system, whereby a large group of people (i.e. the crowd) invest online in innovative projects that interest them. In particular, public events are making increasing use of this technique. If it is not possible to collect sufficient funds to allow the event to take place, the donors' money is returned. As an organiser, this means that you only put your own time and energy into an event when you know that there is enough visitor interest to make it worthwhile. What could be better than that?!

- **Membership**
  If there is a recurring theme in your events, set up a structure for their running that will allow people to become members. Ask for payment of a membership subscription, in return for which they are granted free or reduced price access to the events. Combine this with some external sponsoring and you are well on your way to event success!

- **Mix**
  You still feel the need to sell tickets? Then why not combine (or alternate) free and paying events? Free events are usually an excellent way to promote your activities. It is also a good idea to make the free events

large-scale and the paying events more limited. Use social media to create interest and to transfer the goodwill effect of your free events to your paying editions.

✓ **Sell extras**
Being able to wander around in the VIP zone is always cool. Many people are willing to pay more for 'extras' of this kind. Sometimes a lot more. This is particularly the case, for example, for a 'meet-and-greet' with their idol (but always discuss this in advance with the artists/speakers you book). Offering this kind of privileged treatment allows you to charge premium prices for those who are willing to pay. Companies also like to invite their business relations as VIPs to prestige events, so make sure that you offer them special VIP packages that include things like a private own bar and reception area.

✓ **Content creation**
Crowdsourcing – whereby the public contribute towards the development of an event – has already become a reality. You can use this 'wisdom of crowds' to develop shared knowledge and create unique content. Combine this with the newest technologies and then sell the resulting product in video, audio or text format.

✓ **Franchising**
Why not try and franchise your event concept? Who knows, there may be interest from abroad. Consider, for example, the success of TEDx, which organises events all around the world on the basis of franchising.

✓ **Merchandising**
If Mickey Mouse can do it for Disney, why not do the same for your event by selling cool T-shirts and gadgets? The range of possibilities is almost limitless.

SPONSORING

Sponsoring is unquestionably the most widely used method for reducing the cost for event participants or for increasing the margin of event organisers. As an organiser, you go in search of sponsors who are a good match for your event, in return for which you seek to develop ways in which you can activate the sponsor's brand among your target group. The aim is create a close partnership that not only works for you, but above all is a good fit for your sponsor's business strategy.

But how exactly can you do this? Most organisers make use of an event presentation or sponsor dossier to impress potential clients/investors with exciting details of all the fantastic ideas that will capture the imagination of the event's participants. Organisers also promise that the sponsor's logo will be prominently visible on all flyers, tickets, brochures, etc. After all, that is what sponsors want, isn't it? Sadly, no. Unless you are organising the Tour de France with its millions of viewers on television, the limited visibility that you can offer them is of little benefit to the vast majority of sponsors. If you want them to invest in your event, you need to give them something more – for example, speaker slots or the possibility to host the event's after party.

Of course, you will also need to prepare your own presentation folder to attract your sponsors in the first place. This should contain all relevant facts and figures about your event. For repeats of existing events, you can make use of the data from past editions. For new events, you need to try extra hard to convince potential sponsors of your professionalism and ability. How can you guarantee them that your event will be a success? What are the reasons that make it unwise for them to ignore your event? For smaller events you can also work with a rate card and sponsor packages, but when larger events and budgets are involved you need to sit around the table with your sponsor to find out what promotion options are best for him (or her) and what value those options can offer for both of you.

Here are a number of tips that can help you to create value for sponsors that you can valorise:

- ✔ **Help your sponsors to find potential customers during the event**
  Try to develop ways that will allow sponsors to come into direct contact with potential buyers/clients. At mass events, you can achieve this, for example, with original sampling sessions. If you are organising a B2B event, you can arrange meetings between sponsors and their prospective targets. In this case, bear in mind that you might need to incur additional travel and accommodation costs to persuade some of these targets to

attend your event, but this is well worth it if it allows you to attract more sponsors. The sponsors themselves will also be willing to pay more if they know that more of their targets will be present. In the professional jargon, this is known as a 'hosted buyer' programme.

- ✔ **Design a powerful promotion platform for your sponsors**

    As I have already mentioned, offering logo visibility is of little value for sponsors. To make them interested, you will need to develop a different approach. For example, it is a good idea to make time available in your programme planning that will allow the event's participants to experience at first hand things that are closely related to your sponsor's products. If a virtual reality company is helping to finance your event, find ways that will immerse the participants in a different dimension. If your sponsor is a car manufacturer, make it possible for the participants to have a free test drive somewhere nearby or, failing that, use the brand's vehicles for all your event transport, especially when collecting participants from stations or airports.

- ✔ **Promote your sponsor's content**

    Another way to offer value to your potential financial backers is to increase the number of visitors to their website. You can do this by publishing their content (articles, e-books, blog posts, white papers etc.) on your own event website and social media. In this way, you can help to boost your sponsor's online presence and promote their brand.

- ✔ **Invite your sponsors to speak at your event**

    Give your partners the opportunity to take part in your event as speakers. This offers them the possibility to explain their product and to project their brand vision to a large public. Of course, what they say will need to be relevant and interesting for the event's participants! No one is interested in listening to boring promotional blurb. One way around this is to use an interview format, so that the moderator can intervene if the sponsor's message becomes too overtly commercial.

BUDGET CHECKLIST

Drawing up an event budget is a complex and wide-ranging task. As a result, it is easy to overlook certain items of expenditure. The following checklist – which is by no means 100% comprehensive – will help you to make your budget as detailed and as complete as possible. Once it is ready, remember to run through the budget with your team members at regular intervals, in order to make sure that nothing has been overlooked.

✔ **Communication**
- ☐ Website
- ☐ Printing (see checklist Chapter 8)
- ☐ Marketing (advertising, promotional material, etc.)
- ☐ Mobile applications
- ☐ Social media
- ☐ Ticketing (fixed cost or commission?)
- ☐ ...

✔ **Location/tent**
- ☐ Hire of function room/hall
- ☐ Cloakroom
- ☐ Stage/dance floor
- ☐ Furnishings, tribune, etc.
- ☐ Decoration and embellishment
- ☐ Changing facilities
- ☐ Direction boards and signposts
- ☐ Parking costs
- ☐ Toilets (and their attendants)
- ☐ Heating/air-conditioning
- ☐ Cleaning
- ☐ ...

✔ **Catering**
- ☐ Catering
- ☐ Drink
- ☐ Crew catering

- ☐ Cutlery, glassware, crockery, table linen
- ☐ Bars, buffets, etc.
- ☐ ...

✔ **Activities**
- ☐ Entertainment
- ☐ Guest speakers
- ☐ Activities (workshops, teambuilding, etc.)
- ☐ Children's entertainment
- ☐ Music
- ☐ Copyright
- ☐ ...

✔ **Audio-visual support**
- ☐ Projectors
- ☐ Plasma and LCD screens
- ☐ Microphones
- ☐ Sound systems
- ☐ Lighting systems
- ☐ Video-recording and photography
- ☐ Special effects (fireworks, snow, etc.)
- ☐ Wi-Fi network
- ☐ Hybrid events (live streaming, etc)
- ☐ Event app
- ☐ ...

✔ **Personnel**
- ☐ Floor and event manager(s)
- ☐ Safety coordinator

- ☐ Hostesses
- ☐ Parking attendants
- ☐ Security
- ☐ First aid team
- ☐ Stagehands/technical staff
- ☐ Catering staff (waiters, barmen, etc.)
- ☐ Cloakroom and toilet attendants
- ☐ Translators/interpreters
- ☐ ...

✔ **Diverse costs**
- ☐ Postage
- ☐ Give aways
- ☐ (VIP) transport
- ☐ Hotel costs
- ☐ Permits and insurance
- ☐ Possible theft and damage
- ☐ Electricity, water, other utilities
- ☐ Waste disposal
- ☐ Logistics
- ☐ ...

✔ **Organisational costs (internal and external)**
✔ **Event planning software**
✔ **VAT and taxes**
✔ **Unforeseen expenditure (allow 10%)**

 If you are planning to put on a spectacular show, remember to make sufficient provision in the budget to cover the rehearsals; not only for the time of the artists, speakers and acts, but also for the extra hire of the venue and the additional requirement for technical back-up.

Date, duration and time

When you organise an event, you naturally hope that lots of people are going to come. Choosing the right date, time and duration can be a major contributory factor towards the successful realisation of your objectives.

DATE

Target group

When selecting a suitable date for your event, take account first and foremost of the people you intend to invite. Does your target group have certain wishes or expectations? The following factors may play a role:

- ✓ **Partners and/or children**
  For events without partners, you are probably advised to choose a weekday. Tuesday, Wednesday and Thursday are the most suitable. Events with partners are better organised on a Friday evening. If the children of the guests are also welcome, you really need to opt for a Saturday or a Sunday.

- ✓ **Religious convictions**
  For the practitioners of some faiths it is simply *not done* to organise an event on a day of rest; for example, the Jewish Sabbath. Also take account of religious festivals, such as Ramadan, Yom Kippur, Chinese New Year, etc.

- ✓ **Internal**
  Check the diaries of your internal guest list. Does the CEO have an important appointment elsewhere? Are the members of the board available? Are key staff away on training or engaged in a crucial project? Your guests will expect these important officials to be present. So if you are organising an internal event, make sure that the whole company team is available.

✓ **External**

An important VIP? An international artist that you desperately want on your programme? Their agendas will also play a role when it comes to choosing the best moment for your event.

✓ **Press**

Does your event have a PR objective? If so, you will need to take account of the publication dates of the relevant professional journals that are important for your own or your client's sector. In this respect, summer is traditionally the quiet season. If you can link an interesting story to your event, this will significantly increase your chances of attracting press attention at any time of year. Have you already built up good contacts with influential journalists? Check to make sure that they are free for the date you have in mind for your event. You wouldn't want them to miss it!

Unsuitable periods

Take account of people who are likely to refuse your invitation during the following periods:

✓ **Winter periods** with snow and ice can cause logistical problems. Many people do not want to take the risk on the roads, certainly over long distances, and others may arrive late.
✓ It is wise to avoid organising business events on or around (inter)national **public holidays**. Other holiday periods, particularly in the summer, should also be avoided, if at all possible.
✓ A long weekend is an ideal moment for a short holiday or a city trip – so avoid the so called **bridging weekends** (made possible by a public holiday on a Thursday, Friday, Monday or Tuesday), unless you are organising a leisure-based event.

 Children are welcome? If so, take due account of exams or other busy periods at school.

Which days?

Depending upon the kind of event you are organising, some days might be more suitable than others. The following list is useful as a guideline, but remember that exceptions often prove the rule!

- In general, **Monday** is not a suitable day for a (B2B) event, with the possible exception of activities for specific groups (hairdressers, caterers, etc.), who often have their normal closing day on a Monday.
- On **Tuesday** you can usually organise your event with a reasonable degree of confidence that people will turn up.
- **Wednesday** is also in general a good day, but remember than on the continent there is no school in many countries on Wednesday afternoon, so that many parents stay at home or work part-time.
- **Thursday** is an ideal day for almost any kind of event. In particular, it is highly suitable for events which are scheduled to last late into the evening and to which partners are not invited.
- A lot of two-day congresses are organised on Thursday and **Friday**. Friday evening is the ideal time for an event with partners.
- **Saturday** is well suited to festive events or family days with partners and children.
- **Sunday** is also traditionally a day for events with partners and/or children. But don't forget that many people like to reserve this day for some quality time at home with their partner and family. It is probably better to give Sunday evening a miss: the start of a busy, new working week is just around the corner.

If your target group works nights or in shifts, it is sometimes difficult to find a time and date that suits everyone. However, in some companies it may be possible to adjust the work schedules. Ask and see!

Competition

Take due account of other local and (inter)national events that are also focused on your target group: sports events (World Cup, European Championships, Super Bowl, Olympic Games, Tour de France, etc.), trade exhibitions, cultural events, etc. You can find most of the information you need in various online calendars (tourist boards, sport federations, cultural organisations, etc.).

In addition to having an impact on your number of participants, competing events can also have an influence on your potential costs. During busy event periods you will often need to pay more for your venue and for the services of your suppliers than you would during the low season. Of course, the timing of the low season and the high season also varies to reflect the nature of the event. Wedding venues and festival suppliers tend to be less in demand dur-

ing the winter months, whereas congress locations are more readily available during the summer holidays.

 Draw up your programme in an anti-cyclic manner. Traditionally, there are fewer trade fairs in the summer months, but the people who are still working during this period often have more time and interest to attend. So why not give it a try?

 Is a clash with another event unavoidable? Then why not try to work this other event into yours (assuming that this is not incompatible with your objectives)? There is an important football match being played on the same evening? Then install a giant screen, so that the football fans can watch the game live. But don't forget to arrange payment of the necessary viewing rights!

Once you have found a number of dates that seem to be suitable, first check these with your suppliers, speakers, artists and, above all, your preferred venue. As soon as you have agreed a firm date with all relevant parties, it is advisable to immediately take out the necessary options on that date. It should be possible to get a no-obligation option for an agreed period of, say, one or two weeks. During this period, your venue and your artists will accept no other bookings for your chosen date, but with no binding commitment to eventually use them.

DURATION

Adjust the duration of your event to match the expectations of your target group and following consultation with important stakeholders. Add up the likely duration of the individual elements of your programme, so that you can have some idea of the overall duration. Remember to include travelling time and overnight stays, where appropriate. As a general rule, the longer the duration of the programme, the more likely the guests are likely to cancel. For this reason, it helps to keep the different programme elements relatively short. You should also plan frequent breaks.

TIME

You should not just pluck a starting time and a finishing time for your event out of thin air! Take proper account of travelling time, transport facilities and the location of the venue. Do not plan an event during the rush hour or late on a Sunday evening. Just after work is also a time that is best avoided.

The nature of your target group is also an important factor in selecting the right time. People in executive functions will be more likely to accept an evening invitation than middle managers or civil servants.

You can either ask your invitees to arrive punctually at a given hour, or you can tell them that they are free to arrive at their convenience after a given hour or between the hours of x.oo and x.oo. Make allowances for possible latecomers and plan on a buffer of at least twenty minutes.

> Do you expect your guests to attend your gala event in evening dress? If so, allow them sufficient time to go home and change. In other words, make sure your starting time is not immediately after office hours.

> Plan the start and end of your event to coincide with the hours that public transport is readily available. This will persuade more participants to leave their car at home. Make sure, however, that you stick to your published timings. If your event overruns, there is a risk that your guests might quite literally miss the bus!

Concept and programme

A well-constructed programme takes full account of the target group. It goes without saying that the different elements of your programme can be creative and original, but you must never lose sight of the objective of your event. Choosing a particular theme can give consistency - a leitmotif – to the proceedings. Do you want your event to truly live on in the memory of the participants? This means that you will need to develop a concept that provides your invitees with a 'total experience'.

PROGRAMME ELEMENTS

Event programmes are more about emotions than logistics. The general mood – and therefore the experience – of your participants is determined to a large extent by the way you structure your programme of activities. If you are not careful you may end up compiling a programme that is boring, tiring or confusing for your guests – no matter how 'cool' your event might be!

Meeting design starts with an assessment of expectations, the mapping out of information processes, an analysis of content, and so on. As the director of your event, you need to orchestrate all the different parts into a seamlessly coherent whole, just like a movie director does with the different scenes of his film. Meeting design is a specialist skill and, as the term implies, has the biggest impact on the organisation of congresses. But a strong programme and perfect timing have the ability to raise any business event, festival or celebration to a higher level.

Develop an approach in which your participants are always central. After all, it is for them that you are planning this event! Try to imagine what they will feel and how they will react/behave once the event has started.

Build your programme around different highlights and ensure that these are balanced and properly spread. After an element that requires careful listening, throw in a lighter element or plan a break, so that people can give their minds a rest. Try to find the right blend of information, entertainment, relaxation, networking and culinary moments. In this way, the participants can recharge their batteries, so that they will be better able to remember the information they receive during the key sessions of your event.

Do not reach the climax of your programme too soon. If your event has a spectacular start, it may be difficult to sustain this level of interest throughout the remainder of the programme. This can lead to disappointment – and disappointment means that you will not achieve your objective. Build up the tension gradually, with regular pauses, before moving on to the next peak.

Make sure that you do not overfill your programme with too many activities. Minimalism – less is more – is always a smart option, even if your first inclination is to try and give your participants value for money by offering them as much as possible. You don't need a whole army of speakers and an endless series of sessions to organise a memorable event. An over-ambitious programme can often be overwhelming and/or confusing for the people you are trying to reach. No one can concentrate hard all the time. So, give them a break: don't overload your programme with too many different elements. Fewer activities means less stress and will allow your visitors to enjoy your event all the more.

Put the 'less interesting' elements of your programme first; otherwise you can spoil the build-up to your 'grand finale'. Have you given your invitees the option to arrive over a longer period? If so, plan your timetable of activities in such a way that the latecomers do not miss any of the essential elements.

Never forget that your participants will sometimes have an agenda that is different from your own as organiser. You might want to launch a new product at your event, whereas they might be more interested in networking. These different expectations are not necessarily incompatible, but always seek to achieve the right balance between them. The most important thing is to show that you recognise their wishes – in this example, by leaving enough time in your programme for network opportunities. Perhaps you can even arrange a specific networking activity. And no: networking is not possible while your DJ is blasting out the decibels through your sound system! Organise a quiet location where people can mingle and talk at their ease.

You can also seek to engage your participants more fully in your event by working different types of event dynamic into your programme. Instead of a whole day of monotonous round-table discussions, try to inject a little variety: campfire talks, speaker panels, question and answer sessions, TED-like presentations, etc. But don't over-elaborate. Always remember to keep things simple. What you need is a well-structured programme with different session formats that will prevent everyone from getting bored by too much of the same thing.

Each event has its own different points of emphasis. Even so, there are a number of elements that are common to almost all events. The most important ones – with an estimate of their likely duration – is given in the following list:

- Parking time and walking to the venue: 10 minutes (sometimes longer, if you are using shuttle buses)
- Welcome and registration: 30-60 minutes
- Cloakroom: 5-10 minutes
- Welcome drink: 15 minutes
- Introduction and announcements: 5 minutes
- Speakers, entertainment, presentations: a *maximum* of 1.5 hours without a break
- Coffee break: 15-20 minutes
- Lunch: 1 to 1.5 hours (or 2 hours with networking)
- Reception: 1 to 3 hours
- Aperitif: 30 to 60 minutes
- Dinner: sitting 1.5 to 3 hours, walking 1.5 to 2.5 hours
- Party: 3 to 5 hours
- Entertainment or performance: 20 to 30 minutes
- Departure: 30 minutes

To get a good idea of how long your programme lasts and how it 'feels', you need to try out the different programme elements in advance. Check the duration of each act, make clear arrangements with the speakers, follow the same route that your guests will have to follow (but remember that big groups walk more slowly!), etc.

Try to visualise each separate aspect of your event from beginning to end. Even so, it is sometimes difficult to judge certain elements with accuracy and the unexpected can always happen. This means that on your big day (or night) you may find that your programme is running late or early. If so, try to compensate for this by adjusting the length of your planned breaks, making them shorter or longer, according to the circumstances.

In chapter 13 I will look in more depth at how you choose, furnish and decorate your event venue, but at this stage suffice it to say that your approach to these matters plays an important role in determining the mood and reactions of your participants. It can also have a significant impact on the communication dynamic. A round-table layout encourages people to talk and increases their sense of involvement. By contrast, a theatre format creates a less social and less interactive vibe, resulting in more passive behaviour during the event. In other words, the way you style the venue is linked one-to-one with your event programme.

> 📌 If you find that you have a serious structural shortage of time, make your next break a little shorter and try to adjust the remaining elements of the programme. Never scrap breaks or shorten them excessively: your guests need them to process the previous programme elements – and absorb your message.

> 📌 Ensure that the transition between the different parts of the programme or the different speakers/performers is completed smoothly. I was recently at a festival where it took half an hour to set up the drum kit of the next band on stage. The atmosphere in the crowd evaporated in minutes. So why not bring a mobile DJ booth onto the stage while everything is being made ready for the next act? Solutions of this kind are not difficult to find – if you think about it.

> 📌 Make sure that you have enough staff in potential 'bottleneck' situations: in the cloakroom, at the bar, guiding people to their seats or to/from the car park. These are all elements where considerable time can either be lost or won.

> 📌 Keep your presentations short, interesting and to-the-point. Long PowerPoints and boring speeches can easily ruin the atmosphere surrounding your event.

> 📌 One of the most important elements in the design of a great event programme is to make sure that you provide your participants with all the information they need. If the different sessions are held in different places, don't forget to indicate this clearly in the

> programme notes. Also remember to always put the starting and finishing times of each session. It is crucial that your programme does not create doubt or confusion. Make everything as clear as possible.

 Although people go to congresses and business events to learn, they also possess valuable knowledge of their own. Create opportunities that will allow them to share this knowledge. For example, in teamwork sessions where the participants can talk and exchange ideas with each other on different subjects.

Do you want to attract and hold the full attention of your participants? One of the best ways to do this is to intersperse the 'intellectual' sessions with a little bit of exercise that will get a healthy portion of fresh air into their brains. Back this up with light and healthy catering, which does not leave them feeling overfull. At a congress, you can plan these exercise moments into your programme as separate sessions or short intermezzos; for example, when there is a brief lull between speakers. These moments should be low threshold and not too intense: no one wants to spend the rest of the day sitting in sweaty clothes! Short yoga sessions, breathing exercises or tips for better body posture are all possibilities. And why not: perhaps even a massage workshop? Alternatively, you can take your participants outdoors for an open-air brainstorming walk. All these options freshen up both body and mind. As a result, everyone will remain more alert during the subsequent sessions. The real no-no is to offer them too much sugar-rich food in the course of the day. This is almost guaranteed to send them to sleep (more about this in chapter 10).

THEME

To strengthen the objective of your event, you can choose to work with a central theme or story line, which links the different elements in the programme. It takes time and creativity to develop an original theme of this kind, but it is certainly worth the effort, if you can pull it off. If you have an interesting story to tell, you will stand out from the crowd – and will therefore be able to distinguish yourself from your competitors.

Through the use of certain emphases, you can insert your chosen theme into each aspect of your programme. Are you organising an event on a boat? If so, it might be a fun idea to send out invitations in the form of a boarding pass. And you can give a similarly nautical flavour to your music, acts, decoration, use of colours, catering, etc.

A theme contributes to the participants' overall experience of your event. Just how far you wish to take this depends on a number of different factors. It is self-evident, for example, that an 'only white' party (all-white attire) will immediately create a unique atmosphere of connectedness among your guests. And if you transport them back to the Middle Ages or into the world of Harry Potter, they will soon feel part of a story that will be talked about for a long, long time.

Having a specific theme also makes it easier to bring clarity to your event programme, because it means that you can instantly see whether a programme idea matches this theme or not.

> Events agencies are not only good at taking work off your hands; they are also past-masters when it comes to developing and implementing creative ideas. In this way, you can avoid stale concepts and boring clichés.

EVENT CONCEPTS
AND VISITOR EXPERIENCE

To create a really strong event, which can satisfy even the most complex and demanding objectives, you will need to show a little more daring and imagination. A well-filled programme with an original theme is not always enough. In order to really get through to your audience, you need to provide them with a genuine experience, an experience that will linger long in their memory. If you are able to engage people's emotions in this manner, you will be better able to build up long-term, sustainable relations and they will be quicker to pick up and accept your message. The art of creating this kind of experience consists in the development of a total concept with a high WOW!-factor.

Create a total experience to truly convince your target group.

But what is an 'experience'? The Oxford English Dictionary describes it (amongst other things) as 'a discovery' and 'an inner transformation'. In other words, an experience occurs when our senses are stimulated in a certain way. Experiences can arise spontaneously in everyday life, but they can also be orchestrated during an event in a deliberate manner which plays on the senses of the participants to achieve a particular reaction or objective. Over a longer period, all the experiences developed around a particular product or brand will to a large extent determine the **image** of that product or brand.

In order to create an experience of this kind, it is necessary to follow a number of basic rules. First and foremost, an experience must **stimulate the senses**. This will provoke a physical reaction amongst the audience, such as laughter or amazement. The experience must also induce a sense of **involvement** and **commitment** amongst the audience. Just how **impressive** the experience needs to be will depend on the nature of your target group and your objective. It is important that you have a good understanding of how the group thinks and feels, so that you can judge what kind of reaction might work with them. Finally, an experience needs to be an **exceptional happening** or series of happenings, which momentarily transports your target group away from the reality of everyday life.

A strong concept seeks to play on the imagination of your target group, exciting their sense of fantasy and exploiting the zone of uncertainty which exists between curiosity and confusion. The gradual build-up of tension and excitement ensures a lasting effect. Once you have experienced something of this kind, you are not likely to forget it in a hurry! Even so, remember to keep your own feet firmly on the ground. Your experience needs to be spectacular, but it must also be capable of practical implementation. It is also important that the experience is in keeping with your company culture and the image you are trying to project.

> 📌 Check what kind of events your company has already organised in the past. Never try to repeat the same 'stunt' a second time. Also keep an eye on what your competitors are doing. You obviously don't want to do the same thing, but you will need to do something that at least reaches the same level of experience.

> 📌 More and more guests are expecting the organisation of 'green' events, which take account of the need for sustainable and socially-responsible enterprise. By consciously opting to minimise the ecological footprint of your event you will – in some circles, at least – enhance the image of your company and underline your message in a positive way. Nowadays, this is a 'must'. Although first and foremost, of course, you should be doing it for the environment…

Do not forget that a good event experience also depends on little things, such as the smoothness of the registration process, the warmth of the initial welcome, and so on. Is there somewhere I can leave my coat safely? Can you call a taxi for me? Taking account of all these seemingly 'minor' aspects is known in the event sector as User Experience Design or UX Design for short.

▶ www.eventplanner.net/book/tv-uxdesign

Don't just think in visual terms, but try and find ways to stimulate all the senses, particularly with smells and sounds. Particular fragrances and music have been shown to influence purchasing behaviour, whereas others can stimulate hunger and thirst. These are all elements you can use to create a unique visitor experience.

The hero's journey

To turn an event into a truly unforgettable experience, you can make use of a template derived from literature. In the 1940s, Joseph Campbell discovered that the most powerful and most memorable fairy tales and stories were all based on the same model. He called this model 'the hero's journey'. Even today, a variant of this template is still used in Hollywood to increase the impact of modern films, with *Star Wars*, *Harry Potter* and *The Lord of the Rings* amongst the most recent examples. If it is possible for films, which only appeal to two of our senses (sight and hearing), to transport people to a different world and immerse them in a powerful experience, this opens up huge possibilities for events that are able to work on all five senses.

Campbell's original model consisted of 12 stages. I have combined two of these stages in 'the return journey' to make the template slightly simpler for events. Here are the remaining 11 stages:

ACT 1

1. **The ordinary world**
Every hero has an ordinary world in which he lives. Superman is a journalist. Harry Potter lives amongst 'muggles' (people without magic powers). This normal world should be recognisable for your event participants and must stand in stark contrast with the wonderful world in which the rest of your event story will unfold. In an event, your guests are the heroes and you will transport them to a magical place where special things happen. Think back to the example of Tomorrowland that I mentioned earlier in the book. Of course, this magical place does not always have to be a castle full of wizards and for business events it can certainly be more subtle and restrained. Dreamforce, the annual congress of Salesforce with more than 180,000 visitors, is an excellent example of how you can give a business event an inspiring theme. They opt for a 'camp ground' concept, with park rangers and animals who direct visitors around the site. As a general rule,

however, it is true that the more 'out of the ordinary' the world in which you immerse your participants, the more intense their event experience will be.

2. **The call to action: adventure**
   Something happens that forces the hero to take action. This can be a threat, but also an inner desire that gets stronger and stronger. It does not need to be as dramatic as a gunshot or bolt of lightning. It could be a simple telephone call or unexpected news that throws the hero's ordinary world into chaos. This is the crux of the story, around which everything subsequently revolves. It is the hero's 'why' – or in writer's terms, 'the story question'.

   Can you see the parallel with the invitations you will send out for your event, which will suddenly arrive in the mail boxes of your heroes/guests? For them, it is a call to travel to another place, to enter a new world with people they have never met before. This is where your event experience starts, the moment when you ask your guests to take part in your adventure.

    Try to make the invitations for your event something special. Do something that your guests will not expect. A handwritten note, a package with a small gift, etc.

3. **Refusal of the call: resistance**
   Heroes can also feel afraid and will not necessarily be willing to answer the call/invitation. There is resistance.

   This will also be the first natural reaction of many of your invitees. They will ask themselves whether or not the event is too expensive or too far away. Or whether they have the time. Or is the theme really something that can benefit them. As an event planner, it is important to think in advance about the arguments that you will use to counter these possible objections. Some organisations even go so far as to place a 'convince your boss' section on their website, which potential participants can use to persuade their own managers to let them take part.

4. **Meeting the mentor**
   At this crucial moment of doubt and resistance, the hero needs a mentor who can give him advice, training or perhaps even an important object, like a magic wand. Every story has its Gandalf or Yoda. This is the turning

point, but the mentor role does not have to be a human one. It can be a book, a map or anything else that sparks a change of heart in the hero. Whatever form the mentoring takes, it removes the hero's doubts and fears, giving him the strength to start out on his quest.

With an event, this mentor function can be performed by a video, a website or a folder, as long as its purpose is to eliminate any last doubts your invitees might have and persuade them to finally take the plunge. Whichever form you choose, always ensure that your mentor is clearly focused on its task and sticks closely to your theme and storyline.

ACT 2

5. **Crossing the threshold**
The hero is ready for his adventure. He crosses the threshold between his ordinary world and your new event world. This transitional moment can have even greater impact if he passes through a gateway with gatekeepers who reveal to him the magical secrets of this new world.

The entrance to your event also needs to fulfil this same special function. From the moment your guests arrive, you must lead them into your theme-based décor that will allow them to discover and be enthralled by your new world. Some events begin even earlier than arrival at the venue; for example, when a guest arrives by plane at an airport and is given a special welcome.

6. **Tests, allies and enemies**
The hero has now entered a new world, where different rules apply. He needs to go in search of information and allies. In many Hollywood movies, we see our hero in an old pub, where he learns more about his new environment and meets the people who will become his friends and his enemies. His new situation confronts him with a series of tests that he must successfully complete and will make him stronger for the ordeal that still lies ahead.

At events, your heroes will also go in search of allies in the shape of hostesses, mascots or actors, who will show them the way to follow. During networking sessions, other guests will do the same. In this context, the idea of an enemy should not be taken too literally, but rather metaphorically. For example, one of the most important reasons for taking part in an event is to learn something. To make this possible, however, it is necessary to be open for new opinions and ideas. Your greatest enemy is therefore sometimes yourself and your greatest challenge is to free yourself from your own prejudices and preconceptions. Alternatively – depending on your event story and the extent to which you are able to immerse your guests in it – you can also sometimes give the enemy a concrete form in the shape of a figure against whom all the event participants must struggle together.

7. **The darkest depths**
The 'darkest depths' can represent many things in the hero's story, such as a location where terrible danger lies in wait or an inner conflict that the hero has not yet had to confront. Before he descends into these darkest depths, he makes his necessary preparations. This is a moment when doubts and resistance may once again rise to the surface, serving to make clear the nature and scale of the ordeal that the hero will soon have to face.

As an event planner, you can replicate this phase of the hero's journey in a number of different ways. For a concert, this might be a warm-up band that sets the stage for the main act that is to follow. For a congress, it might be a workshop or a chairman for the day who helps to prepare your guests for the most challenging part of your event.

8. **The ordeal**
This is a dangerous physical trial or a deep inner crisis that the hero needs to survive. He must use all his talents to overcome his enemy. It is only through some form of 'death' that the hero can be reborn, granting him the new power or insight necessary to fulfil his destiny or reach his journey's end. This is the high-point of the hero's story, where everything important to him is put at risk.

This is also the point where you should programme the climax of your event. For example, the spectacular entry of the concert's superstar, who then gives a stunning performance, or a speaker whose radical insights turn your guests' thinking on its head. Alternatively, you can also organise a real 'ordeal'; for example, a serious test (either physical or mental) that your participants need to complete during a teambuilding event.

9. **The reward**
After the ordeal comes the reward. In stories and films, we often see the hero celebrating around a camp fire, sharing the moment with his closest companions and loved ones.

For your event participants, this reward can take many different forms: a book about the congress, a diploma, the new friends they have made, the new business contacts they have met.

ACT 3

10. **The return journey**

The adventure is not yet over. The hero still needs to show to the world how his ordeal has changed him. And sometimes he also requires one last push or must overcome one last challenge before he can return to the ordinary world.

Every event must have a finale, a final act or surprise for your guests. An encore after a concert, a reception after a congress. Once again, small things can make a big difference. At the end of the event, do not simply abandon your guests and let them walk off to their cars, trains or planes. Just as you gave them a warm welcome, always find a way to give them an equally warm send-off. Let the illusion last for a little longer...

11. **Elixir**

This is the final stage of the hero's journey in which he returns home to his ordinary world a changed man. He has grown as a person and acquired many new skills and insights. This is the elixir that he brings back with him. He can now do things that he could never do before.

The elixir of your event might be the new knowledge that your guests take away with them and can share with others once back at home. Or it might be the experience itself, which will always stay fresh in their minds. In my definition of an event earlier in the book, I said that its purpose is to bring about a change in behaviour. This is the moment when that change must occur.

It is up to you as an event planner to choose a theme and decide how far you wish to implement the 'hero's journey' concept in your event. In part, this will be dependent on the nature of your target group and your objectives. But even the most business-like events can benefit from the application of this model, either wholly or partially, because it makes possible the better alignment of the different elements of your programme in an interesting yet subtle manner. True, this will require a great deal of creativity on your part. But this creativity is what separates the truly excellent event planner from the rest. The closer you can stay to a single theme, the easier your task becomes and the intenser the resulting experience will be for your guests. Why not let your event take place in a magical fairy tale setting? Are you afraid to accept the challenge? I hope not! Remember, however, that it

> *Properly implementing the hero's journey demands great* **creativity**, *but that is what separates the truly excellent event planner from the rest.*

will be the way you develop and implement the theme and your attention to detail that will decide whether your story is credible or whether it descends into pure kitsch.

 Provide a (personalised) memento for each of your guests that reflects your theme. Was your event inspired by Harry Potter? Why not give each of them a magic wand with their name on it? Or a series of cards with appropriate sayings or quotes. Mementos of this kind will help your guests to continue enjoying the experience even after the event is over.

 Let your event start from the moment your guests get into their car at home by organising a live radio show with all the latest updates. This will immerse them in your story before they even arrive at the venue, so that they are immediately in the right mood.

You can view an example of how the 'hero's journey' model can be applied to an event in the following video on eventplanner tv:

www.eventplanner.net/book/tv-hero

Gamification

More and more events are making use of gamification to motivate their guests, to involve them more actively in the programme and to increase their overall level of experience satisfaction. This is achieved by using gaming techniques in a non-game environment.

Children are not the only ones who like to play games. Many adults are also fervent gamers, in the broadest sense of the word. Computer games, board games, quizzes: it makes no difference. Competition in all its forms makes us more alert and encourages us to action more quickly. This can also be useful in an event setting.

Gamification can find expression in small things, like the awarding of points or badges when the guests have filled in their profile on your website or in the event app. TripAdvisor and LinkedIn both use this technique to collect more information about their visitors. Of course, more obvious game techniques

can also be used. What about solving a riddle to reveal the 'secret' location of your venue? And once the event has started, the number of gaming possibilities is almost limitless. For example, you can use gamification to stimulate networking at a congress or increase the number of visits to stall holders at an exhibition.

Another popular gaming option is to organise a quiz at the end of each presentation. If you announce in advance that there will be a fun prize for the winner, this instantly increases people's attention for what the speaker has to say. But be careful! Revealing scores isn't always a good idea. This might make a few of the smarter participants happy, but the rest will not want to hear how badly they performed! A short quiz with a quick announcement of the winner is fine. But a general scoreboard that is visible all day will not have the effect you desire. Of course, the quiz does not always have to have a winner. Playing for playing's sake, just to test your knowledge, can also be fun.

Sometimes a boring presentation or the content of a difficult workshop can be replaced by a board game that seeks to teach people the necessary lessons in a playful manner. Because the participants engage actively with the new knowledge and can apply it immediately, the key points are more easily memorised. Having said that, gamification can never compensate for a complete lack of enthusiasm among your public. If your target group has no interest in your message, then even the most fascinating game in the world can do little to change this. In fact, it might irritate them more.

Building play elements into teambuilding is nothing new. Games help to create a strong bond between people. If you give teams a challenging riddle, a complicated puzzle or a difficult obstacle course, they will immediately start collaborating to find the desired solution. People who hardly know each other will join forces to make sure that their team wins.

Remember, however, that gamification must always add something to your event. Using a game just because it is popular or fun is more likely to distract people than to help them understand your message. Think carefully about your public and what you want to achieve. Not everyone can be convinced by playing games.

 Always try out a game in advance on a test public. Is it fun? Is it not too complicated? Does it contain any flaws or mistakes.? Does it achieve the purpose you want? The answers to these questions will allow you to make any adjustments that are necessary.

www.eventplanner.net/book/tv-gamification

Creating concepts

To arrive at such a concept, there are different techniques you can use to stimulate your own creativity and the creativity of your team. The two most popular of these creative-thinking techniques are:

- **Brainstorming**
  Brainstorming is a technique designed to result in a rapid flow of new ideas on a particular subject. Everybody takes part and just writes down on a post-it note the first ideas that spring into their head, without really thinking them through. All the post-it notes are then stuck on the wall, where everyone can see them.

  The basic rules:
  - The ideas generated during a brainstorming must **not be criticised** by others. The wildest ideas are allowed. However crazy they may seem, they make possible new angles of approach and may trigger others to come up with even better ideas.
  - The purpose in the first instance is to encourage **quantity rather than quality**. The underlying idea of a brainstorming session is that by process-

ing as many ideas as possible a single good idea or new line of thought may perhaps emerge.
- **1 + 1 = 3.** By combining ideas, new and better ideas may arise.

It is only after the brainstorming session has finished that you remove all the unusable ideas and rank all the useable ones in order of merit.

✓ **Mind-mapping**
Mind-mapping is a very visual way of brainstorming. You note down a theme or subject in the centre of a piece of paper. Around this theme or subject, you jot down all the words that spontaneously come into your head. In a next stage, you look for new associations between the words that have been written down. Draw arrows between the words you add and the words that have already been written.

Do you need further inspiration? Find it in books and films, read eventplanner.net or use AI to generate new ideas.

HYBRID & ONLINE EVENTS

In our busy modern world, it is not always possible for everyone to be physically present at an event. As a result, it is hardly surprising that hybrid and online events are becoming increasingly popular. In fact, following the corona virus crisis online events have even become the new norm. A hybrid event consists of a live element (the physical event itself) and an online element that people can follow at a distance. With an online event, everything happens (as the name suggests) online.

Before we can talk of a hybrid or online event in the proper sense of the term, it is necessary for the online element to be more than a live video stream. There must also be interaction. The experience that you offer to the online participants must, of course, be based on the fundamentals of your event, but adjusted to reflect their specific expectations. Even with a live event it is not always easy to hold the attention of your participants, but with an online audience the challenge is greater still. In other words, when you are planning a online event it is crucial, from the concept phase onwards, to take proper account of the content and the interactive experience you want to offer to your online participants. This is the only way to focus their attention and secure their commitment.

Why organise a hybrid or online event?

Are you organising an event for invitees from all over the world? If so, the chances that everyone will attend are relatively small. But even with smaller, local events, there will always be some people who are unable to be present. In these circumstances, it may be better to only invite your most important and most interested contacts, providing an alternative and less expensive option (both in terms of time and money) for the rest of your target group. After all, some people might only be marginally interested in the subject under discussion. But people who might otherwise never attend your event might be enticed to participate if you offer them a live feed. This will allow you to reach an entirely new public. And a wider reach is always interesting for potential sponsors. What's more, it can also work the other way around: sometimes it is keynote speakers from other parts of the world who are unable to attend in person. But this is something that can be made possible through a video link.

> **Hybrid events allow you to reach new target groups. Try to be creative. In this way, the extra cost of transmitting your event live on the internet can be turned into an additional source of income.**

One of the biggest fears of the organisers of this kind of event is that all the invitees will participate online and that no one will actually turn up at the event venue. From our experience of many different kinds of events, we can conclude that this type of 'cannibalism' seldom occurs. It is simply not possible to compare the two different forms of participation in an event – live or via the internet. Nowadays, one of the main reasons that people like to come to events is so that they can extend their personal network of contacts. This is not possible if you only follow the event online. After all, cinemas have not closed down simply because DVDs and more recently Netflix are now available on the market! Of course, the cinemas have had to adjust, but there is no reason why events should not do the same. It is the same story with sport. Many people like to watch sporting events from the comfort of their living room armchair, but this does not mean that people no longer go to the stadiums. In fact, precisely the opposite! There are more 'live' supporters than ever before. And this is also true of events. In practice, the organisers of strong events often see that a live feed acts as a stimulus for people to actually make the effort to come to the event venue next time around. It gives the absentees the chance to see what they are missing!

Another advantage of recording your event for live streaming is that afterwards you can offer it for further use (paid or not) in an on-demand environment. In other words, a kind of Netflix for congresses and events. Consider, for example, the popularity of the online video site on TEDx.

Format

If you are looking for a good starting point for the organisation of a successful internet broadcast, you can do worse than to draw your inspiration from the classic TV-formats. Your invitees will be familiar with these formats and this will immediately create an environment with which they are comfortable.

Rather like a chairman at a live event, your presenter can guide your virtual audience step by step through your programme. The difference with a classic TV show is the level of possible interaction. Online viewers can vote, ask questions, interact with each other and lots more besides. And except for small events, it is a good idea to also set up a separate online team that can not only monitor all interactions via chat sessions, social media, etc., but is also responsible for the technical aspects of the internet link. Making television is a job apart, so make sure you use specialists!

While the guests at your live event are enjoying a coffee break, you can conduct a screened discussion with your speakers or ask some of the live participants to comment on what they have already heard. Online guests seldom follow the full programme, but tend to pick out the elements that are most interesting to them. For this reason it is useful to make a programme guide that details which topics will be discussed and when, just like a TV magazine. In this way, your virtual participants will know exactly when to tune in and tune out.

 Remember to ask your speakers or performers for their permission to broadcast their contributions online. Many big names are reluctant to do this.

There are different types of hybrid event:

- ✔ **Individual.**
  Online participants follow the event individually or in small groups, seated in front of their computers.

- ✔ **Pod/remote location.**
  You can also opt to organise your event at different locations, which you can then link via a live transmission. Most applications of this technique involve a main event and a number of subsidiary local pods, although that does not always have to be the case. Various different forms of interaction and communication between the different locations are possible.

✓ **Studio.**
You can also broadcast recordings where no live public is present. With this option, people participate in the event in a 'remote' mode, so that the professional quality of the recordings is more important than with the previous forms.

> 📌 Do you really want to score with your live stream? You will need to launch a separate marketing campaign to attract the necessary viewers.

> 📌 Why not also give your online guests a digital goody bag? For example, you can share a Spotify list with the music of your event, interesting downloads and/or voucher codes. There are plenty of options.

Interaction

As with 'classic' events, such as congresses, interaction usually creates an added value both for and with the public. If you are working online, you have various interactive tools at your disposal. For example, there are chat options that will allow online viewers to ask questions. By imposing certain limits, you can keep the discussions manageable and can also allow questions to be asked by both people at the actual event venue and by people who are participating online (for example, through an online presenter). X and other social media are also ideal for giving feedback for hybrid events. You can even use the same #hashtag as for the live event. But if this is too confusing, a separate hashtag for online participants is also possible. See chapter 7 for more information about choosing the right hashtag and monitoring social media.

> 📌 Live streaming demands plenty of specialised technical know-how. For this reason, it is better to use the services of a specialist company.

PRACTICAL EXAMPLE

The organisers of an international congress in Poland were thrown into confusion when a plane carrying the Polish president crashed, followed a few days later by the eruption of the Eyjafjöll volcano in Iceland, which completely disrupted international air travel in Europe. All the speakers and participants in the congress were grounded, so that almost no one could get to the physical venue. Fortunately, the organisers were smart enough to quickly develop an alternative plan. Just a few days before the congress was due to start, they moved the entire event into a virtual environment, so that the participants could follow the programme on their computers and the speakers could give their presentations via their webcams.

Business model

'Online' does not necessarily mean that everything must be free. If you have a strong programme in terms of content, people may well be prepared to pay to follow your event online. There are also numerous possibilities to create extra visibility for your sponsors, for which they will be prepared to pay good money. Try to be creative. In this way, you can turn the extra cost of broadcasting your event online into an extra source of income.

Briefing

The briefing forms a bridge between the plan and its implementation. The briefing contains all the information that your suppliers and service providers need in order to carry out their tasks correctly. Make sure that you provide sufficient detail, so that everyone knows exactly what you require. In this way, you can avoid unpleasant surprises. Set the relevant information down on paper in good time – otherwise your suppliers will not be able to start!

A briefing helps to make a number of matters clear, but must be more than just the issuing of a set of military-like commands. If you give them room for initiative, your suppliers will often use their wide experience to come up with new and surprising ideas that can take your event to a higher level. For this reason, it is important to send them your briefing sufficiently far in advance and involve as many of them as possible from an early stage. The speakers and/or acts for your event, who you normally invite later on in the preparation process, might also have some excellent ideas for your programme.

Four elements

A good briefing contains information about your company, the event, what you expect from the suppliers and (last but definitely not least) the budget. If you have put your event fully in the hands of an events agency, you will only need to draw up a general briefing. If you have allocated specific elements to several outsider suppliers, you will need to do a separate briefing for each supplier. Make sure that the information is clear and complete. If you fail to do this, there is a real risk of misunderstandings and unnecessary loss of time.

COMPANY

In the first part of your briefing, give the supplier a short summary of general information about your company. Your annual reports and info-folders say much about your mission and vision, as well as adding practical details about the number of employees, main products, core tasks, etc. Also provide insight into your marketing and communication strategy. What is the style and tone of your company? What image are you trying to project? The more background information you can give, the better.

If you have chosen to use an external service supplier, and certainly if you are working with an events agency, it is useful to invite them for a guided tour of your company. By chatting to your colleagues and getting a feel for the atmosphere of the place, the supplier or agency will be able to better tailor his/her proposal to your objectives.

EVENT

In this section of the briefing you must provide all necessary information about the planned event. Give a short summary of the preparations which you have made in accordance with the guidelines discussed in the previous chapters. The supplier must be given answers to the following questions:

- ✔ What is your '**why**'?
- ✔ What is the **objective** of the event?
- ✔ Who are the **target group**? What is the profile of the target group?
- ✔ When will the event take place? **Date, duration and time**?
- ✔ What is the **central theme**, the red thread of the event?
- ✔ What does your ideal event programme look like?
- ✔ What **communication** is foreseen? Which channels (internal/external) are available for use?
- ✔ Has a **venue** already been chosen; if so, where?

SUPPLIER

Every supplier needs a clear picture of what you expect from him. Tell him the things you consider to be important, but also tell him what you do not want.

If possible, avoid giving a simple list of resources, conditions and ideas of your own. This will limit the creativity of the supplier and means that you will almost certainly not get an out-of-the-box idea as a result. Instead, offer a description of the atmosphere, quality and style you are looking for. Give the supplier the opportunity to come up with one or more ideas of his/her own. Then you can decide the final direction you want to take.

 Appoint just a single person to liaise with the supplier. If you have multiple suppliers, appoint a person to be responsible for each of them. In this way, you will avoid the possibility that the supplier will receive conflicting information from different people. In return, ask each supplier for a SPOC (= Single Point of Contact).

> Set clear deadlines and provide the suppliers with a clear timetable. Watch out for a domino-effect. If your tent-builder turns up late, the rest of your planning will be at risk.

When you are preparing a briefing for an event bureau, wedding planner or event decorator, a mood board can often help you to get your ideas and expectations across more clearly. With our eventplanner.net software you can make simple mood boards that you can share with your team and on which you can work with them or other partners. You can also collect and share all the event venues, suppliers, articles, posts and even internet links listed on our platform.

www.eventplanner.net/book/eventsoftware

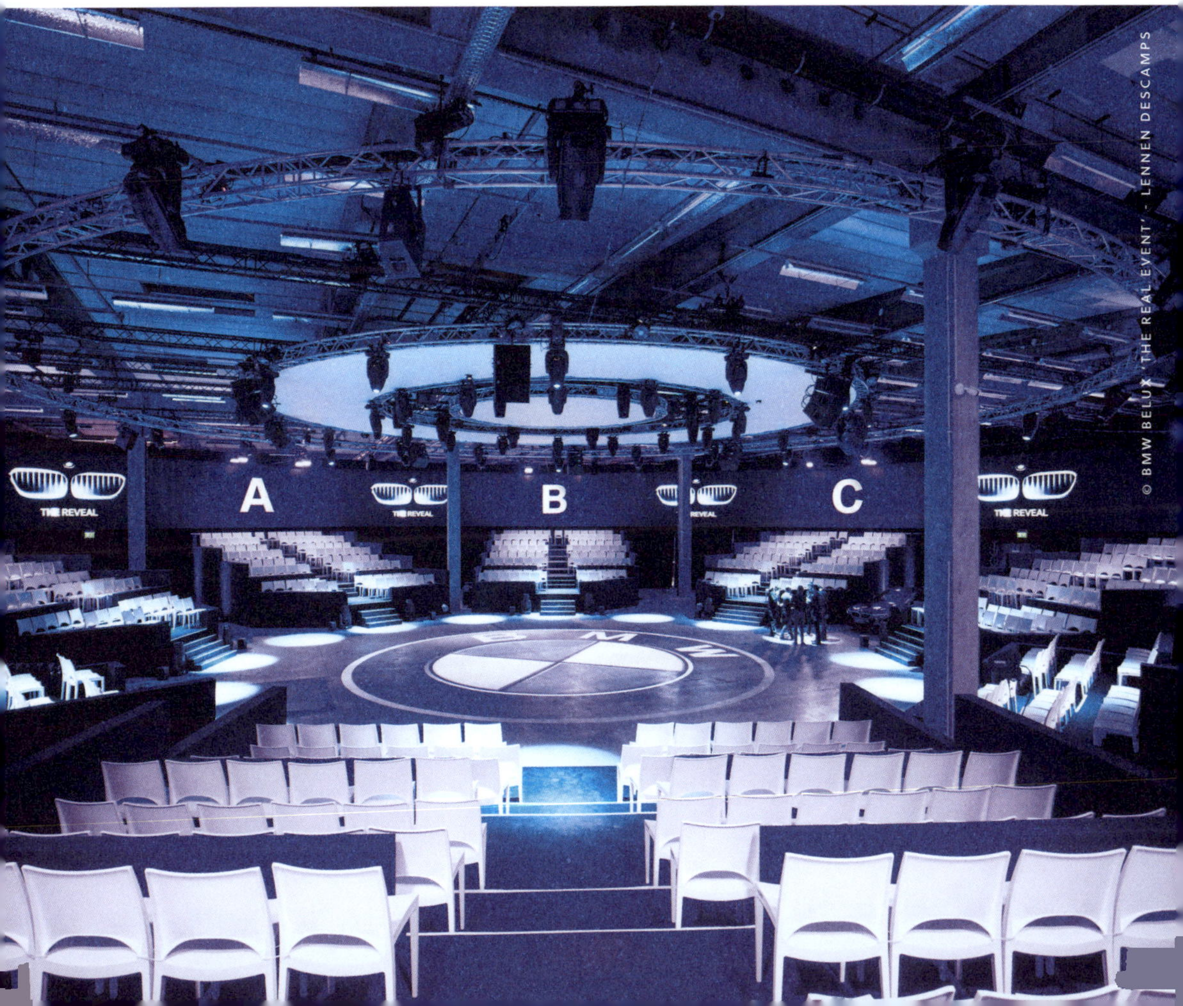

© BMW BELUX 'THE REAL EVENT' - LENNEN DESCAMPS

BUDGET

Do you book Coldplay for your event or are you happy with the local brass band? The way you put together your programme is not only a question of creativity: it is often a question of money. Be open and honest with your suppliers about your budget. A realistic budget assessment can save you plenty of time and disappointment ('This is a bit expensive. Can you come up with something that costs 7,500 dollars less?'). If you are giving a briefing to two or more potential suppliers, it is impossible to make a valid comparison without proper budget details.

 Don't forget to mention the internal project number that you are using for the event.

EVENT BRIEFING

Even after you have chosen your event suppliers, further briefings will still be necessary. These often relate to practical information that you wish to share in addition to your action plan, such as security arrangements or the behaviour that you expect from your event personnel. Once again our eventplanner.net software can help you to prepare these briefings, including generic sections for everyone involved in the event, specific sections for specific partners (for example, 'all caterers') and even individual additions. A clear briefing with all relevant information but without unnecessary detail will help to ensure a better and safer event.

Promote your event

People's appointment books get full very quickly. This not only means that you need to launch your marketing campaign and send out your invitations well in advance of the planned date of your event, but also that these elements must persuade the invitee to make some of his valuable free time available in order to attend. The first impression that your invitation makes, that first telling glance, can make all the difference between a positive response and the dustbin. For this reason, you need to devote considerable care to the design of your invitation card and/or campaign. They need to excite people's interest and curiosity. After all, invitation is part of the art of seduction and, as previously mentioned, it also marks the effective start of your event experience!

One glance can mean the difference between acceptance and the dustbin.

GUEST LIST

Are you organising an event for invitees only? If so, your first task is to draw up a guest list. Compiling guest lists is time-consuming work. However, you cannot afford to make mistakes. It is an unforgivable sin to forget someone who should be invited. Ask the help of other departments when you are putting your guest list together. Check with marketing, sales and purchasing. Who do they want you to invite? And don't forget your prospects! If you are organising an internal event, ask the opinion of the human resources manager.

Use your target group description as the basis for your selection. For example, who are 'loyal customers' and who are not. Be consistent in your choice. If you fail to do this, you will soon have an 'out-of-control' guest list with far too many people. This can have serious consequences for your budget.

 If you are organising an internal event, don't forget retired staff, part-time workers, freelancers and even former employees. Try not to forget anyone: cleaners, drivers, etc.

📌 Has your factory recently been rebuilt or radically altered? Why not invite local people and local officials to come and have a look? Perhaps they were inconvenienced during the building works? If so, this is a good way to repay their patience and build up some goodwill at the same time. Open communication can help you to counteract the negative effects of rumour and gossip. You can approach action groups in exactly the same way. Giving people the chance to look behind the scenes at what you do in an informal context can often work wonders.

📌 If you have built up a relationship with journalists of one kind or another, it is better to invite them personally. If you do not yet have the right contacts, send an invitation to the editorial desk of potentially relevant newspapers. Even so remember to be careful when dealing with the press. When you issue a press statement or call a press conference, you always have the strings firmly in your own hands. However, during an event your guests have the opportunity to talk more freely. This means that they can influence the atmosphere more easily, so that you can quickly lose control of your message. This is not necessarily a bad thing, but you need to be aware of the possibility.

📌 Some organisers make a back-up guest list. This is a list of people who can replace people on the A-list, if these are unable to attend. This can be useful, for example, if you are organising a congress, when it always makes a much better impression to have a full hall.

Make the style of address in the invitation as personal as possible, but ensure that the details (titles, names, gender, etc.) are all correct. A mistake in matters of this kind comes across as being very unprofessional and will negatively affect the way the invitee looks at your invitation. Where possible, be aware of and avoid impinging on personal dramas. Do not send a 'Mr. & Mrs.' invitation to a colleague who has just lost his wife. Obviously, it is more difficult to check this kind of information for external contacts, but it is unforgivable to make this type of error for internal events. It may be wise to ask the HR manager to have a last look at your invitation list before you put the envelopes in the post.

INVITATIONS

A good invitation must be eye-catching, intriguing and exciting. Try to persuade your target group with a combination of rational and emotional arguments. Why should they come to your event? How can you persuade them to give up some of their precious free time? Some guests will only take part if there are good networking possibilities; others are partial to expert presentations by leading professionals in their field. You should also try to play on their emotions, but this will only work if you do it in the right manner. It has been mentioned before, but it bears repeating: you must know how your target group thinks and feels! Invitations differ according to the function of the people you are trying to attract. An invitation for an executive will not be the same as an invitation for a sales rep. Remember to adjust the form, style, tone, language and colour to suit your target group and the story behind your event. Never promise anything you cannot deliver.

 A short and clear message always works best. Avoid too much text. Emphasise the date and venue as eye catchers.

 Use the framework of the previously mentioned 'hero's journey' for your invitation trajectory. Provide a 'mentor' who can remove all doubts and objections.

While you obviously need to stress the importance of the event itself, also explain why the presence of the invitee is so crucial to its success. Your guests need to feel important. But don't be too blatant with your flattery. Subtle hints are better and make your event seem more exclusive. Also emphasise what's in it for them. What is the direct benefit that they can gain from the event? Knowledge? New contacts?

Your creativity and originality should already start with the envelope. An elegant invitation does not belong in a boring impersonal envelope. Are you trying to attract people who you know have a busy professional life? Send a warm-up letter or a 'teaser'. If their curiosity is aroused, this allows them to keep the date free in their diary. Or you may prefer to send a 'save-the-date' message by e-mail. Always use the same style and layout. It is important that all your communications can be directly and visually linked to your event

For some events, it can be useful to place a list of the people who are planning to attend on your website. This might encourage others to come. Some of your invitees will only be interested if they know that some of their key contacts or competitors are likely to be present. First make sure, however, that you have permission from all your guests to publish their personal details!

Essential information

The amount of information contained in your invitation will vary from event to event. However, some information is so essential that it always needs to be included. You would not be the first event planner who forgot to mention the date of the event! (Yes, it has really happened.)

- **Who?**
  Who is organising the event? Who is receiving an invitation? What kind of public will be present (trade, press, etc.)?

- **What?**
  What can your guests expect? What is on the programme? Unless, of course, this needs to be kept as a surprise. Even so, always try to arouse the invitee's curiosity.

- **Where?**
  Where is the event taking place? How do you get there and where can you park? Include a map and a route plan, which takes account of people approaching from different directions.

- **When?**
  What is the date of your event? At what time are the guests expected to arrive? Is there an official closing time?

- **Why?**
  What is the purpose of the event?

- **Response**
  How can you register your attendance? By what date do you have to do this? To whom should the invitees address any questions they might have (telephone number, e-mail address, contact person)?

Is there something out of the ordinary about your event? Do you expect something extra from your guests? Remember to mention it on the invitation.

- Are **partners and/or children** invited (or not)?
- Is a particular type of clothing desired? What is the **dress code**?
- Is the invitation a **personal** one, or can it be passed on to a colleague or (business) partner?
- Admission charges, conditions, etc.

Is it necessary for your invitees to let you know whether they are coming or not? If so, make this clear on the invitation. Even though it is essentially a matter of politeness to reply to an invitation, not everyone will do it. You can encourage the type of response you want by using one of a standard series of abbreviations. You may need to bear in mind that not everyone will be familiar with the meaning of these abbreviations, so sometimes you will have to spell it out more literally, depending on the target group concerned.

- **RSVP (Répondez, s'il vous plaît).**
  This requests a reply from the invitee, to confirm whether they are coming or not.

- **Regrets only.**
  This is used when only negative replies are necessary.

- **RFSVP (Response favorable s'il vous plaît).**
  This is used when only positive replies are necessary.

 Do not underestimate the influence of partners on the decision of invitees to attend – or not. You must take this factor into account when planning events outside normal working hours.

No-show

It is the day of your big event: everything is ready, hundreds of people have promised to attend, the doors open and… you suddenly discover that half of your invitees have not turned up! To reduce this notorious 'no-show' percentage to a minimum, you can apply the following useful suggestions:

- Send out your **invitations in plenty of time**. It is much easier to persuade people to make time free for your event if they have plenty of warning, so that they don't need to cancel or rearrange other commitments. The ideal moment is four to six weeks in advance. Send a reminder two weeks later to those who have failed to reply (but not, of course, to those who have already replied favourably).

- Make the **registration threshold as low as possible** by using online registration. Also provide an alternative for specific target groups, such as senior citizens, who may not (yet) be familiar with the use of computers. Post is one option. Telephone is another. But don't forget to provide an address or number!

 Provide a personal code for registration purposes. This means that if an invitee is already in your database, he/she does not need to fill in his/her personal details all over again. Also keep your answer form as simple as possible: this mean less administration – for everybody! Or simply use the eventplanner.net software for your guest list.

 Always give your invitees the chance to confirm that they will not be attending.

- Have you received an acceptance registration from someone? Send them an **acknowledgement of receipt**. This is not only polite, but also helps to fix your event more firmly in their memory. The more often you bring the event to their attention, they more committed towards it they are likely to feel. It is therefore a good idea to communicate with them regularly about further updates. Having said this, avoid overkill! Don't overdo it by bombarding them with mails every five minutes!

- Always implement an **active no-show policy**. Some organisers project the names of invitees who have failed to turn up on a large screen during the event, in order to focus attention on this problem. If you think that this is too confrontational, another option – and one that is applied at the networking events of eventplanner.net– is to deny the no-showers access to your following events for a number of months. This approach has halved our no-show percentage from 30% to less than 15%.

Because the no-show problem has now reached dramatic proportions, particularly for free events, more and more organisers are now asking for payment of a deposit (for example, via your credit card). If you turn up, this deposit is refunded in full; if you fail to show, the deposit is retained. Or there is an even subtler alternative: why not ask the no-showers to make a donation to a good cause? Publish your no-show policy clearly in advance, since this is the only way to bring about the much-needed change in invitee behaviour.

▶ www.eventplanner.net/book/tv-noshow

- ✓ Two weeks before the event **telephone** all your invitees who have not yet replied, so that you can invite them again personally.

- ✓ **Personal and informal invitations** are popular and often successful. If you bump into one of your invitees, let him know that you are counting on his attendance. Ask all your colleagues to do the same thing. After all, account managers and reps probably have more daily contact with your customers than you do. They are therefore the ideal people to give this kind of informal invitation.

- ✓ Announcing important **'firsts'** at your event or promising **gifts** and **incentives** are both good strategies for reducing the 'no-show' percentage. Providing, of course, that you communicate them in advance.

Medium

Sending your invitations by e-mail is fast and cheap, and also has the added advantage that it usually arrives at the right person. Moreover, it is a simple matter to link a registration system to an e-mail invitation. The disadvantages, however, are equally obvious. Your invitee probably receives dozens of e-mails every day. What is going to make yours stand out from the crowd, so that it doesn't end up in his virtual dustbin or the spam folder? You are likely to receive a much higher response rate with a personal, printed invitation, sent to a private address. The more original and eye-catching the invitation, the greater the likelihood of acceptance. In other words, you should not use media such as e-mail and/or social media platforms as an exclusive channel of communication, but as a supportive one, which you can include as part of a wider invitation process. Each medium has its own specific target group: for example, e-mail works better on specific target groups than on a scatter group of private hotmail addresses.

> 📌 If you work with a professional e-mail system, you can see who has opened your mail and/or logged on to your registration site. It can sometimes be worth the effort to send a second mail to people who have already shown interest in this way but have not yet registered.

> 📌 Are you sending your invitations by post or courier? Always send one invitation to yourself, so that you can see if for any reason the delivery of the invitations is delayed. This allows you to take corrective action promptly and efficiently.

> 📌 Try to make your invitation stand out in a creative manner. For example, you can send a video invitation on a USB stick or you can place a personal film with your spoken invitation on the Internet. Or you can go old school: handwritten invitations are once again gaining in popularity and can give your event a little extra cachet.

The use of SMSs of WhatsApp messages is also becoming more popular as part of the invitation support process. These channels can easily be integrated into your marketing automation software. For example, you can send a personal access code to the registration site by SMS or issue reminders to your invitees on the day before the event.

Dress code

In most cases, your guests will be free to dress as they please. In most cases – but not always. Sometimes, a particular type of clothing will contribute to the atmosphere of your event or may be necessary because of specific (weather) conditions. For this reason, it is always advisable to refer to the dress code in your invitation. This puts your guests at their ease: they know what you expect and it eliminates the risk that they will arrive inappropriately dressed. But remember never to make unreasonable demands on your guests: there is no point in inviting your factory workers to an event, but then insisting on full evening dress. This simply creates a threshold which increases the likelihood of a non-registration or a no-show. At the same time, it is worth remembering that 'special' clothing can sometimes raise your event to a higher level of sophistication and/or enjoyment. For example, themed clothing or black tie will have an immediate impact on the atmosphere and the intensity of your event experience.

Some of the most common dress codes include:

- ✔ **Evening dress**
  The classic dress code for formal occasions. This means a suit or dinner jacket for the men, and a long dress or two-piece for the ladies.

- **Black tie**
  This gives women the choice between a cocktail dress and a long evening dress, whereas the men are obliged to wear a black dinner jacket with a white shirt.

- **White tie or gala**
  A super-formal dress code, which is only used on very exclusive or ceremonial occasions. The ladies will wear a long gala dress with long gloves, while the gentleman will sport a dinner jacket with a white shirt and a white bow tie.

- **Tuxedo**
  The name says it all. Very similar to black tie. The men must wear dinner jackets and the women a stylish evening dress.

- **Jacket and tie**
  One of the most frequently used dress codes. The men dress in lounge suits (or, as the name suggests, in jacket and tie) and the women dress in a two-piece or an elegant but sober ensemble.

- **Cocktail**
  A fashionable dress code that requires fashionable clothes. Women will opt for a frivolous designer outfit, exuding class and femininity, whereas the men will go for a dark-coloured suit.

- **Festive dress**
  Both men and women wear less formal clothing, but without becoming too casual; a 'well-groomed' look is still required.

- **Casual or informal**
  A more or less wear-what-you-like occasion. This helps to put your guests at their ease, but may detract from the standing of your event.

- **Themed dress**
  Themed dress can be fun. Disco outfits, fancy dress, bal masqué, medieval banquet: there are plenty of possibilities. If you go for this option, make sure that it actually adds something to the event and is a perfect fit with your 'hero's journey' story. In this way, you will be able to reward your guests for making the effort with a truly unique experience.

- **Special dress**
  Rainwear, warm clothing, a change of clothes, etc.

More and more organisers are moving away from traditional dress codes and are opting instead for 'smart casual', 'a touch of red', etc. This is a fun idea, but make sure that your guests properly understand what you intend.

> 📌 Do you want to work with a theme for your dress code? If so, ask the serving staff, the DJ and even the artists to stick as far as possible to the same theme.

> 📌 Not all your guests will arrive fully dressed to match your theme and some guests will not have made the effort at all. Make sure that you always have plenty of accessories on hand, such as hats and boas, that they can use to get them into the right party mood.

> 📌 Nothing is quite so embarrassing for a guest as a tear in a gala dress or a button that comes loose. Check that the receptionists or the toilet attendants have a sewing kit available, so that essential minor repairs can be carried out on the spot. A supply of basic cosmetics in the toilets – hairspray, deodorant, etc. – is also much appreciated.

🔗 www.eventplanner.net/book/attire

CHECKLIST FOR THE INVITATION TRAJECTORY

This checklist with guidelines for timings is ideal for classic business events and private celebrations. For a congress or public event with paid ticketed entry you will need to start your marketing campaign much earlier. You will also need to bring the timings forward when you are organising an event abroad for which your participants will need to travel or when your event is scheduled to take place during a busy and/or holiday period.

> 📌 Do you have any international invitees on your guest list? Take account of the fact that invitations sent abroad will take longer to arrive – and therefore longer to be replied to.

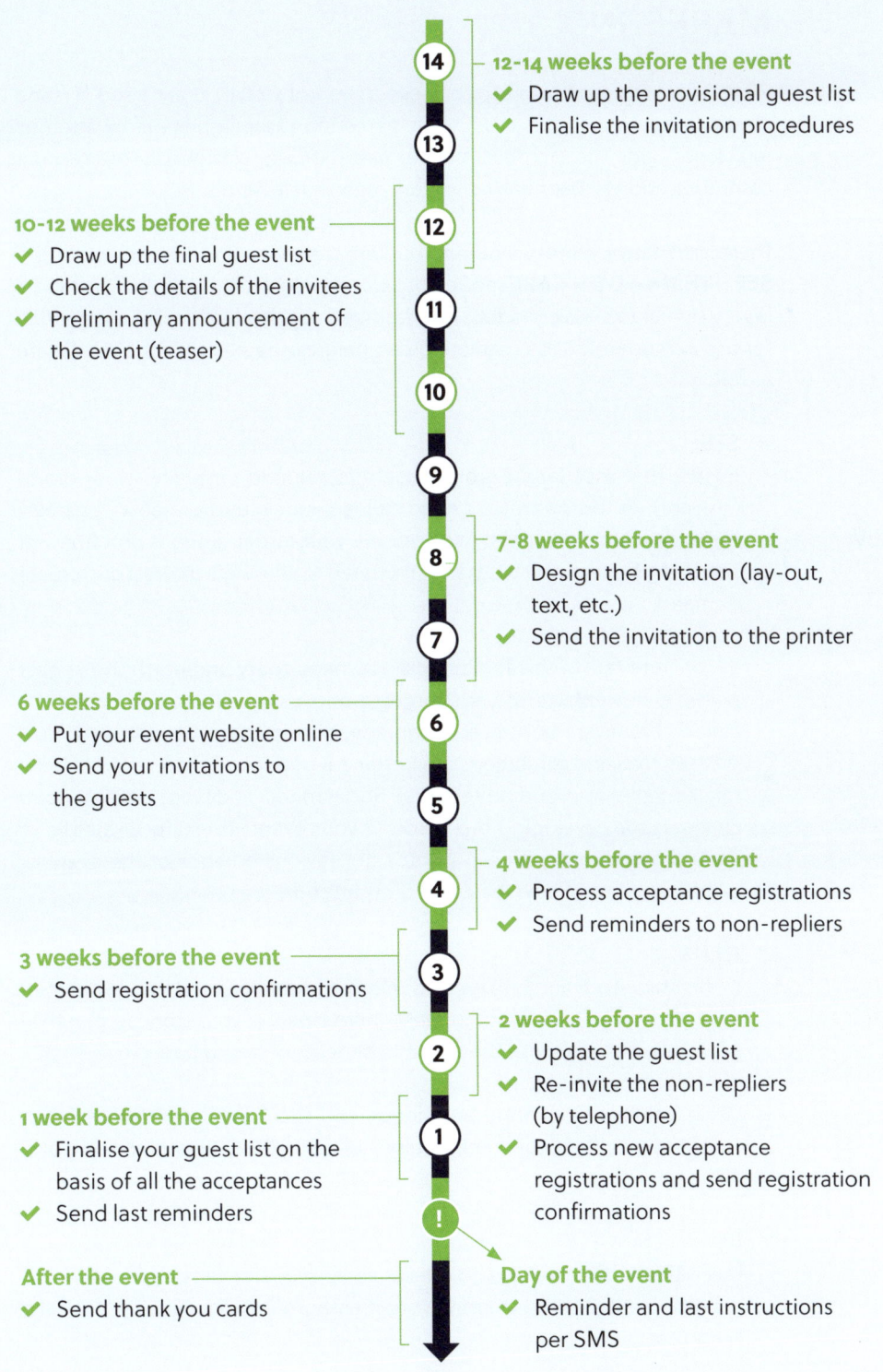

MARKETING

When you are organising a public event, you obviously don't need to send classic invitations. In this case, your marketing campaign starts by attempting to persuade the members of your target group to attend. In this respect, communication is essential: no visitors means no event!

There are many different kinds of marketing models. I like to work with the **SEE – THINK – DO – CARE** model that was developed by Google. This model is very similar to classic models, but has been adjusted to make it compatible for use in modern online marketing campaigns. The basics of the model are as follows:

- **SEE**
  Ensure that your target group is able to see and remember your brand (= event). In this phase you need to load your brand as heavily as possible to develop awareness. At this point, your target group is probably not searching for an event to attend. You need to stimulate interest and create demand.

  In concrete terms, this means that you need to try and reach the largest possible percentage of your target group using all relevant communication channels. Public events can advertise in the national media; congresses, fairs and exhibitions are better advised to use professional media related to the appropriate sector(s). Social media and blogs are also good channels for developing buzz around your event. Think, for example, of entertaining blogs with fun photos of previous editions of the event or backstage films of how the event is organised.

- **THINK**
  In this stage your aim is to help your target group to understand your message (your 'why'). You want to make them a part of your story, so that they gradually start to realise the possible benefits of taking part in the event.

  Using influencers, sharing knowledge and circulating short films of your speakers are all ways of helping to stimulate a FOMO (fear of missing out) feeling.

- **DO**
  This is the moment when you effectively change the behaviour of your target group and convert them to your message. You mobilise them to take action.

Your target group is now ready to open their wallets. A clear call to action to buy tickets or a temporary promotion offer can often give them the final push they need. You can also use paid social media campaigns that are focused on your specific target group or on people who have shown interest in your earlier communications.

- ✓ **CARE**
  By providing excellent customer service and a faultless experience you create a cadre of loyal customers who will also come to your event next year. You convince them to become brand ambassadors, who will promote your event among their friends and acquaintances.

Sadly, it is an illusion to think that with just a single contact moment or e-mail you will immediately start selling all your tickets. It is only after multiple touchpoints that you will be able to convert your prospects. One of the most common marketing errors is to focus exclusively on the touchpoints that achieve direct results.

Imagine, for example, that you see a Google AdWords campaign that is generating plenty of ticket sales. There is a huge temptation to devote your entire marketing budget to this channel. But if you look into the matter more closely you will find that the purchasers first saw a banner for the event, followed by an article in the press, a poster in their favourite bar, an online blog from one of the event's star performers and finally an invitation to like a post from one of their friends who has already bought a ticket. It is only then that the purchaser becomes convinced to attend the event himself, at which point he searches the internet for more information and is directed to your advert in Google AdWords, where he buys his own ticket. Does this mean that Google AdWords is primarily responsible for this sale? Not at all! Without the banner, article, poster, blog and online post, there would never have been a sale. Every touchpoint is important and together they are known as the customer journey.

If I am called in as a consultant by an event or company to 'fix' their (online) marketing, the main problem is almost always the failure of the event or company to take sufficient account of this model, so that their 'why' is not authentic and/or their marketing plan is not geared to the target group and their touchpoints. Getting a misdirected campaign back on track is extremely difficult and sometimes even impossible. Organisations that opt to embrace the SEE – THINK – DO – CARE model increase their chances of success significantly.

Marketing plan

As with your event as a whole, you must also start your communication by first working out an appropriate plan. In this marketing plan you should not only describe your target group (again) and your message (based on the authentic 'why' of your event), but should also develop a customer journey and identify the touchpoints you want to use.

Using consumer research, try to discover what things are important for your target group. What really matters to them, where do they search for information about it, how do they communicate about it and how can you reach them most efficiently? Your budget will determine whether you recruit a marketing bureau to conduct this research or whether you enter into direct dialogue with your target public, using your own staff and resources. Whichever option you choose, the essence of the matter is to find out how you can best attract the attention of your public – and convince them to attend. This information will later help you to define your media plan, but will also guide you in setting the right tone of voice for your communication. It goes without saying that you need to address a group of business leaders in a different way than a group of hip youngsters!

This research may reveal that it is necessary to split your initial target group into sub-groups, if it becomes clear that some people need a different approach to the majority. If the definition of your advertising target group is too wide, your reach and response will be less effective.

After you have decided precisely what you want to achieve (ticket sales, name recognition, image creation, etc.), you can start the development of your creative campaign. Ensure that this is always in keeping with the objective of the event. What message do you want to put across? How are you going to package this message? What call to action are you going to use? Will there be TV advertising?

> Super-creative campaigns are fun but they are not always the most effective. Be critical and constantly re-evaluate your campaigns. Is this slogan working? Is this image eye-catching enough? If not, change them!

📌 Attracting new visitors costs far more time and money than convincing past visitors to attend your event again. Make sure that you give all your visitors a good time and a great experience, so that they are happy to come back next year. Perhaps you can give your loyal customers some kind of bonus or even involve them in the preparation of the event.

Media plan

Depending on the nature of your event, you then need to track down the channels most frequently used by your target group. Consider advertising in the traditional media (newspapers, magazines, radio and television), but also in specialised professional journals and niche media. And don't forget the online options offered by search engines and social media. Online advertising allows you to focus accurately on your target group at super-low cost.

Your campaign might be brilliantly innovative and creative, but if it fails to reach the eyes and/or ears of your target group its effect will be minimal. Channels with too much background 'noise' will not give you an efficient return for your money. Perhaps your target group watches a commercial television station, but if this group only represents 10% of the total reach of the station this will not be a good investment of your budget.

In other words, when selecting your media always take account of the reach and the target group of the media in question. If you have a very broad target group, you can probably work with national media. If, however, you are organising something more specific like a marketing congress, you will need to search for media that have a narrower reach but are ideally positioned in your niche. The more credible your chosen medium is regarded by the target of your message, the better the result is likely to be.

The success of a campaign stands or falls with good media planning. In your media plan, which is part of your marketing plan, you must define (based on accurate market data) your target group, your objective, your advertising message, and the media you will use (what, how and when). The media plan gives tangible shape and form to the media you will employ, expressed as a time planning.

Good marketing is all about repetition and (as we have already seen) the creation of a cascade of touchpoints. In the media plan, this is generally referred to as 'contact frequency': how often you come into contact with the same person during your campaign. Launching the campaign with a single big bang might seem tempting, but in reality it is much better to work with a succession of waves.

Achieving the desired level of reach and the desired contact frequency always comes at a price. These costs are often expressed in terms of a CPM (Cost Per Mille or the cost of reaching one thousand people in the target group) or as a GRP (Gross Rating Point, equivalent to the cost of reaching 1% of the target group). The communication capacity of a medium is the extent to which that medium can effectively transmit your message. Television, for example, is ideal for showing your product (festival, sports event, etc.) to a mass audience, whereas a printed medium is better suited to the communication of product specifications, etc. Online combines the best of both worlds and makes everything measurable, providing you go about it correctly.

> 📌 Because everything is measurable when you are working online, there is a tendency to judge every channel in terms of its conversion rate. But as we saw earlier with the SEE – THINK – DO – CARE model, you also need touchpoints that boost your brand recognition and match your designated customer journey. In other words, you should not judge a banner campaign by the number of clicks or conversions, but by its level of reach within your target group. Stick to your plan!

> 📌 In general, a diversified media mix works better than the use of a single medium, unless your budget is small. In that case, you need to choose a limited number of media or perhaps even just a single channel. Otherwise, there is a risk that your message will become fragmented, so that too few touchpoints will reach each prospect.

Content marketing

I am convinced that content marketing is the basis for every good marketing campaign. By 'content' I mean every text and image in whatever form that you create and share via whatever medium: folder, video, (e-)book, drawing, podcast, etc. With content marketing, you develop and disseminate valuable, relevant and consistent content for your specific target group in a strategic manner. The ultimate purpose of this content is to persuade people (customers) to choose your event or products, but the process is indirect rather than direct. It is achieved by first telling the story of your company or event and by sharing knowledge. In this way, you eventually position yourself, your company, your product or your event as the expert in the market. You establish yourself as an authority and it is this that allows you to convince people in your favour. This strategy does not mean that you always have to create your own content. If appropriate, you can also use existing content from the professional media, relevant blogs, and so on. You make a selection of the best available content in the knowledge domain that interests you and your target group – and then you share it. And keep on sharing it.

Are you organising a lifestyle exhibition? If so, you may find it useful to share articles and videos that offer your target group concrete tips about healthy living or a list with all the hippest wellness addresses. But the same can apply equally for a customer event or festival. These too make it possible to use content to share your story and your 'why' with the world. What kind of content?

Perhaps the success stories of existing customers or videos of some of the top acts from previous festival editions.

In his book *All Marketers are Liars*, Seth Godin rightly concludes that people are not really interested in pure facts. They want to believe in a story. All the more reason, then, to make sure that you have a powerful story to tell.

An event is actually a form of content marketing in itself. Each type of event, even a wedding celebration or a party, has its own story and is an expression of content. The entire marketing trajectory, the event itself and the communication about it afterwards are all aligned, so that they project a consistent message. Montages of keynote speakers or top acts can subsequently be shared and form the starting point of the content marketing for the next edition of your event.

If you have a good marketing plan, it should soon become clear on which social media sites you should post and for which topics in Google you want to score in order to attract new participants to your event. You have already completed the largest and hardest part of the work when you defined your target group and identified the things that really matter to them.

Last but not least, you also need a content marketing channel, a place where you can bring all your content together. This might be a website, a separate blog or even your own social media channel. However, you can also use other (professional) media to spread unique content, using their credibility as a lever with your target group. Think carefully about which channels you want to use and how you can further promote them. For example, you might decide to write a blog post, which you then redistribute on social media.

Keep on communicating! Repetition is crucial. In a world where almost everyone is constantly swiping on their smartphone, a message needs to be repeated many times before people can be persuaded to take action – like buying a ticket for your event.

 Are you organising a content-based event for a specific target group? A podcast can be a fun way to attract new participants. You can set up your own podcast about the content of the event or take part in an existing podcast as a guest. Or why not ask one of your keynote speakers to do it? Alternatively, see if you can talk at other similar events.

Growth hacking

Growth hacking is the smart use of social media and innovative technology in the most efficient and most effective manner to grow your business – or in our case your event.

The idea behind growth hacking was first developed by internet start-ups that wanted to grow as quickly as possible but had little or no marketing budget. Using smart hacks that often cost very little they were able to convince large numbers of potential users. They did this by looking at their business in a completely different way, combined with the use of the technology that they had available. World famous companies like X, Facebook, Airbnb, Evernote and Hotmail all started in this manner. Of course, they all had a fantastically good product, but they still needed a spark to ignite and perpetuate their rapid growth. Let me give you some idea of what they did – and still do:

- **Hotmail**, at least in its early years, added the text 'PS -I love you' to every mail, with a link back to Hotmail. Understandably, this registered a huge number of clicks and brought in many new users. Even today, Apple uses a similar hack with their 'Sent from my iPhone' text, which tells everyone you know what kind of phone you are using.

- **X** (formerly Twitter) had plenty of press interest in its early years but subsequently noted that many of its users quickly dropped out. Until, that is, X eventually discovered that users with five to ten followers were more inclined to stay for the long term. Since then, X automatically suggests profiles to follow when someone makes an account.

- **Airbnb** attracted lots of users in a short space of time because they went in search on Craiglist for people who offered rooms for hire through online advertisements. True, this was not a wholly 'clean' hack and today they would immediately be blocked as a spammer. But they saw an opportunity, took it – and are now one of the biggest players in their sector.

- **LinkedIn** was the first platform that made user profiles public, so that they would feature prominently in the results of search engines like Google. This was clever – because at some time or other we all look people up by their name.

- **YouTube** displays after each viewed video an embedded code that allows the video to be uploaded on other sites. This is a simple hack, but it ensured that in no time at all YouTube became the world's largest video channel, which it still is today.

- **Dropbox** increased its number of sign-ups by 60% though a smart 'recommend us' campaign, which gave users 500 MB of extra storage capacity for every friend they persuaded to join.

You get the point. And the same applies to events: you need sufficient traction in a relatively short space of time. The good news is that you can use the same kinds of hacks as the people in Silicon Valley. What's more, they don't cost very much, so that you don't need extra budget – just a little bit of creativity. I regularly assist companies with their growth hacking projects and in all modesty, I can say that the results nearly always exceed expectations. So, what is stopping you? Just do it!

Growth hackers list all their ideas for boosting their conversion and promoting their viral dissemination in a backlist. Each idea is given an ICE score, which stands for impact, confidence and ease. Impact is a score that indicates the level of effectiveness that you expect from your hack. Confidence is a score that indicates how sure you are that this impact will be achieved. Ease is a score that indicates how easy it is to implement the hack (the higher the score, the easier it is). You give each of your proposed hacks a score out of ten for each of the three elements, following which you can order your backlist from high to low on the basis of the combined score out of thirty. This gives you a reasonable idea of where your priorities should lay, which is a good thing, because you often have too many ideas rather than not enough.

The result of each experiment with a growth hack should be carefully measured, ideally by using an A/B test that allows you to compare results with and without the hack. If your hack works, you keep it. If it doesn't, you ditch it – immediately.

Below you can find a number of ideas that you might be able to use for your event. But don't just copy them blindly: think carefully about how you can use them creatively in a manner that matches your event as closely as possible. Also remember that a hack which works well for one event might have the opposite effect for a different event.

- It might sound like stating the obvious, but hacking your registration process is always a good idea. Can you make it simpler? Can you make the 'register' button clearer? What if you place the 'sign-up' form for your newsletter at the top of your website instead of at the bottom?

- On-boarding mails. After event registration or a ticket sale, send your guests an interesting tip every X-number of days, telling them something that is important to know about the event. For example, on the first day you might send them a 'welcome' message and a copy of the programme. A few days later, you can send them a mail with information about hotels near the event venue or the diet options that are available for the event catering. A few days after that you can tell them how they can show others that they are part of your event community; for example, by sharing the event on social media or using the event hashtag. You can even use gamification to make this hack more fun. In your final mail, you send your guests information about the accessibility of the venue and how to get there.

Are there other things that you expect your visitors to do, such as making a profile on the event website, registering for specific sessions or making appointments with stall holders? You can also send them mails about these matters. If your on-boarding mails contain useful information of this kind, they will not be regarded as annoying. Quite the reverse. By focusing each time on a single topic or action, you ensure that your visitors will clearly get each message, which is often not the case if you overload them with several messages in the same mail.

If you approach your on-boarding thoughtfully, your mails can even have an up-sell effect. For example, after a few mails you can offer someone who bought a standard ticket the possibility to upgrade to a VIP ticket on special terms.

- ✓ Make your registration viral. Work with 'two-for-the-price-of-one' vouchers. Offer discounts to people who send at least three event invites to friends via your website.

- ✓ Also make use of growth hacking as part of your social media strategy, your advertising and anything else that you think can make your event's promotion more efficient and more effective. Hacks do not always need to be complex and high-tech. Even small things can help to give your event a big boost.

You can find more examples on growthhackers.com. The literature list at the back of this book also contains a number of other books with good tips. But if you want to focus heavily on growth hacking, it is advisable to call in an expert.

Another technique that I use both for eventplanner.net and for client projects is 'design sprint'. In some ways, this name is misleading, because it has little to do with 'design' in the classic sense of the word, but with the development of solutions for complex challenges. The framework was originated by Google and makes it possible over a relatively short 'sprint' of five days to formulate a problem, elaborate solutions, build a prototype and test it on a trial group. If, for example, you are not certain how to make your congress relevant for your target group or what your event website should look like in order to have maximum effect, design sprint can nearly always provide the answer. Although I am happy to offer design sprints as a useful tool, exactly how you should use it falls outside the scope of this book. If you would like to know more, the link below is a good place to start. If, however, you want to implement a design sprint, it is again advisable to work with someone who already has experience of the system.

www.eventplanner.net/book/designsprint

Website

You cannot organise your event or communicate about it successfully without building (or having built) a good event website. It is the ideal tool not only to inform your participants about the event and its programme, but also, for example, to allow them to discover who else will be in attendance. However, the most important reason for investing in a website is probably the **registration and ticketing module**. This makes it possible for participants to register or buy tickets quickly and easily, whilst at the same time providing you as organiser with all the details you need in a database.

> Always make sure that your guests can register with a minimum of fuss and effort and always send them a confirmatory e-mail.

Even for personnel events and private parties it is becoming increasingly common to create a website. Alternatively, small business or staff events can be announced on a separate page on your company website. Larger events always need a dedicated website. It goes without saying that this website needs to look professional and must match the mood and theme that you have in mind for your event. Unless you need something simple, like a blog for your wedding celebrations, it is wisest to leave website construction to the experts.

> Is your communication budget limited? There are plenty of ready-to-use registration applications online, such as the eventplanner.net app. Equally, there are numerous event websites on the market that are readily available and not all that expensive.

Your website must become the focal point – the nerve centre, if you like – of your entire marketing campaign. In many cases, it will fulfil the role of 'mentor' in the 'hero's journey' scenario, as well as being the hub for the content marketing that will take away your potential visitors' last doubts and convince them to sign up for the event. Online videos of speakers (for congresses) or bands (for concerts) can be used to create thought-provoking trailers that will strengthen your message still further.

> By releasing bits of information at different times through your website or other social media, you can not only build up anticipation for the event but also encourage people to visit the website more than once. In other words, multiple touchpoints!

Do not forget that people's experience of your event has already started. This means that your website must be fast and user-friendly. The last thing you want is for potential participants to drop out because they have become frustrated by website functions that do not work properly or because they cannot find the information they want. You need to think very carefully about the usability and functionality of your website. The following videos can help:

www.eventplanner.net/book/tv-usability

 www.eventplanner.net/book/eventsite

Interaction with the visitors to your website strengthens their user experience. Perhaps you can organise a poll for which they need to show their preference for a particular speaker or artist. Or maybe you can post a proposition on one of the subjects that will be addressed during the event and let them discuss it now online.

> Do not try to think for your public, but ask instead for their opinions. Make use of the 'wisdom of crowds' to improve the quality of your event and to respond to your public's expectations. This is also known as crowd sourcing. Do not be afraid of feedback, but have the courage to take account of it whenever possible.

After the event your website is the ideal place to post photos and videos that you can share with your guests. It is also possible, if you prefer, to protect your site with a password, so that the guests are the only ones who can gain access to it.

As I have already mentioned, one of the most important reasons why people take part in live events is to come into contact with others. As well as facilitating on-site networking, you can also stimulate interaction between your participants online. When registering, ask your invitees to add their profile to your website, with a photo and a short description of who they are, what they do and how they can be contacted. You can even devise a Tinder-like app that will allow other guests to swipe left or right to get in touch with potentially interesting 'partners'. Measures of this kind will further stimulate the physical networking that takes place at the event and offers the possibility of reviewing the details of any new contacts they have made via their profiles. You can further encourage your guests to use your website to leave comments or suggestions, send messages to each other, organise meetings or take part in discussion forums. Remember, however, to keep things simple. None of your guests will be willing to spend an hour completing a complicated profile form. And don't forget to always ask for permission to process their personal details. It can help to link your website to existing social media channels, so that your guests can log in with their Facebook or LinkedIn account. This means that they will immediately have a profile that they can transfer to your site with just the click of a mouse, as well as making it easier for them to share your event with their friends and (business) relations, which also works to your benefit.

TICKETING

If you are selling entrance tickets to your event, reliable ticketing software is essential. The very last thing you want is that your visitor registration programme crashes when you start selling tickets, because of the high level of demand. This must be one of your most crucial criteria when selecting a ticketing partner – and it usually pays to go for experience.

Consider the use of mobile ticketing, whereby tickets are 'delivered' direct to the smartphones of your participants. With this system, you no longer need an actual ticket; you simply show your phone at the entrance to the event. Quick, easy and environmentally friendly! NFC (near-field communication) is also becoming increasingly popular. Special scanners can identify that you have bought a ticket, even though your phone is still in your pocket or handbag.

But while this technology is unquestionably 'hip', it is wiser to rely on a system that is efficient in all circumstances and will continue to operate in the event of technical failure.

 Nowadays, nearly all software is offered in the cloud. This is super-easy and super-beneficial, but remember that for your event it is always sensible – if not essential – to have a back-up solution that you can rely on. If the internet connection crashes while you are scanning your guests' online tickets, you must have an alternative that will still allow you to check them before they enter. This applies equally for all aspects of your event that are dependent on the cloud.

The eventplanner.net software offers powerful ticketing tools and a handy app for both Apple and Android. This makes it possible to scan tickets quickly and easily, even if connection with the internet is broken, thanks to an offline back-up system. This ticketing solution is also suitable for RSVP events like weddings.

 www.eventplanner.net/book/eventsoftware

E-mail marketing

If you use your e-mail marketing in the right way, it is one of the most powerful communication channels that an event manager can have. In contrast to what many people are saying, e-mail is by no means dead. Of course, everything begins with building up a high-quality database and that is where the problem so often lies. Compiling a good mailing list is not as easy as it sounds. Far from it.

If you are organising a business event for customers, your marketing department probably has a mailing list that you can use as a basis. But if you are organising a new congress or festival, you will need to start from scratch. Only send mails to people who have **opted-in** (given permission). Spamming people always has a negative effect and also ensures that all your mails, even for the people who want to read them, will end up in the spam filter.

E-mail marketing is all about building up relationships. In contrast to social media, where your message is competing with countless others, an e-mail makes possible a more personal touch. You can communicate directly with your public and gear the content to reflect their known interests and needs. This means that e-mail marketing is a highly effective way of cosseting your leads, stimulating your ticket sales and keeping your community properly informed.

E-mail marketing is also easily measurable. With tools that can record open rates, click-through rates and conversions, you can gain valuable insights into the behaviour of your target group. This data will help you to refine your overall strategy, so that each new e-mail becomes more effective than the previous one.

 With the introduction of European privacy legislation (GDPR), the rules for the collection and protection of customer data have been tightened up significantly. Many other countries in the world are now following the EU example and are implementing similar legislations. If you want to avoid huge fines, make sure you play by the rules. Do not add e-mail addresses to your mailing list randomly and without thought. Also take the necessary steps to protect your system against hacking.

A **clean e-mail database** also ensures that your mails are less likely to be blocked by spam filters. Immediately delete from your files any mails that bounce back because the e-mail address no longer exists. Always use a professional **mailing tool** and never set dozens of e-mail addresses in CC.

When you are compiling your e-mail database, do not simply collect e-mail addresses, but also the names, interests and any known special requirements of your prospects. This will allow you not only to personalise your mails, but also to adjust the content appropriately, which will significantly increase the click-through rate (CTR). Make sure that your e-mails contain something of value for the receivers. Sending a mail every week that simply says 'buy tickets' will not work. In fact, you will lose existing subscribers faster than you will attract new ones. Content marketing can provide the solution. Include in your mails relevant articles, videos and links that will appeal to your target group and share knowledge and tips about your specialist field with them. Of course, this is easier for a congress than for a personnel dinner, but even for the latter it should still be possible to make your communication interesting.

Here are some practical tips for a successful mailing and e-mail marketing strategy:

- **Segment your target group.** Divide your target group into categories based on factors like past attendance, interests and likely level of engagement. Send different mails to new prospects and returning participants. This will make your mails more relevant and increase the likelihood of commitment and, ultimately, conversion.
- **Draw up a content calendar.** Timing is crucial in e-mail marketing. Draw up a content calendar that records precise details of when each e-mail will be sent and what will be in it. Start with a general announcement to generate initial enthusiasm and follow this with regular updates, reminders and post-event thank-you's. Plan your e-mails around important moments, such as the deadline for early subscribers, or important milestones in your event's preparation. This will ensure maximum impact. It is also important that not all e-mails of the same kind are sent on the same day. You need to devise personal e-mail trajectories (journeys) based on specific user actions. For example, you can set up your system so that follow-up e-mails are sent one day, one week and two weeks after a participant's registration for the event. This means that everyone will get all the information they need, but at the moment that is right for them, depending on their date of registration. This approach personalises the participant's overall event experience and guarantees that all your communication is relevant and up-to-date.
- **Personalisation** must go further than simply mentioning the name of the receiver. Adjust the content of your mails to reflect each person's interests and needs. If, for example, your event consists of different tracks or sessions, highlight the most relevant tracks and sessions for each segment of your target group. This will increase engagement and help you to build up a stronger connection with your public.
- Make sure that you have a powerful and thought-provoking **title** for your e-mail, something that will arouse people's curiosity. The title usually determines whether or not your mail will be opened or dropped unread into the waste basket. Use action-oriented language and create a feeling of urgency to take advantage of an opening that will not last indefinitely. Something like 'Don't miss your last opportunity to register for this exclusive event' will work much better and generate more interest than a general introductory title.
- Design a really good **landing page**. Once you have attracted the attention of your reader, it is important that they can click through with a minimum of delay to your website – and to the right part of your website. If you send them a mail that allows them to register free of charge, make sure they arrive directly on the registration page – and not on the home page.
- Keep your e-mails **short and to-the-point**, so that they can be quickly scanned by your readers.

- ✔ Always first send a **test-mail** to yourself, preferably via different mail programmes. This will allow you to check exactly how your mail will look when it arrives in the mailbox of your target public. A good tool for testing different mail clients is litmus.com
- ✔ Make use of **A/B testing**. Good e-marketing solutions support this feature as standard. It is possible, for example, to send off your first batch of e-mails with two different titles. The software immediately measures which title has the best response and then uses this title to complete the rest of the mailing.
- ✔ When you send your mails, use a **personal e-mail address** and name for the sender. This strengthens the relationship with your potential participants much more than a general address like 'info@yourevent.com'. If you receive an event e-mail from a recognisable person, like the event organiser or an important member of the event team, this feels much more personal and credible, which in turn will increase both your open rates and the participants' level of engagement. So instead of sending a mail under the 'info@yourevent.com' address with no named sender, consider something like 'Sarah of Your Event Team' under the address 'sarah@yourevent.com'. This simple amendment will give your mails more the feeling of a direct one-to-one conversation, which will encourage the receivers to open and answer them. It will also serve to cement a stronger bond between your brand and your public, so that a positive feeling of familiarity and trust develops.
- ✔ **Optimise your mails for mobile devices.** Make sure that your e-mails are mobile- friendly. A large part of your target group will read these mails on their smartphones, so it is important to use a responsive design that allows your mails to look good and be easily readable on any device.

Marketing automation

Your communication does not stop once someone has registered for your event and/or bought a ticket. Quite the reverse! Think, for example, of the on-boarding trajectory that we discussed in the earlier section on growth hacking. Marketing automation can take this process another stage further. What the e-commerce sector refers to as 'shop abandonment' can also be relevant for events. Shop abandonment – or in our case event abandonment – is when a potential buyer starts the ordering procedure but does not complete it. If this person was logged in, so that you know his e-mail address, you can automatically send him an e-mail that tries to persuade him to complete the purchase or registration. If he was not logged in, you can try to make use of retargeting. This is a technique that allows Google, Facebook and other advertising networks to make use of cookies to identify the same user on other websites, so that they can show banners for your event on these sites. Zalando uses the same technique whenever someone views a product on their website. Days later, you suddenly start seeing banners everywhere online for the same product! Remember, however, that if you wish to pursue this option for your event, you must ensure that it complies with the GDPR legislation.

Have you sent an event invitation by e-mail but see that after five days the addressee has still not opened it? You can arrange to send him an automatic reminder by SMS or, failing that, an invitation by post. By automating your marketing in this manner, you can achieve greater reach with the same resources.

Data-driven marketing means that you will probably need to work with big data. For example, you can identify which content a visitor has viewed on your website, so that you can send him a more personalised offer. Wearables, iBeacons, RFID and event apps even make it possible to follow the visitors' behaviour during the actual event. This allows you to respond quickly and flexible to their interests. For example, you can tailor your newsletter after the event to reflect the sessions, podia and stands that you know they visited. The possibilities are almost limitless and are set to expand even further in the years ahead! So make sure that you don't miss the boat, but first take the necessary time to discover the best software for your specific needs.

Google

Once you have an event website, it is obviously crucial that your guests can find it easily. Nowadays, everyone is talking about search engine optimisation (SEO) and search engine advertising (SEA). As an event organiser, how can you make best use of these possibilities?

SEO

For many one-off events there is not much point in investing in SEO. It can take months before SEO techniques start to have a beneficial effect on your ranking, by which time your event might already have taken place. It is different, however, for annually recurring events like trade fairs and congresses. In these cases, devoting attention and resources to SEO is much more worthwhile. The best way to do it? The most important tip is 'content, content and more content'.

In the past, getting the best out of SEO was largely a case of having the best technical tricks. Nowadays, it is all about offering relevant content that is written to appeal to your visitors rather than the search engine algorithms. If you want to score on a search term like 'marketing congress', you will need to a make a separate page for your website that concentrates on that specific subject with rock-solid content. To discover which key words you should focus on, you will need to carry out the necessary research. This means mapping the key words used by your target group and identifying which of them have the best search volume. You can do this either by using Google Trends, a simulation tool in Google AdWords, or else by acquiring specialist software.

Although there are a lot of things you can do for yourself, it is nevertheless advisable to hire an expert if you want to take SEO seriously.

SEA

In most cases, SEA is a much more self-evident choice for promoting your event through search engines like Google. On Google AdWords or Bing you can decide for yourself which keywords you want to use for your advertisement to be found and also the maximum amount you want to pay per visitor to your website. Once again, you base these decisions on key word research. Campaigns of this kind are fast-moving and can be set up with a limited budget. More importantly, they generaly give good results. Google also offers machine learning in AdWords campaigns, so that it optimises the settings as the campaign progresses, with the aim of generating the maximum number of conversions for the lowest possible cost. Yet again, you will need the services of an expert if you want to get the best out of SEA. When we are asked to take over the AdWords campaigns of some of our clients, we see time after time that they could have saved significant amounts on their ad-spend if they had only come to the professionals first.

 Remember to also advertise on your own brand name. Perhaps you think that the name will automatically come at the top of any organic search results. And perhaps it will, but there will still be other adverts above it. Normally, there should be little competition on your brand name or the name of your event, as a result of which you can buy in lots of traffic cheaply, which converts well and keeps your prospects away from your competitors. This is a no brainer, but it is one that is still often forgotten.

 www.eventplanner.net/book/adwords

Analytics

Measuring is knowing. There are different systems available on the market to measure the behaviour of the people who visit your website. These systems record not only how often they visit your site, but which pages they visited and how long they stayed there. Be warned, however: not all analytics solutions conform with the privacy legislation. So choose the software that you use for your event carefully.

The most interesting feature of these systems for event organisers is probably the possibility to track conversions. In this way, you can easily see how many visitors register via your website and you can then use these statistics to find out why other visitors drop out. Ask the help of your webmaster to install an analytics tool on your site.

In addition to e-commerce objectives like ticket sales, it is advisable to also programme micro moments as an objective. The downloading of a PDF, the viewing of a particular video, registering for your newsletter, viewing a specific page or viewing five random pages are all pieces of useful information that allow you to see which steps help to persuade your site visitors and later convert them into participants in your event. Tracking these moments with your analytics tool and attaching values to them makes it possible to fine tune the use of your marketing channels like Google AdWords. In particular, it helps you to better assess the quality of the traffic in the SEE and THINK phases of the SEE – THINK -DO – CARE model, so that any necessary adjustments can be made, especially early on in your marketing campaign, when you have too few actual conversions for accurate analysis.

Social media

Social media like Facebook, Instagram, TikTok, X and LinkedIn offer event organisers a wide range of new marketing possibilities. Good, open communication with a strong message can quickly and easily provide you with plenty of word-of-mouth publicity (viral marketing), which is one of the key factors for success. Remember, however, that communication nowadays is becoming more transparent and more direct. This means that it also gives your visitors a platform on which they can share their opinions – not all of which will be favourable – with the world.

Most social media are **multi-purpose** and can be used in a variety of different ways. During the preliminary phase they can be used to generate buzz around your event; for example, via promotional adverts or the sending of virtual invitations. Videos of popular speakers can also be shared via social media, as can other content that is relevant for your target group and followers. Get your potential participants more involved by asking them questions. Once the event starts, you can continue making use of social media to facilitate interaction with your public (X-wall, voting, etc.) or to inform the outside world about the event's progress. Sharing the event via a live stream is also an option. After the event, the same media can be used to share photos, videos and presentations.

The possibilities are almost limitless and new developments are taking place at lightning speed. For this reason, it is not possible to discuss all the many potential applications here. Moreover, by the time you actually buy this book many of these applications will already have been replaced by new and better ones! I will therefore confine myself to looking at the most popular websites and their current application options for events. The fact that this selection is far from complete is not important. What matters is that you, as an event organiser, learn more about what social media can do for you. With this knowledge at the back of your mind, you can then explore the worldwide web for yourself to identify the tools and channels that are most suitable for your target group and event.

Let me start, however, by warning you about a number of potential pitfalls:

1. Social media have a lot to offer (efficiency, relatively low costs, etc.) but should not be used as your sole mode of information sharing and interaction. Do not forget to include the classic media in your marketing mix and always **think cross-medially**. Integrate online and offline communication.

2. Social media are unique. Each platform has its own advantages, limitations and specific characteristics. Make sure that you know what they are before you use them. And never forget that the **basic rules for good communication** continue to apply. If you have done your homework properly, you will have identified your target group, know how best to reach them and how best to communicate with them. For example, LinkedIn is highly suitable for business communication, whereas younger people are probably easier to approach via TikTok. That being said, many of the old boundaries, such as the line between our private and professional worlds, are becoming increasingly blurred, so that nowadays a platform like Facebook is also acceptable for business contacts.

3. Determine in advance the **objectives** that you want to achieve with social media, so that you can use them in a targeted manner and avoid becoming lost in the plethora of services and information that is available. Social

media are time-consuming. Measure all your online activities and learn from your mistakes. Make adjustments, when necessary.

4. If you are not already present on social media platforms, you should not use them. You need to **participate actively** to understand their dynamic and how they can best be used for your event. You want to start? Begin by listening – and listening carefully! What are people saying about you online? Only then can you start to talk for yourself.

5. Conversions via social media continue after office hours. Using these media has **an effect on your entire organisation**. Make sure that everyone is involved and make clear arrangements.

6. **Negative feedback**. Most companies hate negative feedback. Their forced and defensive reaction simply serves to make matters even worse! Never delete negative posts about your event. If you do, sooner or later they will boomerang back in your face. Always acknowledge negative criticism, but devote no more attention to it than is strictly necessary. Do not

allow the situation to escalate, otherwise you will bring the criticism to the attention of other fans and followers who have not yet seen it. Remove all discussion about the negative post (but not the post itself) from your website as quickly as possible. The best tactic is to thank the critic for their feedback and ask them to send you more information about their grievance by e-mail, so that you can try to find a solution. And if you succeed, you will often find that this one-time critic later becomes one of your most fervent ambassadors!

▶ www.eventplanner.net/book/tv-socialmedia

 Nowadays, there are various online tools such as Hootsuite or Sprout Social that allow you to monitor all social media channels from a single centralised dashboard. This saves time and ensures that no relevant messages and posts slip by unnoticed.

X

X (formerly Twitter) can be used in many different ways to support your event, before, during and afterwards. Posting regular updates and newsflashes on X can give a significant boost to the event's promotion campaign. Communicate openly and enter into dialogue with your target group.

 It is important that you have someone in your event team who can feed, regulate and manage your online community.

You can use your company's normal **X account** to promote your event or you can open a special account. In general, a special account is only necessary for (large-scale) recurring events that are a brand in their own right.

Whenever you post something about your event on X, always make sure that you attach a hashtag with the name of the event (#eventname). This will allow you to follow and review all posts about the event created by yourself or your guests. This backchannel can often provide useful information and feedback.

How do you choose a smart hashtag?
When choosing a hashtag, try to take account of the following basic principles:

- ✓ Make it **short**: On X you only have 280 characters in which to get your message across and the number of characters in the hashtag has to be deducted from this total amount. For this reason, it can be a good idea to work with an abbreviation.
- ✓ Make it **recognisable**: One of the disadvantages of an abbreviation is that the name of your event may no longer be recognisable. From a marketing standpoint, it is important that people write about you on X, but they have to be able to find you in the first place. Only then will their entire network also be able to 'discover' your congress or event.
- ✓ Make it **logical**: There is probably a hashtag for your event that is fairly obvious. It might even be being used by some of your participants before you know it! Don't be afraid to use this kind of hashtag, but remember: it is your online community that ultimately decides which hashtag will be used; the best you can do is to try and influence their decision.
- ✓ Make it **unique**: Because anyone can use a hashtag at any time, you need to check whether your planned hashtag has been used before. If it has, this would create unnecessary 'interference' when your participants are trying to find each other.
- ✓ Make it **sustainable**: One way to make your hashtag unique is add the year of the event. If, however, you promote your hashtag successfully, the year date does little to help the long-term sustainability of your event. Moreover, you want your target group to communicate with each other throughout the year, don't you?

> 📌 Once you have found your ideal hashtag, use it in all your communication, both online and offline: on social media, on your event website, in your invitation mails, on your posters, etc. In this way, your hashtag will become firmly established in the minds of your followers, so that they will be more quickly inclined to also use it.

Your participants will also post messages and share photos during the event. Make use of this by integrating what they have to say and show into your event set-up. For example, you can display all the posts with your event hashtag on a large screen in the entrance hall or auditorium of your venue. This is generally known as an X-wall and it offers a number of other interesting possibilities, such as allowing your public to pose questions, or to give their opinions on certain relevant themes, or even to take part in real-time online discussions about the event with one of your speakers (which is known in the jargon as a backchannel).

The disadvantage of an X-wall is that the opinions of your participants are freely available for all to see. Not all of these opinions will be positive, so you need to expect some criticism and be ready to deal with it in a correct and positive manner. Make sure that there is someone in your on-site team who can remove posts from the X-wall, if this is deemed necessary. Although this kind of 'censorship' should be avoided if at all possible, inappropriate or insulting comments – for example, about a speaker – are not acceptable, especially if it is projected on the wall behind him!

 It is easy to project posts about your event by simply selecting the hashtag. If you want an X-wall with high-quality graphic visualisation and/or tools for the moderation of discussions, there are various online options available, which can be found if you Google 'X-wall' or 'Twitter wall'.

 If you want to make use of a live X-stream, make sure that there is also a screen near the podium facing in the direction of the moderator/speakers. If anything out of the ordinary occurs, they will at least be able to see what is being said both inside the auditorium and beyond, so that they can respond accordingly with a minimum of delay.

The eventplanner.net editorial account can be followed on X via @eventplanner.net.

 www.eventplanner.net/book/twitter

LINKEDIN

LinkedIn.com is the social media network most widely used by business people. It is particularly suitable for making (new) contacts, exchanging ideas and sharing knowledge. In contrast to X, it is difficult to make use of LinkedIn during your event, but it can play a useful role both before and after it.

You can use a **LinkedIn group** to bring people together around a theme of common interest, such as your event. Making a group costs nothing and offers a number of tools as standard, including a forum where your invitees can converse with each other.

It is also possible to place targeted **advertisements** on LinkedIn to promote your B2B event. This is particularly useful because it allows you to focus on very specific targets like sectors (car sector, media sector, etc.), individual functions (CEOs, marketing managers, sales directors, etc.) or different combinations of socio-demographic elements.

eventplanner.net also has a LinkedIn group that unites all the professionals from the event industry worldwide. Please feel free to join us at no cost, so that you can make new contacts with clients, suppliers and fellow organisers.

www.eventplanner.net/book/linkedin

FACEBOOK & INSTAGRAM
Facebook is the world's largest social networking site. The platform offers an ever increasing number of possibilities for companies and brands to enter into dialogue with their target group. For public events and festivals, this is certainly the best platform to use.

Like LinkedIn, it is also possible to create a group on Facebook. Alternatively, you can set up a fan page or event page. A **Facebook group** or **fan page** can both be used to share information about your event or to converse with your target group. There are, however, a number of differences between these two options. The main advantage of a fan page is that it allows you to record valuable statistical information and use a simple URL. The main advantage of a group is that it can be made private and also allows you to send messages to all its members. For a brand or commercial event, it is probably better to opt for a fan page. A group is more appropriate for internal or smaller society-type events. Both options allow you to create an event, so that people can indicate whether or not they will attend.

Instagram is a highly visual platform on which you can attempt to convince your target group through the sharing of videos and photos. If you are aiming at a younger public, TikTok is an even better place to focus your attention.

 If you have your own registration system for your event, do not forget to indicate clearly that this is where people need to register their attendance. This will avoid people trying to 'register' incorrectly on Facebook, which may lead to them missing your event altogether!

Share the photos of your event via Facebook. If your participants start to tag them (which they often will), this means that their friends will get to see the photos as well.

 Add a watermark to your photos, such as the logo of your company. You can find plenty of quick and easy-to-use tools on the internet that will allow you to prepare your batches of photos for online posting.

It is also possible to place highly targeted adverts on Facebook that can take account of many different criteria and areas of interest.

YOUTUBE + VIDEO

Nowadays, everyone knows YouTube. This highly accessible platform can also be used to promote and/or support your event. For example, during the early phase of your event preparation you can post a teaser or promo-film on YouTube. A handy bonus is the fact that all your videos can also be uploaded onto your own website by embedding them, but don't forget to tag them sufficiently with suitable key words. Otherwise, people will not be able to find your videos, neither on YouTube nor on Google.

Do you want to post an online video of higher quality via a better player and without advertisements? If so, you can consider using Vimeo.com as an alternative to YouTube. The advantage of this is that you have greater control over the 'distribution' of your film. The disadvantage is that the viral spreading of your video message will be slower and less wide ranging, while your total streaming costs will soar.

Afterwards, you can upload a video report and presentations on YouTube that capture the atmosphere of your event. But be careful: this material can be seen by everyone all around the world! Make sure that you do not reveal any confidential information or show images that might be embarrassing for certain individuals. If you did not film your event's presentations, it is always possible to distribute your speakers' slides via SlideShare. SlideShare.com is for PowerPoints what YouTube is for videos.

 Make good arrangements with your artists and speakers and always ensure that you obtain the necessary rights and permissions to disseminate video content. If you want to add background music to these images, you will be directed to one of the

> copyright organisations to pay royalties, unless you have chosen royalty-free music.

INFLUENCERS

Influencers are people with a certain degree of celebrity in their field, who above all have a huge following on social media. These influencers include bloggers, podcaster, youtubers and social media 'stars'. Can you get them involved in your event? If so, they can almost guarantee that their followers will be interested in taking part. There are influencers for every sector and every target group. The trick, of course, is to find the best one for you.

Of course, you will not be alone in trying to persuade these famous influencers to support your event. Others will want their help, too. The following tips can help to persuade influencers to opt for you:

- ✓ **Invite them personally**
  Choose the right moment and the right way to send your invitation. Approaching an influencer through a mass mailing will get you nowhere. Approach him or her personally. If you already know them slightly, this will increase your chances of success. Do some research and use your contacts to try and find out the best moment and the best way to make the approach: by telephone, a personal mail, a stylish invitation card and/or a welcome package by post?

- ✓ **Offer real added value**
  Influencers are more easily inclined to accept an invitation if they feel that their presence at your event will be worthwhile for their followers and themselves. This makes it all the more important to choose the right influencer for your target group. If the influencer can benefit by meeting people from your target group, he/she will be more willing to take part in the event.

- ✓ **Provide an incentive**
  Once again, do some research and use your contacts to try and find out what the influencer would appreciate most. An exclusive gift? A guest appearance as your event host? The mentioning of his/her name on all your invitations? Real VIP treatment, such as being collected for your event by limousine? Many influencers have an ego that you might be able to exploit. Give them the platform they desire or pay for their services.

- ✓ **Also involve other influencers**
  People who are aware of their own value as influencers also like to be sur-

rounded by others of equal influence and value. This might be your keynote speakers, or people who have been nominated for awards in your branch, or other celebrities. Consult with your influencer and ask who he/she would recommend or like to have along.

The biggest disadvantage of influencer marketing, as you may have gathered from the above tips, is that it is a very intense form of marketing. It is far more time consuming than classic advertising and also means that you must be willing to accept the influencer's co-creation. If you ask a YouTube star to make a promo-film for your event, they will do it as they see fit. You can suggest ideas, but in the end they will do it their way. You must be prepared to accept this partial loss of control.

On the other side of the coin, the biggest advantage of influencer marketing is that it allows you to put across your message in a much more authentic manner and through a channel that is highly credible for your target group.

SOCIAL MEDIA DURING THE EVENT ITSELF
Integrating social media into your event needs to go much further than simply having an X-wall. There are other useful ways to stimulate your guests to take part in the event dialogue. The five best places to position social media outlets in your venue are as follows:

- **Main entrance and reception area**
  Guests are often enthusiastic when they first enter your event. Make use of this good vibe and place a social media centre in your welcome and reception area. This will excite their enthusiasm even more and motivate them to be interactively-minded right from the very start. This is also where you will have the biggest reach, since all your guests need to enter and leave the venue via this area. It is also the best place to make your event hashtag more widely known and to increase your guests' awareness of your social media channels.

- **Empty walls and hall entrances**
  Position screens with relevant and interesting social media content on empty walls or near the entrances to the various halls where the event sessions will take place. These high visibility locations allow you to share useful information, programme schedules, updates and messages. The most effective social media screens do not show standard images or difficult-to-read X streams, but images that are tailor-made to match your event (house style, design, logo, etc.).

✓ **Podia**
Place social media outlets in clearly visible positions on your event podia, so that your guests can actively take part during presentations. Ask questions that they can answer. If you share social media content in the background, your guests will feel more engaged than if you simply display a static image or logo. But watch out for the pitfalls I mentioned when we discussed X-walls in an earlier section!

✓ **Social media lounge**
Rest lounges and battery charging areas are usually boring and uninspiring places. Transform them into social media lounges where guests can see what is happening elsewhere in the event. They can certainly relax here, but also check in and/or share posts or photos. Make a photogenic corner where everyone will want to have their picture taken. Ensure that your hashtag is clearly visible in these lounges and that a good internet connection is available.

✓ **After parties**
When are your guests at their most interactive? During networking sessions and after parties! They are more relaxed and want to enjoy themselves. Share interesting conclusions with them and pose questions via your carefully sited social media screens. These conversation starters will prompt your guests to become active on your channels. You can also show photos of the guests on the screens. Selfies of new friends or colleagues are a perfect way to create interaction.

Press

Press interest is always good and for some events it is absolutely essential. If for example, you are organising a trade fair, articles in the relevant professional media are crucial to make your event come alive. Likewise, festivals and other public events need the buzz created by the national media to get their event well and truly off the ground. Of course, there are moments when you would prefer not to appear in the press and some (internal) events deal with confidential information that you do not want to share.

 Ask the help of your colleagues in your (internal) PR department when you want to make use of the (professional) press. They will have a reliable list of all the press contacts that are relevant to your event and who should therefore be invited to maintain good relations. The PR people will also know who best to invite in writing and who best to invite in person.

You can opt to send a general press release to all editorial offices or you can work more selectively. The advantage of inviting a large number of journalists is that it makes your playing field much bigger. The disadvantage is that the information you share with the journalists will be less interesting for many of them, so that they will not show up at the event.

The advantage of a selective approach is that you can offer certain 'friendly' journalists a scoop. They will obviously be more inclined to accept your invitation and to report about you favourably and prominently in their media. This also has the added benefit of further strengthening your relationship with the journalist in question. If your select group of chosen journalists is not available, you can always fall back on plan B.

Remember that journalists do not have much time and always work with tight deadlines. Make things as easy for them as you can. Inform them about your planning, so that they know what is going to happen. But do not tell them everything right away. Give them a press folder with all relevant details about your company, new product, etc. and add a press release that they can copy or amend. Agree clearly where and what can be photographed during the event.

> Give journalists the opportunity to question or interview your artists, speakers, CEO, etc. This can be arranged in the form of a press conference. Set up a press room that has a good internet connection and lines of communication.

> Not every journalist will be suitable for your event. Make your selection on the basis on their known specialisations and the relationships you have already built up. Keep your media plans in a proper perspective and avoid overdoing things. If you are organising a small event, you are better off inviting journalists from the regional and/or professional media, rather than hoping for (inter)national press attention.

> What is the best moment for distributing your press folder to journalists? If you do it too early during the event, there is a good chance that the busy journalists will leave straight away. But if you leave it too late, there is also a chance that they will have already left without your relevant information. Make your decision based on the kind of event you are organising and the relationship you have with the journalists in question.

> Are you expecting a camera team? Make sure you provide them with adequate parking space for their satellite vans and take account in your action plan of the time they will need to set up their equipment.

PRESS RELEASE

Journalists receive a dozen or more press releases and invitations in their mailbox each day. They often decide within the space of seven seconds whether or not they will publish your release. This means that if you want to score, you need to make it stand out from the crowd. In short, it has to be newsworthy.

Self-evidently, the content of your press release must be interesting for the journalists. It must contain 'news', something they feel is worth publishing. Be aware of the risk of 'corporate blindness': a story that you think is interesting might be of no interest to a wide public. Opening your new office building is probably a big thing for you and your colleagues, but no one else will really care all that much. If your press release satisfies the following criteria, there is a good chance that your story will be deemed newsworthy.

- ✓ **Current**
  Old news is not interesting. Do not send press releases that contain news that is already outdated.

- ✓ **Different**
  A controversial subject is always interesting. People want to read about conflict and sensation. Everything that is out of the ordinary or deviates from the norm generates interest.

- ✓ **Innovative**
  A new product or event will score if it is innovative. Fresh ideas and creative approaches greatly increase newsworthiness. An 'ordinary' new product or commercial message will not set a journalist's pulse racing.

- ✓ **Impressive**
  The bigger the numbers, the higher the percentages, the larger the area, the more likely your press release will hit the mark.

- ✓ **Impactful**
  A press release is only interesting when it has an impact on the reader or has important social relevance. The more people close to the reader are involved in the story, the greater its subjective newsworthiness.

- ✓ **Credible**
  The reputation, importance and reliability of the origin of the press release significantly increase its credibility. In other words, the image of your company will have an impact on the success of your press releases.

- ✓ **Authoritative**
  A quote from the CEO, an expert or a celebrity will add weight to your message and make it more believable. If possible, place this quote in the first or second paragraph of your press release.

Before sending it, re-read your press release and assess it critically. Will it spark the reader's interest? If it came from another company, would you read it? If you answer 'no' to these questions, the content is probably too commercial and therefore more suited for an advertising message. In this case, you would be better advised to opt for an advertorial. This is a paid advertisement giving information about a product or event in the style of a journalistic article. But be careful! Strict rules apply to advertorials. For example, you need to state clearly that it is an advertorial and not an objective article. The advantage, however, is that you have full control over the content, which is not the case when you hand over a press release to a journalist.

HOW DO YOU WRITE A GOOD PRESS RELEASE?

The essence of your press release should be encapsulated in the first paragraph. You answer the questions posed by the five W's: who, what, where, when and why. In the following paragraphs you offer more explanation about those answers and give additional details. Your press release should therefore be written like an inverted pyramid: the most important at the top, the supporting details at the bottom. Avoid a long introduction. The last thing you write is the title. A good title should be catchy, but must also indicate clearly what the press release is about.

In addition to the press release, provide information about your company, its most important products and any other relevant material. In this way, the journalist has all the right information to hand. Do not forget to include a high-resolution photo that relates to the subject of your press release. Check everything a last time for spelling and grammatical errors before you send it off.

📌 Include your press release directly in the body of your e-mail to the journalists, and not attached in annex. The fewer steps they have to take to read your release, the better. Extra information and/or photos can be added in annex or in a download link. Have you got a YouTube film? If so, make sure to add the embed codes.

📌 It is incredible that many organisations still send their press releases with the title... 'press release'! This is the fastest way to get your release deleted by the receivers. Instead, stimulate their curiosity with a catchy title.

📌 Do not forget to add your contact details to the press release, so that journalists can easily get in touch with the right people if they need more information.

📌 Do not put all the journalists in CC, but make use of BCC. Better still, send each one a personal mail. Otherwise, the 'exclusive' nature of your press release will instantly be lost. Moreover, some of the journalists may not like having their own details shared with all and sundry.

Remember: there is no such thing as 'free publicity'. If you want to gain the attention of the press, you will need to offer them something newsworthy.

Printing and branding

Invitations, posters, badges, programme books, entrance tickets, staff uniforms, banners, flags: every event involves plenty of printing, be it on paper or fabric. In most cases, the type of event and the budget will determine what you have printed – and how. Begin in plenty of time – because you always have more printing work than you imagine – and your printers will also need time to do the job properly.

LAYOUT AND VISUAL IDENTITY

Large companies usually have their own communications department which coordinates printing internally. However, if you are unable to make staff available for this task or if the printing for your event is too voluminous, you can make use of the services of an external graphic designer or a communications agency.

Whether you arrange your printing internally or externally, make sure that all your communications are consistent. There are various options: for example, you can base your event communication on the house style of your company or you can develop a new style specifically for the occasion. In most cases, a combination of both options offers the best results.

> Devote careful attention to your textual content. Employ the services of a professional copywriter. Check the proofs thoroughly for spelling mistakes and other grammatical errors.

VISUAL IDENTITY AND BRANDING

People are highly visual beings. Sight is the principle way for us to observe and perceive the world around us – and the same applies for your event participants. People only remember 10% of what they hear, but when linked to an image they can remember as much as 65%, even after three days. When we talk about the visual identity of an event, we are referring to all the many different visual elements (name, colour, logo, typography, graphic design features, etc.) that are used throughout your venue. Together, these elements form the branding of the event and project a certain image with an easily recognisable and consistent perception of value.

How can you develop a strong branding? Here are some tips to help you on your way:

- **Colours**
Colours can influence the way your visitors think about your event. So you need to be very careful how you choose them. Pick a central colour that best matches the philosophy and message of your event. For example, purple would be suitable for an event about wellness or spirituality. Green is appropriate for events focused on the environment and sustainability. And red is ideal for an event about entrepreneurship.

Would you like to know more about colours and events? Read this article:

 www.eventplanner.net/book/colours

- **Graphic elements**
Always opt for a clean and easy-to-recognise graphic design. Let's imagine that the core element of the visual identity of your event is a composition made up of three interlocking circles. This is the image that your visitors will associate first and foremost with the event. Consequently, you need to make sure that they can see it in lots of different places. There are also a number of different ways you can do this: different colours, different sizes, different configurations, different contexts, and so on.

- **Consistency**
Although these minor variations are possible, you need to be consistent when it comes to respecting the basic design. You can't have three interlocking circles on your printed programme and then use four on your website. Once you have chosen a set of graphic elements, stick with them. Consistency is key. All your event material and all your communication channels must reflect the same visual identity. Otherwise people will become confused and will not be able to recognise your event. Also use the same consistent style in all your photography. And don't forget your social media posts.

From the 'save the date' e-mail to the very final 'thank you for being there' message, it is important that you consciously and consistently display your graphic elements and your visual identity. Apply the same principle to your use of visual elements during the event: programmes, banners, presentations, signs, and so on. In this way, the image of the event will remain firmly rooted in the minds of your participants.

PRINTER

Prices and quality can vary enormously from printer to printer, so ask for price quotations and samples from at least three printers. Make sure you ask for offers based on the same format, layout and print run: you need to compare like with like. Also ask the printer what kind of print work he is capable of providing.

*Fast and cheap is not always the same as **good**.*

You will probably find that the prices you receive differ considerably. The cheapest tender may sometimes also be the best choice, but make sure that this does not conceal a major difference in quality. Nowadays, there are numerous online printers who can do your printing work at knock-down prices. You can upload your design online and download the finished product in just a few days' time. But be warned: fast and cheap does not always necessarily mean good; often the very reverse.

Ask for price tenders as soon as you know exactly what you need in terms of printing. It is important to make arrangements with your chosen printer at an early stage. Last minute printing costs more and makes mistakes more likely. Agree clear and timely deadlines with the printer about when and in what format (specifications) he must deliver your printed items.

 Try and have all your printing done by a single printer. This saves time, because you avoid the need to make several different arrangements. It is also cheaper for large orders and eliminates possible problems relating to differences of quality, colour, etc. between the various printed items. Remember, however, that not every printer does every type of printing.

If the size of your print run is small, you may decide to opt for digital printing. There are no start-up costs and it is often quicker. It is also easier to personalise your print work, providing you have a good database. If your print run is larger, offset printing offers some interesting and creative options. Offset printing is generally of better quality than digital, although the most recent digital printers are giving increasingly good results. Ask your printer for advice – that is what they're there for.

 If you are organising an international event, you will probably need print work in different languages. This can increase the cost of your printing dramatically, since it means that the printer needs to prepare more than one printing plate, which quickly pushes up their number of work hours. In these circumstances, a clever design (for example, all text changes in a single colour) can save you a lot of money.

www.eventplanner.net/book/printers

TYPE OF PAPER

The type of paper helps to determine the style and quality of your printed matter (chic, business-like, exclusive, personal). Discuss the image you are trying to project with the printer or your communications team. Choose the right materials to match each different type of image or different type of product. Whenever possible, try to use recycled paper.

Look at a range of different samples. Ask the printer to provide a specimen model and then choose the right envelope to match.

> 📌 Keep a folder with all the different paper and material samples that you think might be suitable for your event. If you find it difficult to understand the mysterious language of the printing world – paper thicknesses, grain size, etc. – you can just pull the things you like out of your folder. This will make your discussions less technical and easier to follow.

> 📌 Heavier paper means more postage costs. Postal companies will be happy to provide you with information about these costs. Moreover, with the liberalisation of the postal sector there are now a number of new players in the market offering highly competitive prices. Well worth checking out!

> 📌 Some types of printed matter (such as menu cards, programme books, etc.) need to withstand repeated use. Choose a thicker, grease-proof type of paper for these items.

FORMAT

There are two main factors when deciding upon the format. How practical is your preferred format and what are the cost implications?

For example, it can be useful to offer programme books which are small enough to fit neatly into a handbag or inside pocket. Place cards at dining tables can be small, but must nonetheless be big enough and clear enough to be read in dimmed lighting.

The standard paper sizes are usually the cheapest, both for printing and for postage. If you want to send an item of print work in your standard and pre-existing company envelopes, make sure that the sizes match.

 Are you thinking about different formats? Ask Bpost (B), TNT Post (NL) or other suppliers about exactly how much they charge for the delivery of non-standard formats.

PRINTING TICKETS

Although most organisers nowadays prefer to use the 'safe' digital option for their ticketing, there are still events that make use of printed tickets. In that case, it is important to be aware of the possibility of forgeries. However, with a few small measures it is still possible to make your printed tickets reasonably secure. With this in mind, the most common printing techniques are as follows:

- **Digital hologram/glossmark**
  Digital holograms or a glossmark allow you to create a sheen effect. In this way, a particular logo or number can be made 'shiny'. This sheen effect cannot be copied or scanned, which makes forgery of your tickets almost impossible.

- **Micro-text**
  You can print a micro-text on your tickets, using super-small letters that are not legible with the naked eye. These tickets are also difficult to copy, because the resolution of most copying machines is too low to accurately duplicate the micro-text without smudging. This makes entrance control relatively easy. Just look at the ticket under a magnifying glass. Is the text legible? If so, the ticket is an original. If not, ...

- **Barcodes**
  A very popular and frequently used technique is the addition of barcodes or QR codes to tickets. Of course, this means that you need a barcode or QR scanner at each of your entrance points. You should also remember that barcodes can be copied, but only to gain admittance once.

- **UV-printing**
  UV-printing is a technique that allows a logo, text or numbers to be added to your ticket in ink that is invisible to the naked eye. These additions only

become visible if passed under a UV-lamp (blacklight), when they appear in bright blue or white.

- **Infra-red printing**
  This technique is comparable with UV-printing, but works at the other end of the light spectrum. This type of invisible ink can only be read using an infra-red camera and a computer screen.

- **Correlation text**
  You can also have your tickets printed with a text in ink that can only be read under a special filter.

VISUAL IMAGES

It is said that "a picture paints a thousand words". For this reason, you will often want to use pictures as part of your print design. Make sure that you deliver the photographs to the printer in good time, that they are of professional quality, and that they are of a sufficiently high resolution for printing purposes. Remember also to think about possible copyright implications: the commercial use of 'protected' photos can cost you a lot of money afterwards.

Of course, you can always hire a photographer and make your own photographs. They can deliver exactly what you want – but at a price. To keep this price to a minimum, make sure that you give them precise instructions before they start. Don't start improvising on set: time is money!

If the use of a professional photographer is out of the question, you can search for suitable stock photos in databanks such as istockphoto.com, unsplash.com or pexels.com. These offer a huge range of professional photographs on just about every subject under the sun. Once you have paid the necessary fee, there is no problem about using the photographs in your print work.

> Check in good time with your printer or communications bureau to make sure that the quality of the photographs is sufficiently good for what you have in mind. If the resolution is not high enough, the quality of the end product will be greatly reduced. It is better to have no photo than a poor photo. Photographs with a lower resolution are, however, suitable for web applications. Although nowadays you also need to be careful with the use of high-resolution (retina display) screens.

CHECKLIST FOR PRINTING AND PRINTED MATTER

The preparation period for your event is always a very busy time, so it is sometimes easy to overlook things. The following checklist will help to ensure that you do not forget anything important as far as printing is concerned.

Invitation trajectory

- ☐ Pre-announcement/teaser
- ☐ Invitations
- ☐ Answer cards
- ☐ Letters of confirmation
- ☐ Route plan
- ☐ Envelopes
- ☐ Flyers, leaflets, posters
- ☐ Entrance tickets
- ☐ ...

During the event

- ☐ Badges, armbands, name plates/stickers
- ☐ Programme books
- ☐ Hand-outs (or USB sticks with presentations)
- ☐ Ground plan
- ☐ Note books and pens
- ☐ Direction signs
- ☐ Signs for 'reserved', 'no smoking', etc.
- ☐ Menu cards
- ☐ Tables plans, numbers and name cards
- ☐ Napkins / serviettes
- ☐ Food/drink vouchers
- ☐ Press folders
- ☐ Flags, banners
- ☐ Textile printing (caps, T-shirts, umbrellas, etc.)
- ☐ Stage decoration (backdrop)
- ☐ Survey/inquiry forms
- ☐ Action plans
- ☐ ...

After the event

- ☐ Commemorative paper/magazine
- ☐ Photo books
- ☐ Thank you cards
- ☐ ...

Venue (location)

The location will determine to a large extent the atmosphere, attractiveness and appeal of your event. In other words, your choice of venue can make all the difference between success and failure. Above all, remember to consider the practical implications of your choice. How easily accessible is the venue? What facilities does it offer?

CHOOSING A VENUE

The ideal venue takes account of all the factors which you need to combine in order to make your event a success. As we shall see, a number of these factors can have a severely limiting effect on the number of suitable venues from which you can choose. In short, your approach will need to be creative.

The location and the available facilities are the two most important factors. You may have found the perfect place, but is it easy to get to for your guests? If not, you will need to keep on looking or be prepared to lay on (and pay for) extra transport. Remember also to check for adequate parking space and to look at the capacity of the different rooms/halls you want to use.

The charm and atmosphere of the location is another key factor. It needs to create the right ambiance for your target group and to set the right tone for your theme, so that it can support the successful realisation of your objectives.

On eventplanner.net you can find a comprehensive search engine that will help you to track down the perfect venue for your event with minimum fuss and bother.

> An average of 5% of event guests make use of public transport and this figure is growing all the time. How far is the nearest bus stop or train station from your proposed venue? If it is too far, think about organising a shuttle service.

📌 Is the venue difficult to find? If so, place direction signs along the route. You will need to ask the permission of the local authorities to do this, so remember to make your application in plenty of time. Sometimes, you may have to pay a fee and if you want to place really large boards alongside a public road, you may even need planning permission.

📌 Make sure that there are no road works or strikes planned for the day of your event. If necessary, arrange alternative routes or check to see whether or not the planned diversions are sufficiently clear and easy to follow. Take account of the fact that some of your guests may arrive late as a result.

📌 Are you organising a multi-day or late evening event? If so, find out what overnight accommodation facilities are available in the vicinity of your venue. Be ready to provide this information if some of your guests don't want to make the long journey home. You can also communicate this information in advance via your event website or in a mailing.

CHECKLIST FOR VENUES

The following checklist is a useful tool to make sure that your dream venue really is suitable to host your dream event.

- ✔ Does the venue have the right 'feel' for your event? Is this the atmosphere you want? Can you (and will you be allowed to) make changes to create the **right atmosphere**? If possible, visit the venue when another event is taking place, so that you can assess the possibilities and limitations of the event space.
- ✔ Is the venue easily **accessible**? Is the location central and is the required journey time for your guests acceptable? Can the guests make use of their own transport and public transport? What is the situation for guests who may need to make international travel connections? Is the entrance attractive?
- ✔ Is the **maximum capacity** large enough for your planned event? Is the **division and layout of the space/rooms** suitable for the activities you have in mind? Can you rearrange the available space (for example, with moveable partitions) to make it more suitable? Can you enlarge the avail-

able space (for example, by placing a tent against an outer wall)? Also be careful not to book venues that are too large. If necessary, place screens or curtains to make the space seem smaller. Guests often feel lost and uncomfortable in large (open) spaces.

- ✓ Are there enough separate **break-out** rooms to organise parallel sessions?
- ✓ Are **adequate parking facilities** available, either at the venue itself or somewhere nearby? If necessary, can a shuttle service be arranged? Is the parking safe? Is there security surveillance? Are there **battery charging points** for electric cars and bikes?
- ✓ Is the venue **accessible for the physically-challenged**? Are there parking spaces for them near the entrance? Is a toilet available for wheelchair users? Are there obstacles, such as too many stairs? Is there a lift?
- ✓ Are there **enough toilets** in general? You should count on one toilet for every 75 guests. Don't forget to engage toilet attendants and make sure that the toilets do not give off smells which are noticeable in your event space: this can be very off-putting! If this is the case, there are specialised firms that deal with the elimination or masking of such smells.
- ✓ Is there a **cloakroom**? Is it large enough? If not, is there a room that you can transform into a cloakroom? Is there a numbering system?
- ✓ Are catering facilities available (i.e., a **kitchen**)?

- Are you obliged to make use of the venue's **house suppliers** for technical support, catering, decoration, etc.? Do you need to pay an indemnity fee if you want to work with your own suppliers?
- Can you make use of any **tables, chairs, etc.** that may be available at the location. Or do you need to rent these from a specialised hire company? Are the chairs and seats suitable for long periods of sitting?
- Does the venue have its own **audio-visual facilities** and **sound-system** that you can use? Are these installations sufficient for the entertainment you have in mind?
- Are the venue's **acoustics** acceptable? Can you solve potential problems by installing sound-absorbing curtains or screens? Is there any outside noise (train line, road works, etc.) in the vicinity of the venue, which may disrupt your event?
- Check that the event space can be **darkened**, if this is necessary for your planned activity, or, alternatively, that there is sufficient **daylight**.
- Is the power supply sufficient to meet your **electricity needs**? Or do you need to hire in an additional generator?
- Is (running) **water** available? Is there a possibility to install a temporary water supply/disposal system?
- Are all **utilities costs** (use of water, electricity, etc.) included in the basic hire cost of the venue?
- Is there sufficient (atmospheric) **lighting** in and around the venue? Is the parking area well-lit and safe? Does this apply equally to any walkways?
- Does the venue have its own **stage** or is there space to construct a hired stage? Is there a **dance floor**?
- Are there **changing rooms** for both staff and artists? Are there enough mirrors, coat hangers, etc.? Is there a backstage lounge where the artists can relax? Is there easy access between the changing rooms and the stage area (so that they don't need to walk through the audience)?
- Is there a maximum **noise level** or **closing time** of which you need to take account? Is it possible to obtain special permission to get around these limitations?
- Are the **heating** and/or **air-conditioning systems** adequate? When a large number of guests enter a room in rapid succession, the temperature can rise (too) quickly. Ask the advice of a specialist company: they can tell you how to avoid the entrance becoming too cold, while the rest of the room is too warm.
- Is it possible to continually **ventilate** the room(s)? A lack of air can lead to loss of concentration, which is hardly ideal for congresses and seminars.
- Does the venue offer the use of **ancillary services** (secretariat, toilet assistant, cloakroom, etc.) in its price?
- What **first aid equipment and facilities** are available? Is there an automated external defibrillator on site?

- ✔ Does the venue have a (digital) **sign system** to show guests the way from one room to another? Are there **information screens/boards** to show details of the programme and the locations of the various activities?
- ✔ Are there good **internet connections** and a Wi-Fi hotspot which the guests can use? Ask for the access codes in advance and conduct a trial run to verify the quality of the connection. Is the use of these facilities free or do the guests need to buy a voucher? Check that the connection has sufficient capacity to allow all your guests to surf at the same time (which is absolutely essential for congresses and seminars). You can read more about this in the paragraph on the internet in chapter 14.
- ✔ Does the venue have a **location manager** who can help you to think through problems during the preparations and assist in the smooth running of the actual event itself?
- ✔ Are there sufficient **hotel** rooms available in the vicinity of the venue?
- ✔ Are you able to hire the venue **exclusively** or will other events be taking place there at the same time? How can you avoid possible overcrowding or overuse of the available facilities?
- ✔ What facilities exist for the press and for communications in general? Is there a room that can be set up as a **press room** or communications centre? This room must be equipped with electricity and a good internet connection. You may also wish to consider setting up a **production office**, from which you can coordinate the running of the event.
- ✔ Remember to pay close attention to **security**. Are there sufficient emergency exits, fire extinguishers, a first aid kit, etc.? Check that the smoke detectors are not too sensitive, so that they might be triggered off by any smoke effects which might be used by your stage act.
- ✔ Ask about the conditions relating to **set construction and removal**. You can often hire the venue for a few days before and after your event at preferential rates.
- ✔ Is the venue easily accessible for all your **logistical operations**, such as the delivery and collection of materials and equipment?
- ✔ Check that the **entrance doors** are sufficiently wide. For example, it would be a shame to book a venue for a new car launch only to discover at a later stage that you can't get the car inside the building!
- ✔ Is the **load-bearing capacity** of the roof sufficient to support heavy constructions and winching? Are the **ceilings** sufficiently high?
- ✔ When you organise an event at a location of your own (for example, the staff canteen or a storage hangar), check with your insurance company to make certain that you are **insured** against all possible risks.
- ✔ Can you make arrangements for **smokers**? Notwithstanding the ban on smoking in public places, some of your guests will still want to 'light up' during your event. Is there a covered area (outside) where they can smoke or can you rig up a temporary structure with heating units?

- ✓ Always check the **environmental permit** of your event venue. Why? Look back at the reasons we gave in chapter 1!
- ✓ What are the **terms** for cancellation, availability and payment? Are there any other general conditions?

> 📌 Always take a camera with you when you go to scout venues. Photographs can be a useful memory aid later on, when you are working on designs, decoration, etc. back at your office. Also ask for a ground plan of the site and any for any technical information that is available.

> 📌 If you are looking for a venue for a health event, add the presence of outdoor and sporting facilities to your checklist. Can you exit the main building easily? Is there a terrace or garden? Are there wellness options on site or nearby? If so, integrate the possibility to use these facilities into your event programme. As an alternative, go resolutely for the full outdoor option.

ORIGINAL LOCATIONS

Traditional locations such as function rooms, congress centres and staff canteens are very practical, since most of the facilities you need are close at hand. However, these locations are sometimes not very original and are often lacking in inspiration. For this reason, more and more companies are going in search of venues which can surprise, even amaze, their guests. Special venues of this kind are hip!

Do not be afraid to be creative. Any location is suitable for an event.

Do not be afraid to be creative. In principle, any location is suitable – or can be made suitable – for an event: factories, workshops, garages, churches, museums, yachts, fun parks, golf clubs, etc. The disadvantage is that venues of this kind frequently lack many basic facilities. You may need to make your own arrangements for electricity, toilets, heating, decoration, etc. This will cost you money. But the main benefit of such locations rests in the fact that your own creativity is less restricted: for example, your freedom to decide about decoration and layout will be much greater than in a 'standard' location.

📍 Opting to use a special venue for your event must be a conscious choice. Some things will not be as straightforward as at other locations. Does this venue bring added value to your event? If so, go for it! If not, save yourself a whole heap of stress and money by choosing a well-equipped standard venue.

📍 A moving venue such as a boat, train or plane will give your guests a very different (but equally memorable) kind of event experience. The big advantage is that these guests will stay for the whole event. The big disadvantage is that those who want to leave early will be trapped!

Tents

Remember, too, that you do not always need to make use of permanent structures. Temporary accommodation, such as tents, can also be surprisingly comfortable and elegant. They also offer a number of unique possibilities. For example, tents give you the option of holding your event at almost any location: on top of a mountain, in your company grounds, on a floating platform... Bear in mind, however, that using tents in this way is usually more expensive than hiring a classic indoor venue. However, it will create an effect for your guests that few (if any) indoor venues can match.

You might choose a pagoda tent, an alu-hall, a mirror tent, a circus tent or even a tent with different levels. There is a large difference in the 'charm' factor of these different types of tent, just as there are large differences in quality between the various suppliers. If you are placing a white frame tent for your event, make sure that it actually is 'white' – and not covered with mud from a previous event. And don't forget to install a strong floor, which is not only resistant to the cold and damp of the under-surface, but also provides sufficient stability. Different styles of tent 'wall' are also available: some are transparent, while others can be opened during warm weather. Take proper account of noise levels and apply in good time for the necessary permission to erect your tent. Also remember that some form of heating will be necessary during colder periods.

Be careful if you are placing your tent on open ground, where there might be plenty of wind. You might need additional anchoring to guarantee maximum safety. If in doubt, ask advice from a specialist. Professional suppliers will usually ensure that all necessary safety standards and norms are properly complied with and should be able to provide certificates to this effect.

Last but not least, make certain that your tent site is accessible and capable of carrying the heavy traffic that will be necessary to install your tent and supply your event. If necessary, you can use steel ramps to prevent lorries from turning your chosen venue into a ploughed field! Even so, bear in mind that the erection and removal of a tent can take a number of days – so build this into your planning. If your chosen site is not on level ground, the tent constructor will need to take account of the height difference. A difference of 40 cm or less should be no problem. Anything more will probably need a special construction.

📌 Visit your chosen site in advance with your tent supplier and check for any potential difficulties. Relatively small problems can sometimes have major financial implications. For example, an immoveable hedge or fence around your chosen site may mean that you need to hire a crane or perhaps even that all the material needs to be carried in by hand.

📌 Whenever you choose this kind of temporary venue, always install emergency lighting and make sure that there are sufficient emergency exits. Adjust your sound system to take account of the poorer general acoustics in tents and make proper waste disposal arrangements for your temporary toilet units.

Open air

If your event is taking place during the summer, you may opt for an open-air location. If so, try and choose an inspirational spot: a wood, a beach, a lake, a fun park, etc. Remember that you will need permission to hold your event in one of these places, so make sure that you apply for the necessary permits in good time. Most importantly, devise a good back-up plan in case the weather gods are not kind to you on your big day! Decide well in advance at what point you will need to take the final decision about whether to hold the event outdoors or indoors (or in a worst-case scenario even cancel it). Build this eventuality into your preparations.

CAPACITY, ROOM LAYOUT AND SET-UP

You can arrange your furniture and equipment in many different ways within your available space. When choosing your layout, you need to take account of the type of event and the required net surface area per guest/participant. The total **net surface area** is the area of your enclosed accommodation, excluding the stage, free-standing decoration and any technical facilities.

Again depending on the type of event, you may need to provide tables, chairs, etc. If your programme includes a presentation, make sure that all the guests have a good view of both the speaker and the presentation screen. Don't place chairs behind supporting columns or anything else that might block people's line of sight. Are you organising a congress with relatively long sessions? If so, opt for comfortable chairs and arrange them so that there is plenty of leg room. Adjust the layout in accordance with the possibilities offered by the available space.

 Do you want to arrange your seating in a theatre layout? Use chairs that click together, because they are much safer. If something happens, so that the room needs to be evacuated, the seats remain in place and do not block the safe and swift exit of your guests. In some countries and regions this kind of room set-up is compulsory.

Are you planning a seated dinner? If at all possible, try to use round tables. These are not only more pleasing visually, but also increase the pleasure of your guests: everyone can see everyone else, so that talking is easy and no one feels left out. Whether they are round or oblong, ensure that the tables are sufficiently large, so that the guests are not too cramped or have your elegant table decoration hanging over their plates!

Remember to foresee special places for VIP guests and the press. If you are expecting wheelchair users at a performance event, make sure that space is reserved for them at the front of the auditorium.

The following diagrams illustrate a number of classic layouts, with an indication of the required number of square metres (*net area*) per person.

Meetings and congresses

✓ **Theatre layout**
0.5 m² per person

✓ **School layout**
1.5 m² per person

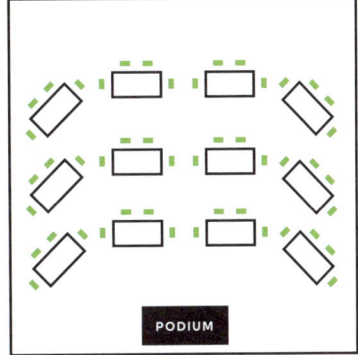

✓ **Cabaret layout**
1 m² per person

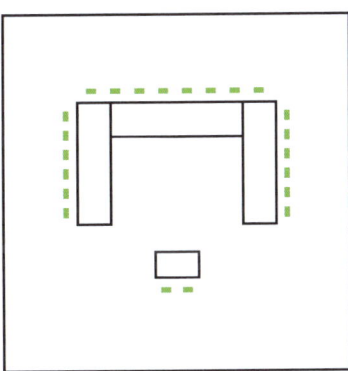

✓ **Square layout**
2.5 m² per person

✓ **U-shape**
2.5 m² per person

Festive occasions

✓ **Reception**
1 m² per person

✓ **Banquet/seated dinner**
1.5 to 2 m² per person

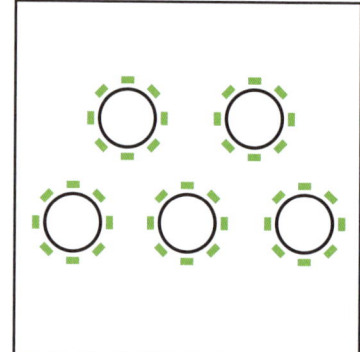

✓ **Party**
1.5 m² per person
Bar: 1 per 100-150 people
Food buffet: 1 per 50 people

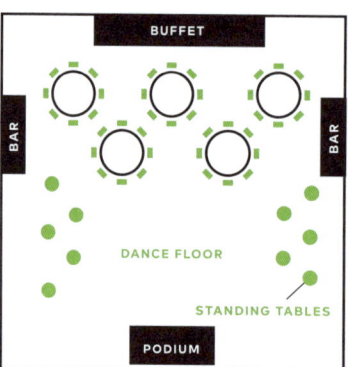

In addition to traditional layouts, you can also devise more creative set-ups. Start, for example, with a 'seated dinner' layout, add a podium and after the meal turn around all the chairs that have their backs to the podium, so that you create a 'cabaret' layout. Or opt for an 'open space' layout, with all the chairs in a circle around your speaker or act in the middle. This reduces the need for other furniture and the resulting lack of obstacles stimulates greater interaction. Of course, the speaker needs to be confident that he/she can deal with this set-up, because it is challenging to talk to a group when half of them are always looking at your back! A 'runway' layout is based on the 'square' layout, but you only use the tables on the left and right sides (and not the top and bottom). This creates two parallel rows of tables, between which the speaker can walk up and down on the 'catwalk'. This makes it possible to present some parts of the programme in a more dynamic manner. You can also play around with various types of furniture: standing tables, seating areas with comfy armchairs, clusters of free-standing chairs, and so on. This can work particularly well in networking zones.

> A dance floor will usually take up between 10-20% of the total surface area.

LINKS
Could you use a bit of extra inspiration to find your ideal event venue? If so, take a look at the following URLs:

- www.eventplanner.net/book/banquethalls
- www.eventplanner.net/book/eventvenues
- www.eventplanner.net/book/meetingrooms
- www.eventplanner.net/book/conferencevenues
- www.eventplanner.net/book/exhibitionhalls
- www.eventplanner.net/book/castles
- www.eventplanner.net/book/tents
- www.eventplanner.net/book/clubs
- www.eventplanner.net/book/concertvenues

 www.eventplanner.net/book/hotels

  www.eventplanner.net/book/themeparks

www.eventplanner.net/book/ships

 www.eventplanner.net/book/theaters

EVENTS ABROAD

Organising an event abroad brings with it a number of extra challenges. A different language, a new work dynamic, local customs that you don't understand…

Here are some other potential pitfalls that you need to be aware of:

✓ **You cannot rely on your usual network**
Where is the technician who you can call every five minutes when you are trying to install his equipment? Where is the IT professional who will drop everything and come to your rescue if your Wi-Fi connection crashes? Where is your regular security team whose protocols you know so well? You will have no close working relationships of this kind when organising an event abroad.

✓ **You are not familiar with the culture**
Imagine that your event starts on Wednesday and you want to print off the final revised version of your programme on Tuesday evening. But you did not know that Tuesday is a public holiday in the country where you are, so that everything will be closed!

✓ **You cannot communicate quickly and clearly**
You cannot speak Hindi, French or Spanish, although your English is good enough for routine business matters. But have you ever tried to speak a different language, even if you know it well, when you are stressed and trying to get your message across as quickly and as clearly as possible?

Fortunately, there are a few things you can do to compensate for these pitfalls:

- ✔ **Make yourself familiar with the country**
  It pays to thoroughly research the country where you are planning to hold your event. Make a list of general questions that you need to take into account. Is this country/city safe? What is the economic and political situation? Is there adequate public transport and how does it operate? What is its gastronomic culture? Are there religious issues that may have an influence on your event? If, for example, you are organising a congress in Dubai during the middle of Ramadan, what impact will this have on you and your guests?

- ✔ **Make clear arrangements with your suppliers**
  In some countries it is not always clear what is included in the price and what is not. For example, some foreign event locations oblige you to work with their own suppliers for catering, decoration, musical installations, etc. Or charge all kinds of supplementary costs for things you never thought of. To avoid these inconveniences, inform yourself thoroughly in advance and make clear arrangements.

- ✔ **Inspect the venue and its surroundings**
  You need to inspect your chosen venue and its surroundings in person. Plan an on-site visit at least a couple of months before your event is scheduled to take place. Check if the location is easily accessible and whether your participants can use public transport.

- ✔ **Analyse the local event landscape**
  You cannot run an event without the help of multiple suppliers. Before you even set foot in your host location, draw up a list of local suppliers that you think can help you. Contact them by phone and/or arrange an online meeting. If you reach provisional agreement, meet them face to face during your on-site inspection visit or when you arrive in the country to set up the event.

- ✔ **Build up a professional team**
  Equally, you cannot run an event in a foreign country without the help of a local team. You need experienced people you can rely on. Surround yourself with local planners and advisers who can assist you to deal with the special event planning requirements of their country. Ask for their guidance to find out how things really work. It is also a good idea to contact and work with the local tourist office and other event-related organisations.

In some countries, such as the United States, it is compulsory to work with local labour for the construction and dismantling of your event site. Check what the local regulations say on these matters and comply accordingly.

- ✓ **Make sure you have good insurance**
  In some countries, event venues and suppliers ask for an insurance certificate as a form of guarantee. Make sure that you are always insured for a sufficiently high amount. In the US, for example, people are much more easily inclined to litigate for perceived damage and injuries.

ACCESSIBILITY

When discussing the checklist for event venues earlier in the book, I briefly mentioned the need for parking space and good access for wheelchair users. Of course, making your event truly accessible for people with a limitation requires much more than that.

This is an issue that is still often overlooked by event planners or else it is eliminated from their thinking because of the extra cost it involves. This is short-sighted. You need to make your event easily accessible not only for the physically challenged, but also for the elderly, people with young children in prams and even your own suppliers. It is estimated that one person in four has some form of limitation, so you cannot afford to ignore 25% of your visitors!

Providing basic accessibility is not as complex or as expensive as people often think. There are a number of relatively simple conditions that make it easy to achieve:

- ✓ Provide clear information about the accessibility arrangements for your event. Mention specifically in advance if some areas are not (easily) accessible. You can do this on your website.
- ✓ Make sure that people with a limitation can park nearby.
- ✓ If there is a podium for your event, make sure that wheelchair users can see it properly by giving them a place at the front or on a raised platform. Clearly indicate these places with pictograms on the ground.
- ✓ Ensure that the location as a whole is accessible. Are there steps up to the entrance? This can often be solved by hiring in ramps (for a maximum gradient of 15%). Are there unmetalled or gravel paths? Cover them with some form of plating (steel or plastic). This will not only help wheelchair users but also make things easier for other visitors. All accessways must be at least 90 cm wide.

- ✔ Allow assistance dogs at your event. For example, those used by the visually challenged.
- ✔ Arrange that there are enough people or volunteers on hand to provide assistance to those who need it.

If you want to take things a step further, you can recruit a sign language interpreter for the benefit of those who are deaf or have hearing loss. Some locations and organisations even make provision for a hearing loop, which transmits an audio signal directly to users' hearing aid, cutting out background noise and making speech and music clear.

Remember also that accessibility means more than just physical access to the event venue. Is your website simple to use for people with a limitation? Is your use of language (both online and offline) easy to understand?

All these matters are important – so take account of them. Moreover, there is legally enforceable anti-discrimination legislation that covers the reasonable requirements of people with a limitation and the adjustments that need to be made to help them. Make certain that you are in compliance.

▶ www.eventplanner.net/book/tv-accessibility

Catering

They way, so they say, to a man's heart is through his stomach – and this is equally true of events. Catering is therefore very important and – like all the other elements – must be closely attuned to your objectives and the expectations of the target group. Your choice of catering style (seated dinner, walking dinner, buffet, etc.) will depend on a number of factors, such as the culinary impression you wish to make, your budget, the number of guests, the timing and the time available. Catering can be a programmed activity in its own right (for example, cooking workshops or themed dinners), but usually plays a supporting role to other activities.

 At many events, the culinary aspects play a large part in determining overall guest satisfaction. Eating has a direct influence on the perceived experience of the event. It therefore pays to give this important element of your programme the attention it deserves. If your catering is insufficient and/or of poor quality, you will soon notice this in the comments you receive from guests. This is not how you want people to remember your event!

WHICH PARTY CATERER?

Many venues work with one or more fixed caterer. This is useful, since the caterer in question is familiar with the possibilities but also the logistic limitations of the kitchen facilities. On the negative side, the level of cooking and/or the price might not agree with what you had in mind. In some cases, it may be possible to use a caterer of your own choice, providing you pay an indemnity. This compensation is usually a percentage of your budget (between 10 and 35% is customary) or a fixed sum. The same principle also applies to the use of your own drink, where you will need to pay an uncorking fee per bottle.

If you still prefer to go in search of your own (party) caterer, make sure you visit plenty of other events to see your possible candidates 'in action'. Are his cocktail snacks tasty and original? Is the service friendly and well-dressed?

Does the presentation look good? Even if you don't get the chance to watch a caterer at work at a live event, you can always ask to see his own kitchen, where he carries out all his preparations. It is usual for the caterer to cook you a trial meal, so that you know in advance what your guests will be getting on their plates. The cost of this trial meal will usually be deducted from the final price, if the caterer is eventually awarded the event contract.

Check that the caterer works in accordance with the HACCP norms (Hazard Analysis Critical Control Points). This norm sets down conditions for the storage, transport, preparation and serving of food, and therefore offers you a number of guarantees. Additional local norms relating to these and similar matters must also be respected. Most catering companies will be able to boast other quality labels. Even so, take no risks where food is concerned: do your homework thoroughly. The last thing you want is for half of your guests to go down with food poisoning! Also ask to see the qualifications of the serving personnel and, if possible, the selection of uniforms from which you can choose.

If the caterer has never worked at your venue before, it is a good idea to accompany him on a preliminary visit. This allows the caterer to check whether or not the kitchen facilities are sufficient to properly prepare the dishes on your menu. Some caterers have their own mobile kitchen, complete with logistical back-up. Others will have to hire this type of mobile unit. For events with more than one thousand guests, it is advisable to install more than one kitchen and more than one collection/clearance point, in order to cut down the walking distance for the waiters: you don't want your food to be cold by the time it arrives on the table.

Discuss the routes which the waiters should follow to make the service quick and efficient, and agree where the buffets and distribution points should be located. Take account of the need to re-supply bars and buffets: there is nothing worse than a bar without beer or a buffet without food. Moreover, the re-supplying must be carried out in a manner that does not disturb the guests. This applies equally to the removal of empty bottles and rubbish. People do not like standing at a bar that is full of dirty glasses and empty cigarette packets.

 Make sure that there is sufficient working space behind the scenes for the caterer (both for his preparations and for the dirty dishes). A work area that is either too small or badly planned will have a direct impact on the service in the dining area.

📌 Is the power and water supply adequate? Check the caterer's requirements, to avoid unpleasant surprises.

📌 Almost every caterer will arrive at the venue with one or more refrigerated lorries. Make sure that parking space is kept available near the entrance to the kitchen.

Discuss the various possibilities in terms of ancillary facilities (bars, buffets, etc.), decoration, crockery, cutlery, glassware and table linen. These all need to match the concept of your event. Ask if the caterer has a photo-book of the events he has cooked for in the past. This will give you some idea of his overall standard – and of his strengths and weaknesses.

📌 Always serve drinks in the right type of glasses. You don't serve wine in a beer glass and you don't serve cola in a champagne flute.

For relatively small events, where only cocktail snacks are being served, you can probably rely on the services of a local domestic caterer. For all other events, it is probably wiser to opt for a professional (party) caterer.

📌 Don't forget your crew! Make sure that they get healthy meals throughout the event cycle, including the construction and dismantling phases. Chips and pizza are not a good idea. Your crew need to work hard day after day at your event location, so remember that 'an army marches on its stomach'. In terms of numbers, add your artists, speakers and your own team (including yourself, of course!) to the crew list for meal and refreshment provision.

CULINARY CHOICES

Always choose formats and menus that are appropriate for the occasion. A four-course meal during a reception smacks of overkill. But inviting people to a 'dinner' and them serving them a salad sandwich will not go down well either! Think carefully about your event's objectives and pick the format that best matches them. The following are the most common options:

- Tea and/or coffee with cakes and biscuits
- Breakfast (buffet) or brunch
- Sandwich lunch
- Picnic
- Cold/warm lunch buffet
- Cold/warm dinner buffet
- Seated dinner or lunch
- Walking dinner
- Amuse bouche (cocktail snacks)
- Bar snacks (crisps, nuts, olives, etc.)
- Assorted appetisers
- Cold/warm hors d'oeuvres, toasts, etc.
- Barbecue
- Dessert (buffet)
- ...

As you can see, there are plenty of culinary options. If the type of event and your target group make it possible, why not experiment with one of the more unusual ones? Here is a selection of both 'classic' and out-of-the-ordinary possibilities.

SEATED DINNER WITH TABLE SERVICE

This is ideal for formal events like galas or benefits, but also for official occasions with speeches and presentations. The guests sit reasonably still and quiet at table, focusing on the speaker. This set-up is also a good option when you want to give your guests the opportunity for deeper conversation and small-scale networking. The main disadvantage is that you are usually only able to offer the guests a limited menu. You also need a fairly spacious venue. There is nothing worse than being packed like sardines in a tin for the whole evening in a hot room that is too small. Also bear in mind that this is often the most expensive formula.

BUFFET

A buffet is the best formula for larger events where your guests arrive at different times. Other advantages include the possibility to offer a wide range of different dishes that your guests are free to choose, depending on their personal preferences and dietary requirements: vegetarian, gluten-free, low-fat, etc. Good service at events of this kind is crucial: no one likes to stand waiting in queue for minutes on end. So, make sure that you have enough buffet tables that can be approached by the guests from both sides. To facilitate networking, it is also a good idea to have a variety of seating and table

arrangements: low tables with chairs, high tables for standing, comfy lounge corners...

WALKING DINNER
This is the perfect formula when your guests wish to focus 100% on networking, but it also offers two other important benefits. Firstly, your guests do not need to move about to get their food. They can carry on talking at their high tables, while the waiters bring the various small dishes to them. Just as importantly, it is easy to keep your budget under control, because as organiser you can decide for yourself exactly how many different dishes you want to give them. Depending on the timing of the event, you still need to make sure that these dishes are sufficient to satisfy their appetite. You don't want to send your guests home feeling hungry! Also remember that the dishes need to be easily eatable with just one hand, using only a fork or spoon. At events of this kind, the surfaces of the standing tables quickly fill up and you still often see people holding their steak with one hand and unsuccessfully trying to cut it with the other! Choose your dishes to avoid such embarrassments.

LIVE COOKING
This is the most enjoyable set-up for events where you want to create a lighter atmosphere. Depending on the number of participants, it is best to arrange for a number of different stands where various dishes are cooked live. As an

additional advantage, this makes it possible for the cooks to immediately respond to people's culinary preferences and dietary requirements. The fact that your guests can see exactly how their food is cooked is an attraction in its own right and will certainly be a talking point both during and after the event.

FOOD TRUCKS

Food trucks have become an indispensable part of many different events and festivals. In addition to traditional food stalls, you can now find mobile soup stalls, quiche stalls, sushi stalls, oyster stalls and a whole variety of other stalls serving exotic street food. Nowadays, almost every good caterer has his own food truck and they are ideal for events of any size. Whether you are organising a family celebration or a major music festival, a food truck is never out of place. The range of choice is extensive and the quality is usually high. Again, as with live cooking, you have the added benefit that people can watch their food being freshly made. On the down side, guests often have to move to where the trucks are located, which is usually somewhere out of doors, and long queues can sometimes also be a problem, as the cooking and serving space is small. Bear these things in mind when choosing your venue. Try to ensure that the trucks are positioned not too far from the focal point of the event and provide sufficient variety. In addition to original food trucks, there are also a number of other more standard eating options that can serve large groups of guests relatively quickly, so that queuing problems can be kept to a minimum.

> *Do not choose the **cheapest plonk** you can find, but ask the expert advice of a sommelier.*

 There are various ways to liven up your dessert buffet. What about a chocolate fountain or some sculpted ice? In addition, always have enough well-trained staff at buffets to help serve the guests with a minimum of delay.

 Is one of the objectives of your event to improve networking between your guests? If so, draw up a table plan in advance, which partners people who do not (yet) know each other very well. Give all the tables a name and allocate specific guests to specific tables. Numbers are also an option but this can sometimes lead to some guests feeling less valued: who wants to sit at table no. 13 when you could be sitting at table no. 1! If you want to take matters a step further, get your guests to change table after every course.

> This, of course, means that you will need three or four separate seating plans instead of just one. Make sure that this game of 'musical chairs' can be conducted calmly and comfortably, without rush and without crush. You are not at a football match.

The drinks you are planning to serve will also need some careful thought. Do not choose the cheapest plonk you can find, but ask the expert advice of a sommelier. They will tell you which wines best complement your menu and offer the best value for money. Special waters have also become very fashionable in recent years. The choice is huge but making the right selection is not as easy as you might think. For the aperitif you need something with plenty of fizz, and gradually decrease the carbonate level as the evening progresses. The level of salts in the water also plays a crucial role. Once again, you can nowadays consult the advice of a water sommelier. Equally trendy is to serve cocktails freshly mixed by expert cocktail shakers. And for people who drink no alcohol, there is the non-alcoholic version: the mocktail. Or ice teas, if they prefer.

Vegetarian food, allergies and intolerances

Halal, kosher or vegetarian food? Nowadays, most caterers can deal with such requests, providing they are made in good time. You can ask relevant questions as part of the guest registration process: *'Are you allergic to certain foods or do you have a preference for a vegetarian meal? If so, our chef would be grateful to know in advance, so that he can do his best to meet your specific needs.'* In the eventplanner.com software you can easily add simple questions of this kind.

More and more people are conscious about what they eat. Consequently, offering a vegetarian option is always a good idea. This doesn't have to be boring. On the contrary, there are many caterers who can be creative with vegetarian and vegan dishes. Remember that many vegetarians follow their diet for health reasons, so make sure you give them a healthy and tasty alternative. Or why not take things a step further and make vegetarian your standard menu choice for ecological reasons?

Caterers, and you as the event organiser, have a responsibility to take account of food allergies and intolerances and can be held liable if anything goes wrong. You must always clearly notify the presence of allergens in everything you serve to your guests. Those affected by allergies and intolerances will be grateful for this courtesy. The most important allergens are:

- ✔ Cereals containing gluten: wheat, rye, barley, oats, spelt and kamut
- ✔ Shellfish
- ✔ Eggs
- ✔ Fish
- ✔ Peanuts
- ✔ Soya
- ✔ Milk (including lactose and milk proteins)
- ✔ Nuts: almonds, hazelnuts, walnuts, cashew nuts, pecan nuts, Brazil nuts, pistachio nuts and macadamia nuts
- ✔ Mustard
- ✔ Sesame seeds
- ✔ Sulphur dioxide and sulphites in concentrations higher than 10 mg per kilo or litre, expressed as SO_2
- ✔ Lupine
- ✔ Molluscs
- ✔ ...

NUMBERS AND AVERAGES

Nothing is so annoying for a guest as to stand hungrily before an empty buffet that has been plundered by others or to receive a microscopic piece of meat when you feel that you could eat a horse. But the other extreme is not good either: nobody likes to throw away sacksful of food after the event is over. Your caterer should have the necessary experience to avoid either of these scenarios, but the following guidelines may nevertheless come in useful:

Drink

During the first hour of a **reception or party**, you should count on an average of three drinks per guest. For each further hour, count on an average of two drinks.

For an afternoon reception with coffee and tea or for a **coffee break** during a meeting or seminar, count on an average of one and a half cups per person.

During a **dinner** guests drink an average of one glass per course. The main course is good for an average of one and a half glasses.

📌 A happy group of friends will have different drinking behaviour in comparison with the participants at a business seminar. Similarly, the weather conditions, the speed of the bar service, the time of day and the programme content will all have an influence on how much is drunk and how quickly. Ensure that your supply is adequate and agree with your caterer what unused drink can be returned after the event.

📌 Many catering companies work with a fixed price per person for the entire event. By buying your F&B (Food and Beverages) in this manner, you avoid unpleasant budgetary surprises when you eventually receive the catering bill.

📌 Do not let your guests drive home if you see that they are too drunk. Arrange taxis for them instead. Do you want to be certain whether they are sober or not? You can hire alcohol testers which will confirm this beyond doubt. You can turn this into a fun element by putting the testers in the hands of actors dressed as policemen and by rewarding your guests with a small gift when they stay within the legal limit.

Appetisers and hors d'oeuvres

During the first hour of any function your guests will easily consume three hors d'oeuvres, followed by an average of two more during each subsequent hour. During a dinner event, you should seek to achieve a balance between meat, fish and vegetable appetisers. This also applies to other cocktail snacks served before a meal: for example, you should not offer drumsticks during the aperitif if chicken is also your main course.

> If you are planning to move your guests to the dinner table immediately after the aperitif, first give them some nuts, olives or other amuse bouche.

> Before the event starts, work out a plan for the areas of the room to be covered by each member of the catering staff. There is nothing so irritating for guests than to see a waiter passing three metres away but never approaching their table with food or drink. Make sure that your guests don't have to chase their dinner and refreshments, but that these things are brought to them without asking.

Service

Nobody likes to be kept waiting, so you must have enough waiters and service points.

For parties, work on a basis of one bar for every 100-150 people and one waiter for every 50 guests. Are you planning to serve drinks from trays? If so, one waiter for every 40 guests will be enough.

For a dinner buffet, work on the basis of one waiter for every 20 guests. For a seated dinner, increase this to one waiter for every ten guests. Of course, this will depend on the experience of your personnel and the level of service you want to provide.

> Draw up a time schedule for your dinner, indicating when each course should start. Adjust this to match the timings of your entertainment or other programme elements.

> Appoint someone to direct the running of the buffet. Only allow people to approach the food displays in small groups. This avoids gigantic queues and prevents the food from being plundered too quickly.

Number of guests

Your caterer will provide staff, glassware, cutlery, tables, etc. on the basis of your estimate of the number of guests. Make a clear agreement with the caterer and the venue about the date when the final number of guests must be confirmed. Do this in writing. But be careful: this is the number that will be used to calculate your invoice, even if fewer people turn up than you first thought. For this reason, try to delay your notification until the last possible moment: for preference, something like two days before the event rather than two weeks.

HEALTHY AND SUSTAINABLE CATERING

Providing healthy and balanced food at your event will help to make your participants more attentive. At congresses, I often see pastries served for breakfast and croquettes for lunch. This excessive consumption of sugar and fat means that half the people in the auditorium find it hard to concentrate and some of them even fall asleep! You have invested a lot of time, energy and money in your event, so surely it is only logical that you want your guests to hear and understand your message, rather than nodding off into dreamland. Viewed in these terms, any extra cost associated with healthy food seems more than justified.

Nowadays, most caterers have a sufficient number of healthy alternatives in their range. Opt for creative and healthy snacks in between sessions. Instead of coffee and cake, serve a healthy smoothie and fruit. For lunches and dinners, choose lighter meals that will not overfill your guests. Does your caterer cook with bioingredients? Does he provide non-alcoholic variants, such as self-made ice teas? You have everything at your disposal to ensure that your guests eat and drink healthily during your event.

Organic cuisine is no longer the preserve of the woollen sock brigade. Even so, it is still true that food produced and processed in a socially responsible manner is more expensive. Can you perhaps make do with a little less for your event? This saving would certainly help to offset any extra cost. Also make sure that the caterer does not try to pull the wool over your eyes. If he says his cuisine is organic, ask him to show you his biolabels.

As previously mentioned, it is also an option to make a vegetarian dish your standard menu choice, so that fish or meat have to be consciously requested by guests as an alternative. At the moment, things are usually the other way around. A vegetarian menu has the added bonus of a lower ecological footprint.

Again with the environment in mind, avoid wherever possible the use of plastic packaging. Choose local products and keep food waste to a minimum by good planning. If you do have any surpluses, see if they can be donated to organisations that help homeless people or others in need.

Also remember that sustainability is not just about the environment; it is also about people. If possible, give people who are socially disadvantaged or who have a limitation an opportunity to work at your event. There are some caterers who now employ 50-plussers, people with Down syndrome or people who are struggling in the labour market. Why not give them a chance?

www.eventplanner.net/book/catering

www.eventplanner.net/book/cocktailcatering

www.eventplanner.net/book/drinks

www.eventplanner.net/book/foodtrucks

www.eventplanner.net/book/rent-party-supplies

Transport

If you are organising an event, it is in your own best interests that the transport should be properly arranged. As event organiser, this is one of your key responsibilities. Nevertheless, this is an area that is often overlooked. Even if your guests are travelling by their own transport, there are still a number of measures which need to be taken. If the transport arrangements run smoothly, your guests will be less likely to arrive late – and so there will be less disruption to your programme.

OWN TRANSPORT

Most of your guests will travel to the event under their own steam. The car is still the most popular means of transport, although the use of public transport and even bikes is increasing gradually. Whichever means they prefer, provide them all with safe routes and adequate parking facilities.

Route description

Draw up a **clear description of the best routes** to your venue. Take account of the fact that your guests may be arriving from different directions. If necessary, you can place special direction signs to help them during the final kilometres of their journey. Also prepare a travel schedule for guests who are planning to make use of public transport. This should include train and bus times, as well as details of the nearest train station and bus stop.

 If you need a map and a route description, it may be possible to obtain these ready-made from the owners of your venue. If not, you can consult free websites such as **maps.google.com**. Do you also have your own website? With the help of Google Maps you can add an interactive map which will allow your guests to work out their own best route from their homes to your event.

- 📌 Let someone from outside the area test the accuracy of your route plan. You might think that something is an easy landmark to spot, but a stranger might see things differently.

- 📌 Check regularly to see whether or not any road works are planned in the near future along your chosen route. Possible strikes on public transport demand prompt alternative action on your part.

- 📌 As an extra service for your guests who opt to use public transport, you may consider organising a shuttle from the nearest bus stop or train station to your venue.

- 📌 Facilitate carpooling, perhaps by integrating a carpool app into your event website. There are several existing apps, or you can have one specially made to suit your purposes. You can thank your carpoolers by arranging a carpooling parking area close to the event entrance. As an added bonus, people can also start networking in their shared cars.

- 📌 If you are organising a large public event, such as a festival or a concert, it pays to enter into discussions with the public transport authorities at an early stage. They may be willing to lay on additional trains, buses and trams, which will make the journey of your guests to and from the event location that much easier.

Parking

Ideally, you would like a large **parking area** immediately next to the venue. If this is not the case, look for alternatives nearby. Where necessary, make sure that there is a shuttle service to take people to the venue (and back again). When you use a public car park, give the guests free exit tickets, if your budget will allow it.

Parking attendants immediately move things to a much higher level. They guarantee the smooth flow of local traffic and provide general coordination in the parking area. They also increase the feeling of safety for the guests and reduce the level of inconvenience for people living nearby. In short, their use creates a very positive professional impression and makes your visitors feel welcome.

For every 100 cars (good for an average of 175 visitors) on a spacious, enclosed parking area you will need two attendants (one to check tickets or receive money, the other to direct the traffic). For 150 cars you will need a second attendant to show people to the right place. For more than 250 cars, you will need a third.

When cars (up to 100 in number) are parked along the public highway or on an industrial estate, a third attendant will also be necessary to keep a check on the general traffic situation on the roads. Every additional 50 cars means you will need an additional attendant to direct people to vacant spaces.

Make sure that all your attendants are properly briefed and agree a single system for dividing up and using the available area. Only work with experienced attendants. Untrained attendants are often a source of irritation for guests. The basic equipment for the attendants should include weatherproof and highly visible (fluorescent) clothing and walkie-talkies.

Only work with experienced car park attendants. Untrained attendants are often a source of irritation for guests.

- Is your car parking free or paying? Are you using exit cards? Inform your guests well in advance about your parking policy.

- If you are expecting important guests or famous celebrities, make sure that you reserve a parking space for them near the (artist's) entrance. This also applies for the physically challenged and for people who are less mobile, such as senior citizens and pregnant women.

- Check that there is adequate lighting on the parking area and along the walkways leading to and from the event. If necessary, install additional exterior lighting.

- Make sure that the parking area is easily accessible in all weather conditions. A grassed car park can quickly turn into a sea of mud after heavy rain. You don't want your guests getting stuck!

- 📌 If you are using public car parks or garages, ask for information about closing times and pass this on to your guests. 24-hour garages are the ideal choice, if available.

- 📌 During the winter months it is advisable to keep a good supply of salt at the ready, so that this can be used to melt any ice on roads, paths and other surfaces.

- 📌 Electric motoring is here to stay! Make sure that your event venue has a decent number of battery charging points. If it doesn't, there are service providers who can arrange good mobile solutions.

- 📌 If you are organising a high level event or if parking near your chosen venue is almost impossible, perhaps **valet parking** can offer the solution you are looking for. With valet parking, your guests ride almost up to the main entrance, where they hand over the keys of their car to a parking attendant, who then drives the car to a more distant parking area. When a guest wants to go home, the attendant fetches the car and drives it back to where its owner is waiting. This kind of service is perfectly feasible for smaller gatherings, but for larger events – where everybody arrives and leaves at more or less the same time – it can be a logistical nightmare. In all circumstances, additional insurance to cover the possibility of damage to the guests' cars is essential.

- 📌 A thoughtfully conceived traffic plan is by no means an unnecessary luxury. In fact, in some cases it is a condition for being granted the necessary permission to hold your event. If you expect the event to create significant traffic congestion, consult a specialist company that will help you to keep the local traffic moving as smoothly as possible.

- 📌 Do not forget to provide parking space for your crew and for the lorries of your suppliers. Make clear arrangements about who can access the parking areas and when. If, for example, you are organising a congress or trade fair with stands, you do not want the stand holders to block the parking while they dismantle their stands, so that your guests cannot easily leave until they have finished.

Cyclists

Guests who arrive by **bike, scooter or moped** like to know that their 'vehicle' is parked in safety. Provide a (covered) area, where two-wheelers can be kept in an orderly manner. This prevents them from being left near the entrance, which could be a problem if the premises need to be evacuated for any reason.

- Encourage your visitors to come to the event by bike. Offer cyclists small extras, like a free drink, gadgets or even a discount on the ticket price.

- The easiest and cheapest way to create a series of temporary bike racks is to use crowd control barriers with vertical bars. The wheels of between four and six bikes can be placed between the bars.

- Make sure that your traffic signs not only direct motorists to the car park, but also cyclists to the bike racks. In this way, you can avoid bikes being left all over the place.

- Increase the safety and comfort of cyclists by providing security surveillance at the bike racks. Issue two numbered straps when each cyclist arrives, one for the bike and one for the cyclist himself. These can be checked and matched on departure, to make sure that everyone leaves with the correct bike and none are stolen. Other ways to encourage and reward cyclists? Arrange for bicycle pumps and puncture repair kits to be available on site. Or even hire in a bike mechanic. Do not forget that many bicycles are nowadays electric, so that you will need to have a decent number of battery charging points.

Shuttle service

If you need a shuttle service to take your visitors from the car park, train station or some other location to your event, you should bear in mind the following points:

- ✔ Choose a mode of transport that best meets your visitors' needs. Collect as much information as you can in advance about these needs: their age, their level of mobility, their amount of luggage, and so on. Can they all fit in one big bus or is it better to have a series of smaller ones? Will taxis be needed?

- ✔ Provide more places than is strictly necessary. In this way, your buses will not be overcrowded and waiting times can be kept to a minimum or even avoided altogether. This is particularly important when people are ready to go home, because they generally want to leave as quickly as possible. Repeat journeys over the same trajectory help to reduce waiting times, but make sure that you also provide covered bus shelters, so that any guests who do have to wait are not forced to stand in the rain.

- ✔ Keep a reserve bus on stand-by. This is always useful for dealing with any unforeseen eventualities. Do you unexpectedly need to drive a VIP somewhere? Or does a late speaker need to be picked up from the train station? A reserve bus can help you to cope with these situations without upsetting your normal planning.

- ✔ Base your planning on timings and not on distances. Even if the distance between the boarding point and the event location is relatively short, it can still take quite some time – depending on the circumstances – to cover it. Timings allow you to take better account of factors like the weather, other activities in the area, the density of traffic, traffic lights, level crossings, difficult bends, the number of bus stops, how long it takes your passengers to get on and off, and so on. Do a number of trial runs over the trajectory, preferably in conditions that will be similar to those on the day of your event. Use a stopwatch to time the various runs and work out an average.

- ✔ Make a single member of your team responsible for all transport matters, including the necessary communication with drivers and any other assistants who accompany the buses. Give these assistants recognisable clothing, so that your guests can find and approach them easily. Agree with your transport officer that he or one of his helpers will stay with any guests who are waiting for the next shuttle.

- Pay attention to details. Depending on the weather, let the bus warm up or cool down well in advance of the departure time. Ask your drivers to check with the guests over the intercom that the temperature is comfortable. Arrange for suitable music or short films to be played during the journey. Provide bottles of water if it is hot, umbrellas if it is raining and trace the owners of any things left behind on the bus by mistake.

- Provide your guests with clear information in advance about shuttle journey times and the location of the various bus stops.

When your guests register for your event, ask them how they are planning to travel. This will allow you to estimate how many parking spaces, exit tickets, shuttle buses and parking attendants you will need. At the same time, you can send your guests a route plan appropriate for their method of transport.

ORGANISED TRANSPORT

Is the average journey time for your guests relatively long? Is the location a surprise or difficult to reach? If so, it can sometimes be a good idea to arrange organised transport. This can be much more than just a simple means of getting people from point A to point B. For example, you can choose an original means of transport or provide entertainment/catering along the route. This means that for these guests your event will start before they even arrive at the main venue!

There are numerous possibilities; here are just some of them.

Bus

Buses and coaches are ideal for transporting relatively large groups of people over relatively long distances (up to 400 kilometres). The only real condition you need to set is that your guests cannot be allowed to depart from too many different and widely spread locations. Offer them the choice of a limited number of pick-up points, to which they will be expected to make their own way. Take due account of the fact that coaches cannot park everywhere. If the coach is fitted with television, provide a selection of suitable DVD's to help pass the time during the (long) journey. You can even show a light-hearted message or two about your company or event.

Depending upon the size of your group, you can either opt for a single-decker, with space for 50-60 passengers, or a double-decker with room for 70 passengers or more. At the other end of the scale, you can hire mini-buses for as few as eight passengers. There are also luxury VIP variants.

 Ask for a number of different price tenders. The tariffs charged by the coach companies can vary widely.

 When you are organising a large event, it is advisable to arrange your coach requirements through a single specialised company. This company can coordinate all the various routes and pick-up points much more easily than several different companies.

 A coach – even a good one – can always break down. Ask the company how quickly they can provide a replacement in the event of an emergency.

 Always book your transport well in advance!

 www.eventplanner.net/book/buses

Train

It is possible to reserve one or more coaches on a particular train. This means that your guests will be the only people allowed to travel in these coaches. Perhaps this is still not exclusive enough? No problem. Following proper consultation with the authorities, you will probably be able to hire a whole train and have it run (within limits) along a route of your choice. It is even possible to offer catering on board. Remember, however, that the use of these special routes is usually restricted to periods outside the rush hour!

 You can also organise your whole event on a train. Why not enquire with specialist companies about the various possibilities?

Boat

Boats are a stylish means of transport, but can also be very practical. In busy cities they can help you to miss the rush hour or avoid the delays caused by road works or accidents. Like coaches and trains, boats can be so much more than a mere conveyance: they are perfect for organising your entire event, providing your plans are not too large scale. There are special party boats, which are fully equipped and offer all necessary facilities.

 www.eventplanner.net/book/ships

Taxi

Taxis are a useful method of transport for short distances. Their limited carrying capacity makes them well suited for the transfer of small groups arriving from or departing to different destinations. Some taxi companies also have luxury models that are perfect for VIPs or for use as a high-quality shuttle service.

The emergence of services like Uber also opens up some interesting possibilities for event organisers. For example, you can offer your guests Uber vouchers, so that they can travel to the event more cheaply or at your cost.

www.eventplanner.net/book/taxi

Limousines

Having said this, a limousine is still the method of transport for your VIPs. In this manner, your special guests and artists can make an arrival in true Hollywood style!

 Don't forget to put out a red carpet at the entrance. Stepping out of a limo straight into a puddle of water is not the right way to make a good impression.

www.eventplanner.net/book/limousines

Aeroplane or helicopter

For international events, travel by plane or helicopter is also an option. You can make an agreement with a standard airline or a charter company. Arrangements are usually made with a company in the country of destination rather than the country of origin. Be aware, however, of the ecological impact of air travel. Is it really necessary for people to fly in for your event? If it is, try to find ways to compensate for the resulting CO_2 emissions.

📌 Check to see whether it is possible to set up a small reception area at the airport where your guests are arriving. This means that you can meet them off the plane and accompany them on the last stage of their journey.

📌 Small planes or helicopters give national events an extra allure. Choose a regional airport and be sure to make all your arrangements in good time. But don't forget the price tag – which will be high.

🔗 www.eventplanner.net/book/helicopters

Other methods

There are, of course, various other transport possibilities: hot-air balloons, coach and horses, sports cars, quads, etc. The chief criteria for your choice should be practicality and the impression you are trying to create. This must inevitably reflect the objectives which you have set for your event. At a more mundane level, remember that you may need to hire lorries for the logistical side of things.

📌 A horse-drawn carriage is slower than a Ferrari – so take account of this when drawing up your programme.

🔗 www.eventplanner.net/book/ceremonialcars

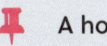 🔗 www.eventplanner.net/book/carriages

🔗 www.eventplanner.net/book/hotairballoons

Entertainment and speakers

A short act to generate some atmosphere or a longer performance, perhaps by different artists? The possibilities are almost limitless. But whether it is in a main role or a supporting role, the key word is always 'entertainment'. This is often the part of the programme that is best remembered by your guests, because it is the part that most engages their emotions. As a result, it is also the part that contributes most significantly to the experience that you are trying to create. Moreover, entertainment is an ideal choice for the main theme or leitmotif of your event.

People love to talk to others about spectacular or memorable acts that they have seen, whereas lifeless acts are dead and buried on the evening of the performance. For this reason, it pays to take things very seriously when it comes to entertainment: take the necessary time and make the necessary effort to find the right acts and entertainers. Also ensure that your choices blend well with the other elements of your programme: you wouldn't want a clown performing at a seminar for undertakers!

Not as easy as you first thought? If you don't really know where to start, it may be worth consulting a professional booking agency. They will help you to find an act which matches perfectly with your event objectives and target group.

> The idea of 'entertainment' is closely related to your target group. Are you really the best person to decide what they might like to see? If you have your doubts, put together a group of people who match the target group profile – and just ask their opinion.

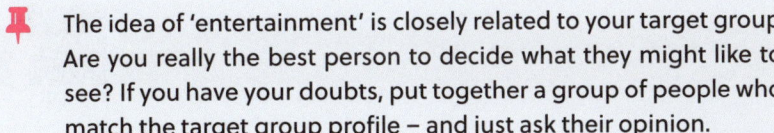
www.eventplanner.net/book/artistagencies

FUNCTION

You don't choose your entertainment 'just like that'. Each different type of act has its own different function. It is therefore important that you select acts whose function contributes towards the objective of your event.

The most common functions are:

✓ **Creating atmosphere**
Atmosphere or ambiance acts are mostly background acts that do not demand the full attention of your guests. Music (piano, violins, etc.), theatre pieces or acrobatics are all possibilities. On some occasions, however, ambiance performances do require the audience to pay attention: otherwise they will miss their effect. For example, you might use clowns, street musicians or comedy acts to brighten up the waiting time in long queues.

✓ **Transmitting your message**
You can opt to use entertainment as a means to transmit your message to your target group. For example, you can employ professional actors to package your message in a comic sketch or a motivation coach who will transform your message into a powerful speech. A second option is to use entertainment to support and underline your message. This can be achieved, for example, through a laser show, a stunt, comedy, etc.

✓ **Networking and teambuilding**
Entertainment is also ideal for bringing people closer together. For instance, workshops are a perfect tool for enhancing team spirit or allowing people to get to know each other in an informal setting. There are many different kinds of workshop: cooking, music, art, dancing, acting, etc. A fun quiz or a treasure hunt are other possible options for forging closer ties between the people in your target group.

% www.eventplanner.net/book/teambuilding

✓ **Providing structure**
You can use entertainment to give structure to your event. For example, you can engage a presenter or a master of ceremonies. He announces the different parts of your programme and ensures a smooth and professional transition from one part to another. In this way, your guests know precisely what to expect.

✓ **Entertaining**

Last but not least, entertainment can sometimes have no other purpose that to entertain. One of the most popular entertainment acts is still a live performance by a (well-known) artist or DJ. Major (inter)national stars will certainly add lustre to your event programme and will guarantee a high turn-out. Only work with famous celebrities, if your budget will allow it. Having said this, it is pointless to spend your entire entertainment budget on a single act. There are plenty of other good and affordable alternatives.

Even though you might be planning a number of acts spread throughout the course of your programme, you will still need a DJ to bridge the intervening gaps or to provide background. You can also use a DJ as a 'warmer-up', someone to get your audience 'in the mood' before the main acts appear. Similarly, a DJ can often provide a spectacular closing 'set' to round off your event in style. Be sure to make clear arrangements with the DJ if he forms a central element in your programme. Agree the types of music to be played and also whether or not you want him to provide verbal links between the different numbers. A DJ might be a bit 'over the top' for a congress, but engage someone to provide appropriate (background) music for intervals and breaks.

The 'show' format is still one of the most popular and spectacular. Why not consider a cabaret, a magic show or even a dinner show, with different acts between the different courses of the meal? At less formal parties, dance acts or drag (transvestite) acts always provide a little something extra. Walk-around acts, like oyster men, champagne ladies, actors, etc., can also raise your event to a higher level.

> Encourage interaction by engaging actors who can perform whilst moving amongst the audience. Make sure, however, that there are clear agreements about what is permissible and what not. What are the limits? How will your target public react?

> Do not allow the DJ to play music that is on the play-list of the live artists performing later in the evening. Also agree with him whether or not he can accept requests from the audience. Too many changes in musical style will often keep your guests off the dance floor.

www.eventplanner.net/book/entertainment

 www.eventplanner.net/book/bands

www.eventplanner.net/book/cabaret

 www.eventplanner.net/book/dancers

www.eventplanner.net/book/djs

 www.eventplanner.net/book/magicians

www.eventplanner.net/book/streetentertainment

 www.eventplanner.net/book/singers

✓ **Children's entertainment**
Children's events require suitable children's entertainment. This means that parents will not then need to be continually occupied with their kids. Circus acts, acrobats, make-up artists, balloon clowns, craft workshops and story-tellers can all be fun and (more importantly) effective. Bouncy castles are also a great favourite. Provide for professional child carers and pay extra attention to child security.

 Try to discover the likely numbers and ages of the children in advance. Provide different entertainment for the different age groups.

 There are specialist agencies which can offer children's entertainment reflecting the main theme of your event.

www.eventplanner.net/book/attractionrental

 www.eventplanner.net/book/balloonsculpture

www.eventplanner.net/book/clowns

 www.eventplanner.net/book/facepainting

www.eventplanner.net/book/childrensentertainment

CHECKLIST ENTERTAINMENT

There is much more to organising your entertainment than simply finding the acts that are appropriate to your objectives, target group and budget. You also need to take account of a number of practical matters. Do you need any permits? What will you do if an artist cancels at the last minute?

Have you really thought of everything? The following checklist will help to reassure you:

It is great to have a good Plan A – providing nothing goes wrong. Try to anticipate problems and make sure you have an alternative Plan B up your sleeve.

- ✔ Include your entertainment activities/acts in your general **action plan**. Indicate clearly when the activities/acts start and finish, and also if there are intervals. Note down who will be accompanying the artists and who will be taking care of stage construction, logistics, lighting and sound, etc. Don't forget to mention how the different entertainment activities/acts will be linked. Practice these hand-overs in advance and keep them as short as possible.

- ✔ Always ask the artists to provide a **technical specification**, so that you know exactly what equipment they will need and who will provide it. Do you need a stage? How big must it be? Do you need to hire sound and lighting gear or does the artist prefer to work with his/her own? And what about instruments: who hires the piano and who tunes it? Make clear arrangements. Some DJ's also have a technical specification, usually relating to the sound installation (although most of them will bring their own).

> 📌 Do different artists need the same instruments and are these instruments difficult to change between performances (e.g., a piano or a set of drums)? If so, it is probably best that you make the arrangements for everyone (this is known in the sector as *'back lining'*). Contact a specialist rental agency.

✔ In addition to a technical specification, most artists will also send you a **'rider'**. This is a list of the personal requirements of the artist and his/her crew. Some artists will want particular types or brands of food and drink. Others expect a chill-out area, a shower, etc.

> 📌 Some top artists will refuse to perform if there is advertising on the stage. They do not want to be associated with particular brands or products. If necessary, remove the offending logos from the set decor.

> 📌 Agree the times and lengths of any intervals, so that the DJ knows when to take over.

✔ Some acts need a strong and reliable **power supply**. Check that the infrastructure of your venue can provide this. If in doubt, hire an extra generator.

✔ It is great to have a good Plan A – providing nothing goes wrong. Try to anticipate problems and make sure you have an alternative Plan B up your sleeve. This will allow you to cope with unforeseen emergencies such as torrential rain, electricity black-outs and sick performers. As far as the latter are concerned, discuss what will happen in the event of a no-show and write this clearly into their contracts.

> 📌 Take account of the fact that some international artists will insist on the option of cancelling their contract at the last minute if an unexpected opportunity to perform on television crops up. Even so, don't let this discourage you from booking top artists. In practice, cancellations of this kind do not happen very often and it should always be possible to negotiate for a back-up act in case of need.

- ✔ Apply for all necessary **permits and permissions** in good time, particularly with regard to noise levels. Inform copyright organisations whenever you are planning to have a musical intermezzo and agree who will settle any **royalties** that need to be paid.

- ✔ Remember to consider the **security** implications of your performance. Famous artists will expect to be guided safely and comfortably to the stage. For (inter)national stars, you may need to take extra security precautions both inside and outside the venue.

- ✔ Do not forget to contact the **presenters/assistants** of any workshops you have planned. Nor should you overlook the need for security. Also arrange transport for your artists at 'free' entertainment activities, such as the children's bouncy castle.

- ✔ Discuss the option of **extending the duration** of a performance. Nothing is so disappointing for your guests as the abrupt termination of an act just when the atmosphere is really starting to buzz. Is the artist prepared to perform a little longer? How much extra would this cost? What effects would any extension have on your action plan?

- ✔ Agree who will look after the artists' **costumes and props**. Is it possible for the artists to dress in a style appropriate to the theme of your evening? Discuss the possibilities.

- ✔ Make sure that there are sufficient **changing facilities** for the number of artists you have booked. Don't forget to provide clothes racks and hangers, mirrors, refreshments, etc. If necessary, ask if they are prepared to share a changing room.

- ✔ Do you want to organise a **meet-and-greet** with the artists for the VIPs at your event? Make the necessary arrangements in advance with the artists concerned. Some will be happy to do this; others will not and some may even ask for an extra fee.

SPEAKERS AND MODERATORS

Speakers can give your event added value in terms of inspiration and learning, but they can also play an entertainment role (for example, presenters or motivation coaches). Once again, you set the tone to reflect your target group and objectives. The above entertainment checklist can also be used for speakers, but here are some specific additional points that you will also need to address:

- ✔ The speakers must be aware of the **content of your programme**. Discuss with them the objectives of your event and the profile of your target group. This will allow the speaker to assess the likely level of their prior knowledge about the subject, so that he can adjust his talk/speech accordingly. Ask if you can have a look at his drafts, so that you can suggest possible amendments, if necessary.

- ✔ Involve the speakers in the **development of your programme**. Agree the running order of the different presentations and the length of time that each should last. Discuss the content of every address with all the other speakers, not just its author. This will prevent repetition or overlapping.

- ✔ Agree in advance with the speakers how you will **let them know when their time is up**. A common method is to set up a discreet light at the back of the room, on which an orange light appears five minutes before the speaker must end, and turns to red when these five minutes have elapsed. Alternatively, you can give a subtle hand signal with a previously agreed gesture.

✔ It can sometimes be very difficult to **keep the public interested** for the duration of your programme. Do all you can to ensure that your guests continue to pay attention. Alternate 'difficult' presentations with less serious subjects. Provide sufficient breaks, so that the audience has time to process the information they have just received. If possible, consider the use of a lighter format, such as a mock tv-show or a theatre performance: this can make your message more digestible, without losing any of its force. An interview setting often works better than a keynote, unless you have a really top speaker. It is also important to have sufficient breaks. Never place more than three speakers after each other without a pause. As already mentioned, your participants need time to digest such a large body of information. After three speakers, the audience's concentration level will be falling and their frustration level increasing!

> 📌 There are very few speakers who are capable of keeping a large audience enthralled for more than 15 minutes. So why do we always allocate them 30-45 minutes? 10 minutes per speaker, with an added 5 minutes for audience interaction, is more than enough.

✔ **Double-check** the presentations on the laptop that is actually going to be used on the day of the event. It is embarrassing if you are unable to start up a funny film or show a clever slide at the right moment, or if the sound fails. Always download films locally, so that you are not dependent on an internet connection.

✔ During the lunch break many participants do more than just eat. They are also busy networking. The **moment after the lunch break is therefore very important**. Most people's energy levels are still low. Programming a difficult subject at this moment will send most of your guests into sleep mode. So choose something light and invigorating instead!

> 📌 Have the slides in your presentation(s) designed by a professional. A poor presentation can be fatal to the standing of your event. Make sure that the styles of the different presentations are compatible with each other and support your central theme. This gives a unity to your message and will enhance its strength.

Turn off the screensaver (and energy saver) on the presentation laptop and choose a neutral background for your desktop. You don't suddenly want to find the photos of your last holiday or your latest Facebook post being projected at the entire audience! Instead of using your own laptop, it is a better idea to have a special laptop for presentations that you only use for this purpose.

Great speakers – and how to find them

If you do not try to find the very best speakers for your event, you are effectively shooting yourself in the foot. Your competitors will certainly want to book these speakers and your guests will expect to be entertained and/or learn something from top performers in their field. So how exactly can you find the best speakers for your next event? Here are a number of easy-to-use tips:

✔ Make a list of the opinion leaders in the relevant professional domain. What is your event about? Which influencers do your potential participants follow? Find out the answers to these questions and then draw up a list of influencers who have something meaningful to say. Check out their specific field of expertise, the latest professional news they have shared and possible subjects that they can talk about at your event. One useful way to track down opinion leaders is to analyse the TEDx list of speakers. Avoid focusing exclusively on a speaker's popularity, but try instead to assess if they can really offer added value for your visitors.

✔ Always thoroughly check the background of your potential speakers. Before you ask someone to speak at your event, do the necessary basic research. For example, do they have experience of speaking to a large audience? Perhaps they have a webpage that lists their past speaking engagements and/or their forthcoming ones. Remember that you are not only trying to find entertaining speakers, but also seasoned professionals who can offer your guests valuable insights or surprising new information.

✔ Use social media to scan for great speakers. Listen to what is being whispered about them on X. Are your potential participants talking to or about certain professionals? If so, perhaps these are the right people to share their knowledge and experience at your event.

✔ You can also hunt for potential speakers on YouTube. Popular YouTube vloggers are almost guaranteed to attract extra participants to your event. If, for example, you are organising a culinary event, you can find plenty of fun how-to-do videos on YouTube, such as knife-sharpening gurus, who not only entertain but can also involve and educate your guests.

✔ Listen to the opinions of others. When choosing your speakers, allow yourself to be guided by the views of potential visitors and/or professionals in the relevant sector. Conduct a survey or post a question on social media, asking who they regard as good speakers in their field or which names they would like to see in your programme. Or why not organise a poll, encouraging them to vote for the speakers they think most deserve a place on your event's expert panel? You will sometimes be surprised by this wisdom of crowds. As a bonus, you give people the feeling that they have helped to add something extra to the event.

www.eventplanner.net/book/speakers

Types of presentation

Depending on what you hope to achieve with your participants, you can choose the most appropriate type of presentation to help you reach your goals. Because some terms tend to be used almost interchangeably, it may be useful to run through the most common types of presentation:

✔ The most well-known form of presentation is the **lecture**. The average duration for a lecture is 45 to 60 minutes, and the number of participants can range from dozens to hundreds. In this type of presentation the subject is dealt with in a narrative manner; this is appropriate, for example, for a historical subject, a philosophical discourse, an adventure story,...

✔ Is your objective to convince your participants of something or persuade them to do something? If so, you will probably opt for the classic **presentation** format. A really strong presentation need only last for 15 minutes. Depending on the subject, however, this can sometimes be extended to as long as 60 minutes (maximum!). Presentations are good for introducing a product, company, theory, good cause, etc.

✔ Like the previous two formats, a **keynote** is also non-interactive. The keynote speaker deals with the main subject of the event and sets out the broad lines for the rest of the programme. This means that the public know more or less what to expect during the remaining hours or days ahead. Alternatively, it is also possible to use a keynote almost as a kind of finale to your event. In this case, the speaker summarises the most important take-aways of the programme, in what is often referred to as a 'wrap-up'. The ideal length for a keynote is 30 to 60 minutes.

- ✔ If the objectives of your speaker are educational, it is probably wisest to organise a **seminar**. A seminar usually lasts between 1 and 3 hours, and is suitable for groups of up to 300 people. The speaker can focus on specific elements of his theme, based on questions he receives from the audience. Because of the size of this audience, this format is less suitable for imparting knowledge or teaching skills to the same level for the whole group. Seminars often have an inspirational purpose and are therefore frequently used in the fields of professional or personal development.

- ✔ A **workshop** is an obvious choice if you need an interactive approach that allows the speaker to discuss specific questions with individual participants. The maximum size for a workshop is around 50 people. The duration can range from 1 hour to a number of days. Workshops frequently issue certificates of competence at the end of the session, to show that participants now possess a particular knowledge or level of competence.

- ✔ A **masterclass** is a very specific format for a very small group, in which each participant has the chance to interact on a one-to-one basis with the speaker on matters relating to the knowledge and skills for which the speaker is an acknowledged expert. As each participant is coached in turn, the remainder of the group looks on. The aim of this 'watch-and-learn' technique is to bring the skills of all the participants to the highest possible level.

- ✔ One of my favourite formats is the **interview** or **panel discussion**. I am often asked to act as the moderator for formats of this kind. And in my opinion they are often more fun and more interactive than traditional presentations, especially if the speakers are less experienced. The interviewer/moderator ensures that the conversation remains interesting, monitors the reactions of the public, and asks supplementary questions when necessary.

Presentation tips

What is the best way to address a group? Speaker, presenter and coach Frederik Imbo offers the following practical tips to those who are about to be thrown to the lions of a public audience. As the organiser, there will no doubt be moments when you too will need to step onto the podium. So these tips are for you as well!

1. **Be prepared**
   If you forget to prepare, prepare to be forgotten! To avoid this undesirable fate, you need to think in advance about the following questions:
   - ✔ What is the background to this presentation?
   - ✔ What is the essence of my message?
   - ✔ Who are my audience?
   - ✔ How can I immediately grab their attention?

2. **Be yourself**
   Do not compare yourself with other speakers or try to copy them. This is not constructive and will put a break on your enthusiasm rather than stimulate it. Compare yourself with yourself and assess the progress you have made in relation to your abilities and potential.

3. **Make genuine contact**
   You cannot surf the Internet if you do not have a connection. This is logical, isn't it? So how do you expect to communicate with your public as a speaker if you fail to first make a connection with them?

   The most important thing that a speaker must do is to build up a rapport with his audience. Rapport involves making contact and building up trust with your listeners. You do this by showing that you are keen to speak to them, that you have something to say that will interest them. But this requires their attention, and this is something for which you must wait. You must give everyone the opportunity to settle down and focus their attention on the here and now. This applies not only to the audience listening to you, but also to you talking to them. One of the biggest mistakes is to be too over-enthusiastic at the beginning, but without establishing real contact. This creates a 'false' impression and will lead your public to see you as an empty box. And empty boxes are usually thrown away and forgotten.

4. **Body language**
   The impact of our communication is determined for 55% by our body language. It is therefore important to take account of the following practical tips:

   - ✔ **Posture and position.** Stand still. Don't fidget and don't change position every few seconds. Your hands behind your back, then at your side and then scratching your nose: this creates a nervous and insecure impression and distracts people's attention from your message. If you have problems keeping your feet still, try to imagine that they are clicked into a pair of skis.

✔ **Change position** every now and then, but do it consciously. Many speakers pace up and down the stage the whole time, in the mistaken belief that this adds dynamism to their presentation. In reality, all it does is distract. Only change position if you are changing subject. Do it deliberately and do it decisively. Dare to use the full width of the podium instead of standing statically in the middle.

✔ **Gestures**. If you need to make a gesture, ensure that it is:
  • large, precise and clear, almost ostentatious and demonstrative;
  • complete (do not pull your arm back half way through the gesture, like it is attached to an elastic band);
  • sufficiently long (keep the gesture going, as long as it bears a relation to what you are saying).

✔ **Eye contact**. Show that you are looking at someone by turning your whole body towards them.
  • If the person is sitting close to you, you can bend forwards towards them, making your posture more one-to-one.
  • If the person is sitting at some distance from you, you can make yourself look taller, by standing on tip-toe and pushing up your chin.

- Hold eye contact until there is real contact. How long is this, exactly? Difficult to say, but at least a couple of seconds. As a general rule, keep looking until it is no longer pleasant either for you or the other person. This is something you will learn to feel. Some speakers judge the length of eye contact by the time it takes to fill a glass of water (or some other tipple of your choice!).

✔ **Mimic**. Some speakers look as though they have been sponsored by Botox! No matter what they are saying, their facial expression remains the same. However, if you want to have an impact on an audience you really need to let them see what you are feeling. If you are happy and enthusiastic about what you are saying, smile and raise your eyebrows. If you want your listeners to think about something complex that you have just said, frown or look pensive.

5. **Silence**
   - ✔ The public sometimes needs a brief period of silence to digest what has just been said.
   - ✔ You can also use silence to build up tension before you say something important. This sharpens the attention of your listeners.
   - ✔ Don't end the silence too soon. A silence of just two or three seconds is pointless. Be bold. You will gradually learn to sense when your silence has lasted long enough to attract everyone's attention.
   - ✔ A silence in which you do not show to the public that you are thinking is a sterile and meaningless silence. Give your silence a clear purpose and explain this to the public by explaining it with comments such as: "Amazing, isn't it?" or "Now I am going to tell you something funny."
   - ✔ Replace your 'ums' and 'ers' with silence.

6. **Be creative**
   Do something creative, something original to attract attention, so that the willingness of the audience to listen to your story will be heightened. Amuse them. Stimulate them. You can do this by:
   - ✔ asking someone in the audience a question;
   - ✔ beginning with a single word or number, leaving a pause and then explaining the significance of the word or number; for example: "four percent... (pause) ... our turnover has increased this year by four percent";
   - ✔ referring to something striking in the current news;
   - ✔ using an object that is surprising in this context;
   - ✔ using a quote or a joke;
   - ✔ knocking people off balance by saying something completely untrue, which you then correct a few seconds later.

If you are presenting an online event or webinar, you can make it all seem far more professional if you invest in a stream deck. This handy device makes it possible to switch quickly and easily between different screens. For example, from your own image to slides. It also simplifies the automation of questions, intermediate screens and various other elements. Make sure, however, that you practice before the event.

Day chairman/presenter

A day chairman or presenter or moderator does more than simply introduce speakers and link all the different elements of the programme together. He can also play an important role in helping you to achieve the objectives of your event. A professional of this kind – whether male or female – can steer debate, facilitate interaction with the participants and exploit the themes that he senses are important to the audience.

Quite often, the director of the company organising the event will put himself forward as presenter. But is he really the best person for the job? Is he neutral enough? An outside presenter can sometimes ask critical questions that it would be difficult for members of the company to ask. And as a 'novice' in technical matters, he/she can ensure that the themes are discussed in a manner that is understandable to everyone.

▶ www.eventplanner.net/book/tv-moderator

A day chairman can also help with the choice of the right form of interaction for your particular audience. Of course, as organiser you must be happy to accept an interactive approach; if you don't play along, no one else will be willing to play along either! Here are the most common forms of event interaction:

- ✔ **Q&A**
  Reserve enough time in your programme to allow speakers to answer questions from the audience. A good presenter will encourage participants to make full use of this opportunity. And he will give them time to think up their own questions by first asking one or two pertinent questions of his own.

- ✔ **Lower house debate**
  Divide the participants into two groups facing each other, like in the lower houses of most parliaments. The presenter then initiates a debate on

the theme under consideration, with one group 'for' and the other group 'against'. If the propositions are well formulated, so that the participants are divided into two 'camps', you can let people change sides at will, so that in this way all possible opinions are aired.

✓ **Fishbowl**
This is a dynamic talk show, in which everyone in the audience can become involved. On the stage there are four chairs. Three of your guest speakers discuss the subject under consideration. The fourth chair is empty. As soon as someone in the audience wants to say something, they come forward and sit on the fourth chair. When this happens, one of the guest speakers vacates his chair, so that there is always one space free for someone else from the audience to join in.

✓ **Voting with your feet**
Asking people to express their opinions physically can be a useful alternative to expensive voting systems. You can do this by asking them to move to a voting area that corresponds with their views or by asking them to move further left or right along a wall in accordance with the strength of their feelings on a particular subject. This method not only creates greater engagement, but also allows you to see at a glance what the group as a whole thinks about a particular problem. Moreover, movement helps to focus people's attention, which is a useful bonus.

✓ **Role-playing and improvisation**
This is an ideal (and often entertaining) way to discuss complex problems safely. Everyone is allowed to make mistakes, so that there are plenty of lessons to be learnt. There is also informative interaction between the discussion leader and the role-play leader. Highly suitable for duo-presentations.

✓ **World café**
The participants move from group to group, thereby taking part in several different ongoing discussions, which often lead to surprising opinions and solutions. For more info, see **www.theworldcafe.com**.

www.eventplanner.net/book/worldcafe

Interaction with the public can help to take your event to the next level, but is often difficult to achieve. It is embarrassing if a speaker finishes his presentation with 'Does anyone have any questions' and there is no reaction whatsoever from the audience! Fortunately, there are a number of things that you can do with a little preparation to avoid such problems. Here are a few useful tips:

- Crowdsource the questions before the Q&A session begins. There are two options. One is social media. Before the event opens, let your followers know that you want to collect questions for your speakers. Or you can use an app for the same purpose. In this way, your shyer and less talkative participants will have the opportunity to interact without feeling exposed to the glare of publicity.

- Give people time to reflect. Your visitors will often need a few moments before they can formulate their questions properly and find the courage to ask them in front of a large audience. One interesting approach is to first let your participants discuss their thoughts and questions in small groups. After this, they will be more ready to interact with the speaker. Of course, it also improves the interaction between the participants themselves.

- It is not a bad idea to ask a few initial questions yourself (or get one of your assistants to do it). This opens the discussion and gets the ball rolling. Others in the audience will soon follow your example and feel encouraged to talk. Moreover, these first few questions also allow you to set the right tone for the subsequent interaction.

- Don't forget the microphone! (Just joking!) However, you can turn the use of the microphone into a fun element by using throwable or app-based microphones. This immediately breaks the ice and creates a more relaxed atmosphere in which interaction becomes easier.

Decoration

Decoration – your decor – is another key factor in helping to determine the standing of your event and your guests' experience of it. Decoration is a question of creating a total atmosphere. Sometimes a good venue can achieve this by itself, but you can always opt to transform the venue by decorating it in a style of your own choosing. Alternatively, you can place a number of 'eye-catchers' to create the right ambiance. Decoration is especially important for events which are linked to a particular theme.

You will probably have guessed by now, but your decoration (like just about everything else related to your event) must reflect the profile of your target group, your central theme and your overall objectives. Based on these factors, you may decide for a décor which is minimalist, modern, exuberant or even a bit kitsch.

A trendy target group always expects a little more, so that a daring, hip, tongue-in-cheek decoration will score well. For a business target group you are probably better opting for a 'less is more' approach, with elegant but largely unobtrusive décor elements. Always consider the expectations of the guests and make sure that your decoration supports rather than overshadows your event.

 Decorating an event is a task which requires great creativity and long years of experience. For this reason, it is probably wisest to make use of the talents of a professional decorator.

 Your decoration must form a clearly identifiable. Work with the lowest possible number of different suppliers and make sure their different elements are all compatible with each other.

LOCATION AS DECOR

Your venue, objective(s) and target group will determine whether you need lots of decoration or hardly any at all. Some authentic locations, such as castles and churches, need little embellishment, because of the strength of their inherent character. Other locations, such as your company warehouse, black boxes, or tents, may need their lack of inherent character to be camouflaged.

> Are you putting up a tent at a breathtaking location? Why not opt for a model with transparent side panels, so that the beauty of the surroundings provides all the decoration you need.

Don't lose sight of the need to divide and use your event space in an appropriate manner. Good layout contributes to the overall success of your decoration. Think carefully about where you are going to put your catering, long tables, high tables, open spaces, easy chairs, etc. Don't overlook important details, such as the colour and quality of your table linen, floral decoration, types of seating, etc.

DECORATIVE ELEMENTS

Sometimes you will need to brighten up your event space even more. The following tips will help you to underline the true nature of your event and make this clear to your guests:

- ✔ Place your decoration **sufficiently high**. At a reception where everyone remains standing, nobody will notice anything under shoulder height.

- ✔ **Good lighting** can bring out the most in your decoration and also increase its dramatic impact (see the section later in this chapter on lighting).

- ✔ **Floral decoration and the use of greenery** add the finishing touch to the styling of your event. Balloons, ice sculptures and other festive decorations can also make valuable contributions towards the overall 'feel' of your venue.

www.eventplanner.net/book/balloons

 www.eventplanner.net/book/icesculptures

- ✓ Always remember that the **safety** of your guests is paramount. Decorative elements must be stable and/or well fixed in place. Avoid sharp edges, loose cables, hot lights, etc.

> 📌 Textiles and plastics (table cloths, Christmas trees, etc.) can be treated with a fire-resistant product to increase safety.

- ✓ Adjust the **use of colour** so that it reflects the house style of your company or event. The aim is to create a harmonious whole, in which all the elements match. Pay attention to details: little things can sometimes make a big difference. For example, it is a good idea to use the colours of the company logo for your carpets, wall decoration, cloakroom numbers, etc. You can also have many of these items printed with your logo, for an even stronger effect ('branding').

- ✓ Give your decorator a **ground plan** of the venue (including any outside areas). Following consultation with the specialists, choose your decorative elements and mark them on the plan. This will save time when everything is delivered.

> 📌 Professional decorators have their own in-house designers, who are able to give visual expression to your creative plans, with coloured-coded ground plans, mood boards and 3D-visuals. This will give you a clear picture of how your event will actually look and feel when it is ready.

Floral decoration and the use of greenery

Say it with flowers! Flowers and plants are not only pleasing to look at, but bring life into your event area, both literally and figuratively. But you won't achieve the desired effect simply by plonking down the occasional bunch of flowers here and there. Instead, you need to follow the rules of floral art.

Floral decoration offers a wide range of **creative possibilities**. The harder elements (surfaces, vases, pots, etc.) and the flowers used must reflect the

event and be appropriate for the event area. Every flower and plant has its own specific character. In other words, there is something for every occasion and every style. From minimalist solitary pieces to exuberant riots of multi-coloured blooms. The creativity of the flower arrangers will determine the level of elegance and charm.

Natural decoration must fit in well with the total visual concept of the event. In addition, the **quality** of the chosen decoration must be first-rate, since the conditions at many events are not immediately favourable for flowers and plants. In particular, the use of lighting and air-conditioning means that the temperature can vary considerably from one hour to the next. For this reason, your floral decoration requires optimal care, especially if your event lasts for more than one day. Wilting flowers will quickly dent your hard-won positive image.

When **choosing** your flowers and plants, take account of factors such as quality, care, colour and fragrance. It is important that they blend well with the other elements of your décor.

Be careful with **lighting**. Good lighting can really enhance the beauty of your flowers, but it can also cause them to wither and die. Remember also that their true natural colours will look different in dimmed light or candlelight: colours in general will be less intense and darker colours in particular will be less easy to distinguish. At the other end of the spectrum, bright colours can be too 'loud' if they are lit by spotlights. For these reasons, you should keep the lighting of your flowers and plants as pure and as natural as possible. For example, you might opt for green-coloured spots, which will give your floral decoration a more 'healthy' appearance.

 Ask the advice of your decorator. Not every flower and plant is suitable for every event. For outdoor locations, don't forget to take account of frost and wind. Remember also to check when particular plants are in bloom.

 Some plants can cause allergic reactions. These should be avoided or removed, if problems arise. Be particularly careful with your choice of species for table decorations.

From your guests' point of view, the natural decoration can start to work its charm **outside**, before they have even set foot inside your venue. For example, you can line the path leading to the entrance with a hedge of small trees or shrubs.

The **entrance** itself can be decorated with ivy screens or fragrant rose bushes.

> The entrance is generally the best place to put fragrant flowers and plants. The fragrance will be lost if they are placed outside, but can sometimes be overpowering if they are placed inside, particularly in combination with the aromas of your food.

Inside, you can use natural decoration to liven up the stage, the buffet, the bar, etc.

Tables can also be made to look more attractive by the simple addition of a small bouquet or floral arrangement. But be careful not to overdo it. There will already be a number of other decorative elements on the tables, such as menus, name cards, candles, etc. Make sure that there is still enough room for the food and also ensure that all these different elements combine well visually, so that the overall effect is one of unity and harmony.

> Do not make your floral elements too large or too tall. This can hamper conversation at the dinner table. Makes sure that your guests can all still see each other! Why not hang the flowers upside down from the ceiling?

> Do not forget to order a bouquet of flowers and a bottle of wine for your speakers. Keep the flowers in a bucket of water in a cool place backstage.

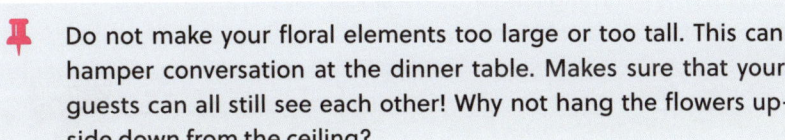
www.eventplanner.net/book/flowers

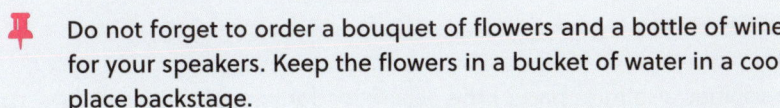
www.eventplanner.net/book/tv-flowers

Themed decoration

A themed event usually requires very specific decoration. You can either rent this or have it specially made. The advantage of hiring standard decoration is that you can usually reserve it easily and at short notice. The design and manufacture of event-specific decoration often takes more time and more money. However, in return you have a series of unique elements which are perfectly suited to the nature of your event.

In addition to accessories, you can also use graphic applications to add decorative charm to your event. For example, you can have banners printed with images or text appropriate to your theme. You can do the same with posters and free-standing panels. With modern graphic techniques, there is no theme which is not capable of being reproduced in a visually attractive manner. For example, why not experiment with 3D holograms.

It is vital to think carefully about your decoration during the concept phase of your event. Do you want standard decoration or do you prefer something made-to-measure? If you go for the latter option, make sure that you begin the design process in good time. If you leave it to the implementation phase, you will already be too late.

The level of quality you require will inevitably be dependent on the target group and the objectives you have in mind. Remember that decorative elements for events lasting longer than a single day will also need to last longer, and so will need to be of better quality.

 www.eventplanner.net/book/decoration

Furnishings

Furnishings also form part of the decoration for your event. Nowadays, you can rent furniture in a wide variety of styles. Hyper-modern design, classic or functional: the options are almost limitless. The choice is yours!

Remember that the correct choice of furniture can be a good way to immediately set the tone and get your guests in the right mood. Think, for example, of cosy seating areas in quiet corners, where the guests can talk. You also need appropriate furniture for your catering zones, entrance hall and even for the interview décor on stage.

Furnishings can also serve other purposes. More and more suppliers now design furniture with built-in sockets and battery charging points for your guests' smartphones and laptops. Cloakrooms also need to have lockers where the guests can store their devices and other valuables in safety.

> 📌 Nowadays, furniture, decoration and technical equipment are usually delivered in large boxes or flight cases. Most suppliers will ask if they can leave these cases at your venue for collection after the event. This saves you extra handling, but make sure that you have enough on-site storage space to make this possible.

> 📌 Do not forget to order the necessary furniture for your changing rooms, the backstage area and your crew spaces.

> 📌 Do not be surprised if you find yourself invoiced by suppliers for damaged or lost furniture and fittings. In fact, this applies to everything you hire, from cutlery to computers. The rule in the event industry is 'you break, you pay!' Make sure that the situation is clearly agreed with your suppliers in advance and check to see what risks you can insure.

Lighting

Correct lighting can transform your venue and its decoration into something magical. By contrast, the wrong lighting can ruin the atmosphere you are trying to create. In particular, poor lighting can make your event look cheap and shabby. Light is therefore an essential element in your décor and makes possible greater depth.

Some useful tips:

- ✔ **Adjust your (party) lighting** to suit the colours of your decor.
- ✔ Place your most attractive decorative elements under **spotlights**. Do not focus attention on unattractive features. Make the lighting of these features more neutral.
- ✔ Lighting must never be **blinding or irritating** for your guests.
- ✔ Be careful for the **effect of shadows**. Sharp shadows cast on the stage or in the public can be distracting. Also check the effect of movement on the shadows in your event area (the shadows cast by the public, the presenter, the acts). A too frequent alternation of light and shadow can be irritating for all concerned. Avoid shadows falling across the faces of your speakers by making sure you have enough white front light.
- ✔ The correct use of lighting can either make your event area **seem bigger or smaller** and more intimate. Never shine bright spotlights on a low ceiling.
- ✔ **Candles** are a great way to create ambiance, but always check that they can be used safely (fire risk). Nowadays, there are plenty of highly convincing replica candles that are hard to tell apart from the real thing.
- ✔ A **smoke or mist machine**, if used in combination with the right lighting, can create a very pleasing decorative effect, but must never cause anxiety or irritation to your guests.
- ✔ Atmospheric lighting can certainly be delightful, but should never hinder staff at work. People need to see what they are doing! Make sure that there is sufficient **working light** in the cloakroom, at the bars, etc.

📌 Lighting is very definitely a matter for the experts. Employ the know-how, technical expertise and equipment of one of the specialist agencies in this field.

📌 Some decorators rent out furniture with built-in lighting features. This can create a stunning effect, particularly in darkened spaces.

📌 The use of LED-lighting is becoming increasingly important in the events sector, particularly for large-scale events. The main advantage is that LED-lights can also work on batteries, so that they can be used without inconvenient and potentially hazardous cables, especially in difficult-to-reach locations.

🔗 www.eventplanner.net/book/light-and-sound-rental

Event **technology**

Every event makes use of equipment and apparatus of one kind or another. In general, the role of technology is increasing all the time, but its use can vary widely from event to event. Sometimes the technological wizardry steals the show. At other events, technical applications are used in a supporting role for presentations and/or performances.

Whatever role you are planning to give technology in your own events, it is crucial to prepare well in advance. Crackling speakers, whistling microphones, badly adjusted lighting or interrupted satellite connections are all potential problems which can have a negative effect on the image of your event.

Technology must always remain subordinate to your central message, and must be put at the service of the speaker or artist, rather than the other way around. Technological magic will not turn a bad act into a good one, but bad technical support can certainly turn a good act into a bad one.

Be aware that event technology is evolving at lightning speed. If you can no longer see the wood for the trees, it makes sense to hire an independent technical producer for your event, who can advise you about making the right choices. This role can sometimes be filled by your equipment supplier or by your event bureau. Remember, however, that the interest of the supplier will often be focused on the equipment that he has available for hire and this might not necessarily coincide with your best interests. Sometimes obtaining a more independent view not only produces a better end result but can also save you money.

*Technology must be put **at the service of** the speaker or artist, rather than the other way around*

 Always work with A-quality equipment and competent professional technicians. Check that your leasing agency has enough back-up material and is available 24 hours a day to deal with any technical problems that may arise. Having someone available on-site is even better.

📌 When you are using high-tech equipment, there will inevitably be a lot of cables lying around. Take the necessary measures to eliminate any risk of tripping, both for staff and guests. Loose cables are not only dangerous, but also unsightly. Collect them together, bind them with tape and, where possible, remove them from view.

📌 Check to see that the electricity supply is capable of withstanding the heavy usage which your event will cause. If necessary, hire additional generators.

🔗 www.eventplanner.net/book/generatorsrental

📌 When dealing with event technology you will often find yourself overwhelmed by all the technical jargon that this involves. Perhaps you are already familiar with terms like 'high definition' and 'kilowatt', but do you know what 'H264 codec', 'impedance' and 'colour temperature' all mean? Of course, this is not always necessary, but you must never be afraid to ask questions about important things that are still unclear to you. Before you know it, you will have taken a decision that can have far-reaching consequences, and all because you did not understand what your supplier was saying.

> 📌 Although all event technology is now computer-operated, this does not mean that it will automatically provide you with a fantastic show at the drop of a hat. Make sure that you allocate sufficient time in your call sheet plan for the programming of all this technical wizardry. Some elements can probably be programmed in advance using special visualisation software.

AUDIO

Sound systems

At some venues you will be able to make use of their permanent in-house sound system. Even so, check to make sure that this installation is suitable for all elements of your programme: announcements, speakers, live performances, etc. In some cases, you will need to hire a sound system from a specialised external company. In making your choice, take account of the number of guests, the acoustics of the event area (height of ceiling, type of wall covering, surface area, etc.) and the space available for the technical equipment.

Nowadays, sound can be modulated in so many different ways that good quality is now possible even in acoustically challenging locations. Many different configurations for the sound system are also available, such as the so called *line-array* (where speakers are hung one underneath the other).

Make sure that there is always a sound technician present at your event, so that he can solve any problems which many arise. Allow sufficient time in your action plan for the installation and the adjustment of the sound system, as well as the need for various sound checks. Run through the programme with your sound people.

For festivals and concerts, but also increasingly for congresses, the control panels for the management of technical elements are positioned in the zone where your public are standing or sitting. This is known in event jargon as FOH (front of house). The FOH should be positioned centrally, so that the sound and lighting technicians have a good view of what is happening on stage and can make any necessary adjustments. Sometimes the FOH is located in a separate room, with the technicians following a video link of the various activities. In this case, however, you run the risk of losing the link. Always make sure that the FOH is properly cordoned off and protected from the public. If necessary, provide extra security. Also take account of any guests who might find themselves sitting or standing behind the FOH. Do all you can to provide them with a good field of vision to the stage. At the same time, it is important to set aside sufficient space for your technical people, so that they can work comfortably and act quickly whenever the circumstances demand it.

> 📌 Some artists prefer to use their own sound equipment and bring their own sound technician with them. Make clear arrangements with regard to the setting up and testing of their system (how, when and where).

> 📌 Remember that your sound system needs to be properly earthed; otherwise, you will be plagued by an irritating buzzing noise.

> 📌 During the live performance of bands or DJ's, it is always a good idea to set up a monitor with the screen facing towards the performer(s). Many artists also like to make use of their own ear pieces *(in-ear monitoring)*, which they plug in to a wireless receiver.

Are you organising an event with multiple break-out sessions in a single large space? If so, wireless headsets (also known as 'silent disco') are an ideal way to listen to a session without being disturbed by other presentations taking place in the same room. These headphones are now increasingly used for keynote sessions at trade fairs and congresses.

Microphones

Choose a microphone that suits both your purpose and the place where you need to install it. Microphones come in various shapes and sizes.

- ✔ lectern microphone: a fixed microphone on a speaking platform or dais (as might be used in a church);
- ✔ table microphone: a fixed microphone on a fixed stand (as might be used at a press conference);
- ✔ hand microphone: a loose microphone, with or without cable (as might be used by a presenter);
- ✔ singing microphone: a loose microphone with or without cable, which is suitable for singing and can also be placed on a stand (as might be used at a musical performance);
- ✔ lapel microphone: a wireless microphone that can be fixed to the lapel of a jacket or a tie (as might be used for a presentation where the speaker needs to keep both hands free);

- ✔ headset: a wireless microphone that can be worn on the head (as might be used by an artist who needs to move about during the performance or by speakers making presentations at congresses);
- ✔ hanging microphone: a microphone on a long sound boom which can be hung over the heads of the artist, speaker or audience from some distance away (as might be used in a tv-recording).

Inform the speaker or artist exactly how the microphone works and test it to see if the resulting sound is clearly audible in all parts of the auditorium. If necessary, adjust the microphones individually.

> 📌 Check the lengths of the cables. Do they give the artist or speaker the required freedom of movement? If not, think about using a wireless microphone.

> 📌 Make sure that there are always reserve microphones available. It is advisable to provide each lectern with two fixed microphones. Having a second back-up for a tie-pin microphone is also sensible. If you opt for a wireless model, change the batteries every day and keep a set of spare batteries close at hand.

> 📌 If you want to interact with your public, remember that you will need either hand microphones or hanging microphones. Or why not opt for a trendy throwable microphone, encased in a soft cube of foam?

> 📌 For large-scale (public) events, provide a number of battery-powered megaphones, just in case the power supply fails and panic breaks out in the public. This will allow you to address the crowd and give them necessary instructions.

Translation facilities

Some (international) events need to be conducted in more than one language. This may require the use of a simultaneous translation system.

The main language used at an event by the chairman/presenter and the speakers is known as the **floor language** (or sometimes the **active lan-**

guage). During relatively simple conferences there will usually be just a single floor language, although other languages may also be occasionally used (for example, during Q&A sessions). During larger congresses there may be more than one floor language. The number of floor languages at an event will determine the number of translators you need.

The languages that the translators can speak are usually categorised as **A, B and C languages**. The A language is the active language and mother tongue of the translator. He translates from his B and/or C language into his A language. The B is the translator's second mother tongue, which he can speak to (almost) the same level as his A language. A translator will also sometimes translate into this B language. The C language is the **passive language** (or languages), from which he translates into languages A and/or B. Congress translators can usually work in more than one C language. For every language your participants speak, you will therefore need a translator that has this language as his own A or B language.

It is a good idea to provide a ground plan of the event area in advance to the organisation responsible for the installation of the translation booths and equipment (which may be the translation agency itself). This will allow them to plan where the cabins and the associated cabling can best be located. Each translator needs a sound-proof booth with a clear view of the act or presentation. Infra-red transmitters send the translation directly to the headphones worn by the participants, who can choose their preferred language using a knob positioned next to each seat. The correct location and installation of the booths is crucial for good translation work. You should try to take account of the following points:

- ✔ Make sure that the translators are in a position where they can have direct eye-contact with the speakers.
- ✔ Translators must be able to discreetly enter and leave their booths and the event room without disturbing the speakers and guests.
- ✔ The different booths must be grouped together in a single location.
- ✔ Ensure that there is sufficient room next to the booths for the technical support personnel.

Naturally, the translators want to do their work as well as they possibly can, but for this they will require your assistance. The more advance information they have about your programme, the easier it is for them to do their job properly. Consequently, it is important to allow sufficient time in your action plan to liaise adequately with your translation team. The most common items of reference material they require are:

- ✔ the programme of activities;
- ✔ the presentations by the speakers;
- ✔ a list of the delegates' names;
- ✔ a list of the participating organisations;
- ✔ a list of branch-specific acronyms, abbreviations and terminology;
- ✔ as much background information as possible;
- ✔ all available hand-outs;
- ✔ previous conference minutes.

> 📌 You need at least two translators per language, since simultaneous translation is very stressful work. Regular change-overs are essential to maintain the required levels of speed and quality.

> 📌 For less common languages, such as Bengali, many translators will not possess a knowledge of these languages as their C language. In these cases, it is usual for the relevant text/speech to be first translated into English, so that other translators can then translate from English into the other necessary languages.

> 📌 Make someone specifically responsible for the headphones used by the participants. This person must be able to explain the use of the headphones, perhaps by means of an illustrated flyer (which will help to limit linguistic difficulties and misunderstandings).

An alternative to translators that is becoming increasingly popular is the live subtitling (and/or translation) of the speaker's text by smart AI software. This software can write in real time on a screen what the speaker is saying and, if necessary, can also translate it. This is particularly useful for people with hearing impairments and for people who do not speak the event's main language. It needs to be borne in mind, however, that the quality of these automatic translations has not yet reached the standard of a professional human translator.

VISUAL **EQUIPMENT**

Projector/beamer

There are different types of projector that can be used to give presentations via a laptop or video projections. To choose the right data-projector, also known as a beamer, you need to take account of the size of the auditorium, the distance between the projector and the screen, and the extent to which it is possible to darken the room. This translates into the required light output and resolution of the projector.

The value of the **light output** is calculated in Ansi-Lumen. In an office setting, 500-1000 Ansi-Lumen will usually be sufficient. With projectors of this intensity, working in dimmed light, you can project onto a screen of roughly 2 x 1.6 metres.

In larger auditoria, where you want to project on a larger screen, you will need a beamer with a higher light output of 2000-12000 Ansi-Lumen. You still need to take account of the distance between the projector and the screen, and the extent to which it is possible to darken the room, since this continues to have an influence on the required level of light output.

The **resolution** of the data-projector is a second important factor. This resolution must be equal to or better than the resolution of the software or the computer that you are using. In recent years 1024 x 768 pixels has been superseded as standard and greater use is now made of Full HD or 1920 x 1080 pixels or even 4K. The higher the resolution, the better the picture quality will be, so that details become sharper and better defined. And don't forget about the image format. A 16:9 **aspect ratio**, such as is used for broadband television, is now becoming more common on presentation laptops, superseding the old 4:3 standard. Remember that terms like SD (standard definition), HD (high definition) and 4K are also important when choosing the right projector.

The key factors are therefore:
1. First determine the size of screen or projection you need.
2. How many people will be sitting in the event room and how far will they be from the screen? Take account of the people sitting on the back row; they need to see everything clearly as well.
3. What is the lighting situation in the event room? This will influence how many Ansi-Lumen you will require. The more light there is, the more powerful your projector will need to be.
4. What resolution and aspect ratio is appropriate?

5. Do you want to project material other than the speakers' presentations via a laptop? Live video images from a camera or a DVD perhaps? If so, you will need an image-switcher that will allow you to move smoothly from one image source to another.

> 📌 Not all projectors are suitable for the display of video images. If you want to show a video, you are probably better advised to use a specially adjusted video projector. However, the most recent models are now capable of dealing with both data and video projection.

> 📌 Do you want a really cool gimmick for the opening of your new company building? Then why not think about *video mapping*. A projection on the front facade can help to make the bricks and mortar come alive! This technique is also being increasingly used at concerts, with the artist interacting with the images projected behind him. Or what about projecting images onto the tables at a formal dinner?

Do you want to project live images from other parts of the world? A satellite connection to beam the video images is probably the best solution. Bear in mind that this will not be cheap and that bad weather (electrical storms) can interrupt transmission. Nowadays, a fast and stable internet connection is a possible – and much less expensive - alternative.

 At congresses, projections that cover the full width of the auditorium are becoming increasingly popular. In addition to slides, live images and extra information can also be shown. In this case, multiple projectors combine to form a single large image.

Projection screen

Do not just project on a white wall, but always use a special projection screen. You lose too much of your picture quality if you do not project onto the right background. There are two types of projector screen. With a front projector screen, the projector is placed in front of the screen and shines onto it. With a rear projector screen, the projector is placed behind the screen and shines through it.

Rear projector screens have the advantage that the projector is not visible and is not standing in anybody's way. In addition, there are no irritating shadows when someone walks between the projector and the screen, and the beam of light is less distracting for the presenter. The disadvantage is that you reduce the space available in your event area for your public, since you need to keep a good distance free behind the screen, in order to ensure the necessary picture quality.

Smart boards

A smart board is an interactive board on which you can make 'live' digital notes or sketches. How does it work? In essence, a beamer projects a computer image onto the screen. You can write on the board with a special pen (or sometimes even with just your finger). The software reconfigures every contact into a mouse click or digital signal, so that the drawing is immediately projected via the beamer onto the screen. Many different technologies are currently used for smart boards: touch screen, electro-magnetic, laser, infra-red, ultrasonic. Often they are used in combination with each other. Remember, however, that the first time you use a digital board – and also after every time that you move it – it will need to be (re)calibrated.

Let your speakers practice with a smart board before they use one in front of a live audience. In the beginning they can be tricky to use, but they can offer you a wide range of interesting possibilities once you have mastered their intricacies.

Plasma and LCD screens

Plasma screens are highly suitable for presentations and video imaging in undarkened rooms. Because the screens are getting bigger and better all the time, they are increasingly replacing the classic beamers in meeting rooms. 75 inch screens are certainly large enough, are easy to use and do not need their lamps changing every five minutes! Moreover, today you also have the option of 4K resolution, which gives you crystal clear images.

 Do you want to make a splash at your event with the excellent quality offered by 4K screens or projectors? If so, make sure that you also have 4K content. Ordinary content on a 4K screen can often have the opposite effect.

Video walls

A video wall consists of a number of separate screens positioned next to each other. Together, they form one large screen and project just a single image. You can be very creative with this kind of wall. You don't need to restrict yourself to the classic 2x2 or 3x3 configurations. Six screens next to each other can be even more impressive! The real challenge is to fill the screens with imaginative content, but recent technical developments mean that this is now becoming an increasingly affordable option.

 The dividing strips between the different screens can be intrusive for presentations with data (text, numbers, graphics). But this is not the case for video clips or ambiance images. Moreover, in recent years a number of seamless screens have come onto the market, allowing you to overcome this problem.

LED screens

LED screens are made up from thousands of tiny LED lights. They are ideal for events which take place in broad daylight (sporting events, festivals, etc.).

Video images and graphics remain clear and well-focused, even on the brightest days. LED screens can also be used to good effect indoors, where their high light output and wide viewing angle offer considerable benefits.

Another advantage of LED displays is the fact that they are modular. This means that they can easily be added to each other to create a single giant screen.

LED is also perfect for bold and innovative solutions, generally known as 'creative LED'. Think, for example, of spectacular stages where LED panels of all different sizes form a background that seems to float in the air, as it projects various images and animations. Creative LED applications are usually based around the use of square LED tiles that allow you to construct just about any shape you can think of. Special mapping software combines these tiles into an integrated whole.

www.eventplanner.net/book/audiovisualrental

LIGHT

In chapter 13 we looked at lighting from a decorative perspective and the way in which it can create atmosphere. However, light also has a more functional purpose as well.

The correct use of lighting can bring certain aspects of your programme to the foreground and push others into the background. The best way to achieve the effects you desire is to hire a professional lighting expert, who will draw up and implement a total lighting package.

Possible applications include:

- lighting of parking areas, paths, walkways and exterior surroundings;
- (atmospheric) lighting in and around the event room;
- specific lighting of special features (for example, the buffets or the registration desk);
- focusing attention on attractive aspects of the decor and removing attention from less attractive aspects;
- full or partial darkening of the event room;
- (decorative) exterior lighting of the event building;
- disco-lighting for the right mood on the dance floor;

- spotlighting of entertainments and performances;
- follow-spots for speakers moving on stage or amongst the audience.

You will need to draw up your lighting plan in collaboration with your lighting expert. Describe to him what effect you wish to create with lighting for each part of your event programme. These different objectives must then be written into a concrete lighting action plan. What equipment will you need? Who will provide it? Where will it be installed?

You will also need a framework on which your lighting can be mounted, often known as a 'rig'. For this reason, the person who constructs this framework and attaches the individual lights is called a 'rigger'. Pay particular attention to safety procedures during the construction and removal process. This is an element of event management where accidents can easily occur. Always double check every light to ensure that it is securely held in place: you don't want a 20 kilogram spotlight falling on the head of one of your guests!

> 📌 Be careful! Theatrical lighting is very different from the lighting for television recordings. Bear this in mind if your event is being filmed or televised.

> 📌 Have a number of gobo's (glass plates) made with your logo and install a number of moveable spotlights (scanners, moving heads...) to project them. When using digital projection spotlights, all you need to do is upload your logo.

> 📌 Make sure that riggers and other crew members working at height are always secured by a safety harness.

🔗 www.eventplanner.net/book/light-and-sound-rental

PODIA

Some venues will have a permanent stage of their own but in other cases you will need to hire and construct a stage specially for your event. A raised platform for a speaker or an indoor stage for a band can quickly and easily be made from modular elements. These elements are adjustable in height and can be joined together to create any shape and area you desire. Your sound and light experts will probably be able to help you find the right supplier. For larger structures, such as for outdoor concerts, you will need to hire a specialist stage constructor. This will probably need planning permission, so make sure that you submit your application in plenty of time.

In the first instance, your stage will need to meet the technical requirements of your artist(s). These requirements are, however, negotiable. An artist who insists on a stage area of 12m x 9m can probably be persuaded to accept 11m x 8m. Check the floor height and adjust your lighting plan to take account of the roof-bearing capacity of covered stages.

When the initial construction has been completed, take the necessary time to check the entire structure thoroughly with the leader of the construction crew. This will allow you to make any necessary adjustments immediately, without the need for return journeys and additional travelling time.

 It is by no means a luxury to appoint a safety coordinator to monitor the construction and removal of a large-scale stage. He must ensure that every aspect of the construction complies with the applicable safety standards. Ask for a stability test to be conducted by a recognised testing agency (the costs to be paid by the

📌 event organiser). Draw up a detailed safety plan and insist that it is respected to the letter by all your suppliers. Avoid, where possible, that two suppliers should be working at the same location at the same time.

📌 You should not compare apples with pears. No two stages are the same; on the contrary, there are often huge differences in terms of load-bearing capacity, rigging capacity, wind resistance, required permits, etc. Take account of this when comparing the different price tenders you receive.

📌 If you are building a stage in a difficult location (in water, on a slope, above stairs, part indoors/part outdoors), it is essential to make a preliminary site visit with your stage constructor. Moreover, the location must be accessible in all weathers for the heavy lorries which will transport the stage elements. Take appropriate remedial measures, where necessary (steel ramps, telescopic loaders, etc.).

🔗 www.eventplanner.net/book/stagerental

SPECIAL EFFECTS

Special effects were originally developed in Hollywood, but they can also turn your event into something really special, making a major contribution to your guests' experience. As always, of course, they need to be in keeping with your event objectives and the profile of your target group. A sudden flash of fire on the podium adds little to a congress presentation, but it can whip up excitement amongst the public at a concert. Within these parameters, there is an enormous range of choice: smoke effects, laser shows, fireworks, foam cannons, confetti canons... These are just some of the many examples to help you on your way.

🔗 www.eventplanner.net/book/audiovisualconcepts

Spraying snow or confetti all over your public? Think twice about the wisdom of this and if you go ahead make sure that you have all the necessary safety permits. It wouldn't be the first time that members of the public have suffered skin irritation from substances in the coloured powders in which they are sprayed. Safe products are usually not the cheapest ones on the market, so don't cut corners.

Laser show

A laser show offers you an almost certain guarantee of spectacular results. Supported by the right music and the right sound effects, these results can be enhanced still further. The public sits more or less in the middle of the show, surrounded by lasers with a dazzling array of different colours. You can even project texts and logos.

In theory, you can hold a laser show either indoors or outdoors. However, for the very best effects you need a darkened space.

 Work exclusively with professional laser artists. They are the only people with the right equipment and therefore the only people capable of producing a show of the required level of sophistication and safety. Incorrect use of the wrong lasers can cause serious eye damage.

Video show

Video shows have become increasingly popular at events in recent years. A VJ *(video jockey)* mixes a series of images, texts and video fragments, and projects them onto a large screen in a live act, set to the rhythm of carefully selected music.

A creative, professional video show can package your message in an original manner. You can exploit your own theme, other current news themes and a wide range of other subjects. A good video show is really a piece of visual art – and will stay fixed in the memory of your guests for a very long time.

Agree with your VJ in advance which elements will play a prominent role in his mix. For example, the logos of your sponsors. Obviously, this means that he will need to be fully aware of your event objectives!

 Do you want to include a fragment from a DVD or a television programme in your mix? This is possible, but you will need to ask the necessary permission and pay the necessary royalties.

Fireworks

A spectacular fireworks display can provide a unique finale for your event. For example, you can time the beginning of the display to coincide with the *moment suprême* of a product launch or at the highpoint of your main act's performance. Remember that you can use fireworks both indoors and outdoors – but this use is subject to very strict rules. You will need to take account of important safety measures, such as evacuation routes, distance to the public, presence of the fire brigade (otherwise you will not be granted the necessary permission). And, of course, the fireworks that you use will be determined to a large extent by the size of your budget and the nature of the location.

For 'light' fireworks (fireworks that can be purchased by the general public) there must be a minimum distance of 15 metres between the display and the spectators. For 'heavy' fireworks (only available to the professionals) you need a much larger distance, sometimes as much as 300 metres. Always check the local regulations, because these can vary from place to place.

Only officially approved fireworks companies are allowed to use professional fireworks. Make sure that all necessary permits are applied for and received in good time. Discuss the safety aspects with the company and with the local police and fire service.

 www.eventplanner.net/book/fireworks

Recent developments

During recent years, a whole range of new techniques have been developed to create spectacular and surprising effects. What do you think, for example, about a full 3D video show or a presentation given by a hologram projection? Or perhaps drones fitted with LED lamps, flying in formation to create a sensational air show? This would certainly be a spectacular alternative to fireworks! Look for something that can play on all the senses of your audience, including the possibility of working with fragrances.

Special effects can also be functional. Think, for example, of a mist of water on a water curtain, which can also serve to cool your guests at events in tropical heat.

(LIVE) PHOTOGRAPH AND VIDEO CAPTATION

Don't forget to hire a photographer and/or a video crew. You can give them a roving assignment at your event to wander around and capture all the best moments on film. Once the event is over, photos and video images are not only great souvenirs for your guests, but also a useful tool for promoting subsequent editions of the event.

By directly transmitting 'live' images onto a screen, the public can see – and experience – everything that is going on both front stage and backstage, or even on other stages. Images of the public (for example, on the dance floor or arriving on the red carpet at the entrance) are also fun to project. And with live streaming, everyone everywhere can enjoy the same images on the internet.

With online or hybrid events, in addition to a camera team or remote-controlled cameras, you will also need a director's unit, where all the different images can be monitored. It is the director who decides which of these images will be used.

> Are you planning to show your speakers in close-up on a large screen? If so, you will need a make-up artist to apply basic TV-style make-up. Under the glare of spotlights, make-up can work wonders and ensure that your speakers' faces don't shine like polished billiard balls!

Like all your suppliers and service providers, the photographer and the cameraman need a good briefing. Otherwise, there is a risk that the results of their efforts will not live up to your expectations. Here are some of the main points you should discuss.

- ✓ Make clear what your **objectives** are. Do you want their photos and clips to concentrate on the public or the entertainment? Do you want general shots or close-ups? Tell them what you are planning to do with the resultant material. Will it be used for promotional purposes, live projection or as a souvenir?

- ✓ Agree **how long** the video clips should last and **how many** photographs you need and in what sizes. You can also describe **the type of shots** you are looking for: a full room, laughing faces, well-dressed people, specific moments. If possible, show them some examples from previous events (a so-called mood board).

- ✓ Make clear agreements about the **editing** of the video images. Do you want them set to music? Will you use 'free' music? If not, who will pay the royalties? Do you want guests or acts to be interviewed?

- ✓ Should the photographs be in **black-and-white** (which is now hip again) **or colour**?

- ✓ Run through the **programme** with the photographer and/or cameraman, so that they know where they must be and when. Make clear which elements of the programme you want them to emphasise.

- ✓ Discuss the possibilities offered by the **location**. Where can the crew put their equipment? What lighting is available? Can they plug into the sound system?

- ✓ What **dress code** do the photographer and the cameraman need to follow? They can hardly wear jeans at a gala ball! Do you want them to be noticeable or would you prefer them to work **incognito**?

- ✓ What are the **deadlines** for the production/delivery of the images? You need to tell your guests clearly when and where they can see or collect the results. For example, at a multi-day event you may want to put out a video report at the end of each day. This requires a very precise action plan, which must be strictly adhered to. The plan must contain details of the desired text, images and music, so that these only need to be fitted in during the editing process.

- ✓ Agree with the photographer and/or the cameraman who will own the **intellectual rights** of their work. Also agree the uses to which the images can be put. It would be a pity to have some fantastic pictures of your event, but not be able to use them for further publicity or PR because your photographer has put his own ugly watermark all over the front of them to promote his own business. Also ask for the rough source material: this can often come in useful at a later stage. If you do decide to use it, it is good practice to employ the same photographer or cameraman for the task. Also bear in mind that some photographers never share their source material or expect additional payment to release it.

> Even the most professional equipment can cause problems. Make sure that the photographer and the cameraman have back-up material at their disposal.

> Take account of your guests' right to privacy. Give people the opportunity to say whether or not they are willing to be photographed/filmed. You can make this clear with a simple notice or announcement at the entrance to the venue.

> When artists or celebrities are appearing at your event, you will need to take account of portrait rights. It could cost you dearly if you just use an image without thinking (not only the retrospective payment of the rights, but also possible compensation, destruction of printed matter, termination of an advertising campaign, etc.).

www.eventplanner.net/book/photo

 www.eventplanner.net/book/video

www.eventplanner.net/book/live-video

Drones

Spectacular aerial images that make the video report of your event complete? Nowadays, this is child's play with the use of drones. These small, versatile and unmanned quadrocopters can fly almost unnoticed above heads of your public. Result: unique aerial shots of your exhibition, event, congress or teambuilding.

There are, however, a number of matters that you need to bear in mind if you want to use drones at your event:

- ✓ **Make a script**
   What images are you expecting? Which are the shots that you absolutely must have? Discuss this in advance with the drone pilot and make clear agreements, on the basis of which you then draw up a script. This is the best briefing you can give.

- ✓ **Be careful: drones can be disruptive and/or irritating**
   Drones make a buzzing noise and create a gust of wind as they pass. You need to take account of this in your script. For example, taking an aerial shot of a charismatic speaker with a drone is not a good idea. If you really need the shot, think of alternatives, like a camera crane.

- ✓ **Safety first**
   The use of drones is not without risk, especially if there are a lot of people in the vicinity. Discuss the possible risks with the drone operator. Make sure he knows the areas where he can fly with safety and the areas he should avoid. Inform him about potential obstacles and also about aerials and other objects that might cause interference with the drone signal. Insist that the operator always maintains eye contact with his drone.

- ✓ **Take account of relevant rules and regulations**
   Complaints about the use of drones often relate to breaches of privacy or the disruption of airspace. Many countries now have legislation and codes of practice that regulate these matters. In most cases, professional drones can only be used by certified pilots, who need to undergo strict medical, theoretical and practical tests. If you wish to make use of a 'high-risk' drone activity, such as flying over a large public, you will first need special permission from the relevant aviation authority.

INTERNET

Nowadays, people expect to have internet access at all times and in all places – including your event! However, this is not always as easy to arrange as it sounds. Many events still do not provide an internet connection for their participants. If there is one, it often works slowly or you have to pay a small fortune for an hour's surfing. This is no longer acceptable in our modern world and will certainly have a negative effect on your participants' experience of your event.

Capacity?

One of the most important challenges is to accurately assess the required capacity or broadband width of your internet connection. To do this, you first need to know what your participants intend to use the internet connection for.

Is it just so that delegates can check their e-mails? Or is there a press room where journalists want to send live video images through to their editorial offices? The transmission of simple text messages via X requires relatively little band width. But if you attach photos and videos to your message, this changes matters completely. In addition to types of use, you will also need to assess how many people will actually make use of your network. This will depend on the type of people in your target group and how many of them will want to communicate with the outside world at the same time. To some extent, this last point will be dependent on your programme. If you have a full programme, there is a strong likelihood that everyone will want to use the internet at the same time; for example, during the coffee breaks and lunch pauses. You will need to take account of these peaks of use.

*At many events there is still no internet connection, or else it works **very slowly** or you have to pay a small fortune for an hour's surfing. This is no longer acceptable in our modern world*

To make matters more concrete, you may find the following simple calculation useful. Imagine that you are organising a congress for 100 delegates. You expect that 75 of them will want to make use of an internet connection and that two-thirds of them will want to be online at the same time. If you anticipate that this will mostly be 'basic' internet use, there is no need to go overboard when making your band width calculation. 1Mbit (megabit) per person of downstream band width for the downloading of data and a ½ megabit upstream per person should be more than sufficient. But for 50 simultaneous online users this means that you need 50Mbit downstream and 25 Mbit upstream. A standard ADSL-connection, which is already present at many locations, will never be able to cope with this level of use – and this is just for a relatively small event of only 100 people! If you have the option to choose a venue that has taken the trouble to invest in a fibreglass internet connection, don't hesitate! All your problems will be solved and you can offer your guests a trouble-free internet experience.

> 📌 The patterns of expectation regarding internet speed are often based on the type of device people are using. With a laptop you expect superfast internet, whereas with a smartphone you may already be used to things working a little slower. If your network only has a limited capacity, it may be a wise move to allocate less band width to smartphone users.

When the participants at your event are often likely to be looking at the same internet page – for example, the programme of the day on the event website – you can save on broadband use by installing a proxy server in your network. This allows you to save the pages that are surfed by the participants for a limited period of time. If another person wants to look at the same page within, say, the next ten minutes, this person does not need to access your network; instead the page in question will be uploaded from the local cache on the proxy server.

Finally, it is important to remember that it is not only the effectiveness of the internet connection to the outside world that determines the quality of the internet experience. Your local network apparatus is just as important. Average common-or-garden routers, which regrettably are still used at some events, can often cope with no more than five people online at the same time. The capacity you need can only be provided by professional routers. So don't cut corners: it doesn't pay in the long run. Also make sure that you have sufficient IP-addresses. This is not a problem that frequently occurs, but it can happen from time to time. So don't let it happen to you!

Do you still think that a strong and secure internet connection is an unnecessary luxury, something on which you can save money? Perhaps these figures will help to convince you differently. The world's largest events pour terabytes of data through their internet connection in just a few hours. Of course, this connectivity and broadband comes at a price. The Super Bowl saw 70 million dollars go up in smoke when the unique devices of some 35,000 supporters used 7 TB of data during the game. The Las Vegas Congress Centre invested 18 million dollars in a network with 2,100 access points that could support up to 100,000 concurrent users. And last year the North American Car Show paid 2 million dollars for 3 TB of data for its 14,500 participants. True, most of you reading this book are unlikely to come up against such extreme limits, but if major event organisers and venues of this kind are prepared to spend such huge sums of money, it is because there is a very good reason to do so. The good news? These examples are all a few years old and, fortunately, the prices for data use are now falling rapidly.

It is also worthwhile (and interesting) following the latest developments in the field of 4G and 5G internet connections for smartphone users. This is not something you will be able to exploit in the immediate future, but within a few years it is probable that everyone will have their own personal broadband connection in their pocket or handbag. This will shift your event requirement away from Wi-Fi hotspots and towards the need for sufficient 5G transmitter masts in the vicinity of your event location.

For large events, provide separate internet connections for your participants and the press. Also add an extra connection for the use of your own organisation. In this way, you can shape your internet access to reflect the differing needs of the different groups, whilst at the same time ensuring that your own staff remain in online contact with the outside world during moments of internet overload.

If there is no fixed, permanent internet connection at your event location, it is possible to have one installed temporarily – although this will cost a lot of money. Alternatively, you can rely on a satellite connection. This is less expensive, but also less reliable, particularly in bad weather. It also has a number of other limitations.

Why not try and find a sponsor for your participants' internet access? You can name the network after your sponsor, so that everyone can see exactly who is allowing them to surf for free at your event. Or else you can make a landing page on which everyone automatically arrives. You can even add useful commercial elements: e-mail address (with an opt-in), questions to be answered before access is granted, etc.

There is also a legal aspect to providing free internet access. As the provider, you are obliged to formally register with the relevant telecommunications authorities. You are also responsible for whatever happens via your network and are required to keep your traffic and location details for a full six months. There are a number of possible loopholes, if you only offer passive internet for a clearly defined target group. But to keep things as safe and as simple as possible, it is probably wise to obtain an internet connection via an experienced ISP (internet service provider), who will assume this responsibility on your behalf.

📌 As far as possible, try and limit the number of external signals that might interfere with your internet connection. For example, Wi-Fi signals can be reduced or distorted by mobile phones, microwaves, high-tension electricity cables, etc.

📌 Do not forget to protect your network and make it secure! The last thing you want is for the network to be hacked during your event. Engage the services of a professional to manage the network for you.

Remember that you need internet access for more than just a data network. Nowadays, more and more events also depend on a stable network for various other production elements. Think, for example, of camera surveillance, digital signage, crowd control screens, cash tills, payment facilities, etc. All these systems also make use of your IP connections. Although Wi-Fi is usually very stable, it is better to use cables for your business-critical applications. If your budget allows it, arrange for your internal network to be completely separated from the public network. This is safer and guarantees network priority for security and emergency services if anything should go wrong at your event. If separate physical networks are not an option in your case, you can use firewalls and virtual networks to separate the data streams and determine priorities on your single main network.

You will not get very far *with the standard ADSL-connection available at most event locations.*

📌 For large events it is wise to appoint a coordinator for all wireless connections. Wi-Fi (and wireless technology in general) has its limitations. There is only a limited set of frequencies that can be used within the same zone. For this reason, make sure that your frequencies will not disrupt each other and make the necessary arrangements to avoid this well in advance. Remember that Bluetooth applications, access control and several other features offer all operation in the same frequency band.

INTERACTIVE VOICE SYSTEMS

Interaction with the public is becoming increasingly important. Consider, for example, the growing interest in the use of remote-control devices, SMS or even your own event app for the casting of votes during congresses, as well as the growing use during events of social media such as X. The results are immediately available on screen.

EVENT APPS

Nowadays, almost all your guests will have a smartphone that they seem to be consulting almost non-stop! This provides you, as the organiser, with a number of possibilities to make your event more interactive. Apps can replace entrance tickets, programme books, maps and diagrams, and so on. The main advantage for organisers is the possibility to make and communicate last-minute changes via these apps.

But you can go much further than simply replacing printed matter. For example, you can integrate numerous other features into your app, such as interactive voting, the viewing of slides, background information on your speakers, locating your friends via GPS, networking, and so much more.

The big disadvantage of mobile apps is that they are expensive when they need to be developed from scratch, especially as you require a separate app for each different kind of smartphone. Fortunately, there are now companies that offer 'plug and play' solutions that are significantly cheaper.

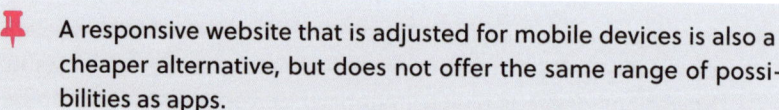

A responsive website that is adjusted for mobile devices is also a cheaper alternative, but does not offer the same range of possibilities as apps.

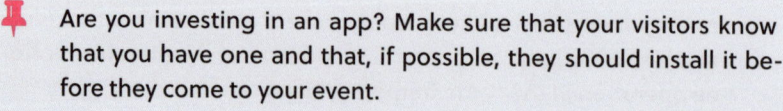

Are you investing in an app? Make sure that your visitors know that you have one and that, if possible, they should install it before they come to your event.

How do you choose an app that you can be confident your visitors will really use? Here are a few tips that will help you to make the right decision:

- ✓ **Test that app and assess its user-friendliness**
  Before buying an event app, always ask for a trial version. You don't need to be an expert in mobile app development to decide whether or not an app is easy to use. Put yourself in the position of a visitor and ask yourself the following questions. Is the app simple to install? Is it intuitive? Is the interface easy to understand and to navigate? If you become irritated because everything takes too long or fails to work in a clear manner, your visitors will feel the same. In other words, this is not the app for you.

- ✓ **Know exactly why you want an event app**
  The event sector is inundated with apps for an amazing diversity of different functions. Knowing exactly what you want from an app can help you to find the perfect match.

- ✓ **Avoid event apps that offer too many options**
  It can sometimes seem as though the best approach is to pick an event app that has multiple options and offers a platform for almost everything.

However, a more minimalist approach is smarter if you want to ensure that your app is widely used by your visitors.

✓ **Check the data use of your app**
As already mentioned, it is not always straightforward to get sufficient internet capacity to run your event without the need to make data choices. If you opt for an app that guzzles data, you might soon find yourself in difficulties. Most apps continue to work satisfactorily even if the internet connection crashes, but it is risky to always assume this.

www.eventplanner.net/book/eventapp

VIDEO CONFERENCING

A video conference brings together people from different parts of the country (or world) through the magic of audio and video-telecommunications, without the need for them to travel to a single location. A video conference can be a simple discussion between two people in different offices (point-to-point) or with several people at several different places (multi-point). You can also exchange documents or allow the other participants to view your own computer screen. The advantages of these online meetings are obvious: huge savings in travelling time and costs.

 Test the necessary connections in advance. Agree with your conference partners what you will do if the connection is broken.

 An important meeting? Make sure that you always have a good IT technician on hand!

Security, first aid and hostesses

Bringing a lot of people together at the same place creates a number of risks and logistical challenges. Consider carefully the risks that are attached to your event and make sure that you have a good security and safety plan. This starts with the professional 'meeting and greeting' of your guests at the point of arrival. If you can add to this the correct and friendly provision of help and information, you will have already gone a long way towards setting the right tone for your event.

SECURITY AND SURVEILLANCE

A first form of security is the manner in which you draw up your guest list. Who do you include and who do you leave out? Guests who have no place at your event can also be filtered out by using the invitation as a kind of entrance ticket: no invitation = no admittance. Alternatively, you can tick off their names on the guest list as they arrive.

 It is best to arrange your guest list in alphabetical order, based on family names. This is the quickest way to search for individual guests when they arrive.

At a large event the best way to keep tabs on your guests is to issue them with a badge or wristband. This allows them to move freely around the entire event area without the need for further checking.

 Not everyone is happy to 'spoil' their nice new outfit by pinning a badge to it. In some cases, the pin might even cause damage to fine fabrics. In other cases, a too noticeable badge can ruin their elegant festive look altogether. Consequently, you should consider

> the various alternatives, such as lanyards, textile stickers, magnetic badges and wrist bands. Also take a look at more ecological options.

Certain elements of your event will require special attention. The cloakroom, the parking area and the box office are all sensitive areas, where you would be wise to add extra security. Also keep any other valuable materials under lock and key. Tents should not be left unattended during the night. You can hire security personnel to do this work, but the use of security cameras and good locks are an added deterrent to potential thieves or vandals.

> If you are planning to use cameras, check carefully to see what the law will allow! You must inform your guests in advance that cameras will be used at the event and must take full account of the legislation relating to privacy.

Personal security

Some events can be high-risk and therefore require competent and comprehensive security. There are a number of different factors that can increase the risk level of your event, such as the presence of particular (unpopular) groups, famous artists or controversial speakers. The total number of guests is also of importance. The greater the number of people at a single location, the higher the risk.

> The political and/or religious opinions of the organisers, speakers or artists can often cause controversy and therefore increase the risk profile of an event.

If you think that your event is risk-sensitive, you are probably best advised to engage the services of a professional security firm. They will conduct a complete risk analysis of your programme and on this basis will determine how many security personnel need to be employed and what other security measures may be necessary. As a general rule, you will need one security guard per entrance, with two at the main entrance. Don't forget the emergency exits, unless these are electronically operated. If your event is a festive one, and in particular if people are drinking, you will need a mobile team of two additional security agents for the first 500 guests. Add an extra agent for every additional group of 500 guests. For a seated dinner, a two-man team will be sufficient to cover 1,000 guests. Also remember to arrange car park security (parking attendants cannot carry out security functions) and a night watchman (if necessary).

 Involve the security firm in your arrangements at an early stage. They can give useful advice relating to the selection of the right venue, the layout of the event area, etc.

At large events, the use of **walkie-talkies** is essential to ensure good communication between the organisers and the security staff. Radios will also need to be present in the reception and backstage areas. It is unwise to rely on mobile phones as an alternative. The cost can quickly mount up and you are dependent upon the quality of the mobile network, which is not consistently reliable. The signal masts near your location may become overloaded at peak moments. For example, if a crisis occurs, all your guests will probably want to use their mobile phones, which may cause your communications system to break down at the time when you most need it. Walkie-talkies have the additional advantage that you can communicate with more than one person at the same time and that the transmissions remain clear and easily understandable, even in noisy locations. You can also hire 'hands-free' sets for walkie-talkies, which can be useful in emergency situations.

 Check that the batteries of all walkie-talkies are fully charged before the start of your event and test their transmission range (especially in concrete buildings) at all crucial positions.

 Radio equipment allows you to operate on different frequencies, so that different groups of staff can each communicate on their 'own' channel. For example, you can use one channel for logistical staff and another channel for the emergency services and the police.

You can choose between equipment that requires a user-permit or does not. The systems that are permit-free are generally cheaper, but have a more limited range and can be listened to (and talked over) by any members of the public who tune in to your frequency. With a permit, you are granted your own secure frequency. But if you want 100% security, you should opt for one of the digital variants. Moreover, these latter systems make it easier to set up larger networks with greater flexibility.

Depending on the level of perceived risk, you may need to involve the local **police** in your preparations. For low-risk events, it is probably sufficient simply to inform the police that the event is taking place and to tell them what risks are present. Good arrangements with the emergency services can help to save time in the event of accidents or problems. Security firms have an obligation to notify the local police when they are operating in their area. This means informing them about the number of staff they will be using and for what purposes.

For large **public events** (such as festivals and concerts) with a high risk, it is advisable to involve the police in the drawing up of your safety and security plan and to request their presence in and around your event venue. In some cases, this will even be compulsory. Plan one or more security meetings with all relevant security partners (see the box on security meetings).

You must certainly ask the advice of the police when your event is being attended by important **VIP's** (such as members of the royal family, politicians, international artists, etc.). These people will usually arrive with a small army of their own personal bodyguards and will also have their own demands relating to minimal standards of security. Make clear arrangements with all concerned.

You can either choose between 'visible' or 'invisible' security. Security guards in uniform have a preventative effect. It will also give some of your guests and performers a feeling of greater safety. Security guards in civilian clothing are less intrusive and threatening. Your guests will not have the feeling that they are 'being watched' and will be free and more spontaneous in their behaviour. The use of stewards or hosts/hostesses can be a good intermediary solution. Remember, however, that stewards cannot perform any security tasks: legislation decrees that such tasks can only be carried out by trained security personnel in possession of the necessary permits.

▶ www.eventplanner.net/book/walkie-talkies

Security meetings for (public) events

Who to invite?
- police
- local authority
- emergency services (fire brigade, Red Cross, first aid team, ...)
- your own security firm
- security and safety coordinator for your event
- operations manager for your event
- communications manager for your event
- ...

Possible points for discussion:
- reason for/purpose of the event
- practical information about the event
- expected number of people present
- is it necessary to inform local people in advance?
- extra traffic measures (e.g. no parking zones, closed streets, etc.)
- arrangements relating to noise levels, finishing time, ban on the sale of alcohol, etc.
- who does what in an emergency situation?
- fixing the security perimeters
- planning an evacuation exercise (if necessary)
- planning and discussing the briefing of all relevant parties
- discussing the internal communication procedures for the event
- planning the final safety check by the fire service
- planning the final check/approval of the electrical installations
- agreeing the necessary signalisation for visitors and personnel
- arranging for emergency lighting (via a separate electrical circuit)
- agreeing the evacuation plan (evacuation of the public zone/staff areas)
- agreeing radio procedures
- ...

Crisis team to deal with any emergency situations:
- security and safety manager of the organisers
- representative from the fire service
- representative from the police
- representative from the local authority
- representatives from the other emergency services
- representative from the security firm
- technical crew
- communications manager (and spokesperson)
- ...

CRISIS COMMUNICATION AND DISASTER MANAGEMENT

Sadly, when things go wrong at an event, they can often go seriously wrong. If this happens, as organiser you need to keep a cool head. You also need to have good crisis communication, so that you can either limit the damage or put things right.

Speed of reaction is crucial. Information must be given quickly and accurately, both internally to your participants and externally (for example, to the press). You want to keep the crisis within reasonable bounds and (at all costs) avoid chaos. Chaos arises when people, in the absence of reliable information, begin to speculate about what 'might' have happened: have people been hurt, is there still a risk, etc. By reacting quickly, you can eliminate speculation of this kind before it even starts. This is more necessary than ever nowadays, when news can be spread at lightning speed via social media, without any real thought for its authenticity.

In addition to speed of communication, accuracy is also paramount. Your information must be both clear and correct. Say precisely what has happened in simple terms that cannot be misunderstood. If there is something that you do not (yet) know – for example, the exact number of victims or precisely what has happened – admit this openly and honestly. Do not avoid issues or hide yourself away; make yourself available and state clearly the action you have taken to obtain more news about the situation. Ask people to remain calm and to follow any instructions that may be given. As organiser, you must accept responsibility for the actions that are necessary to deal with the drama, but in no circumstances should you immediately accept responsibility for the drama itself. Don't apologise in public and certainly not in front of the cameras. You may come to regret any such admissions at a later stage, when it becomes necessary to apportion real liability for what has happened: some people may see this as an admission of guilt, which may have legal consequences.

 In an emergency situation, such as a fire, it is important to realise that the common assumption that people will panic and behave irrationally is often not true. In fact, research has shown that in general people collaborate effectively and that the real danger lies in delaying or slowing down the evacuation. This can sometimes happen if, as organiser, you hope to prevent panic by not telling people honestly what is happening. For this reason, open communication is crucial during an emergency situation. Explain to the public clearly what is going on, where the emergency exits can be found and what they need to do. This gives people confidence and also the necessary information to respond correctly, so that the likelihood of casualties is significantly reduced. For further advice on this important subject, take a look at the interview with expert John Drury, professor of social psychology at the University of Sussex:

▶ www.eventplanner.net/book/tv-crowdpsychologie

Just as every organiser must have a call sheet, so he must also have a crisis plan as a standard element in his event toolbox. Who calls the emergency services? Which routes and emergency exits must the participants use? These are questions that you must answer before the event even starts. Your crisis communication must also be in place (and tested) beforehand. What will you do if the power fails or the sound installation is out of action? How will you communicate your information? In these circumstances, 'old-fashioned' technologies, such as walkie-talkies and megaphones, can work wonders. And don't underestimate the role that your staff can play. In particular, appoint one reliable person who is responsible for liaison with the press and can keep them informed about the latest developments.

In an ideal world, you will have a plan ready to deal with every conceivable disaster that could happen at your event. What if a storm makes your outdoor event venue unsafe? What if panic breaks out? What if there is a medical emergency? Although no plan is perfect, whatever you have worked out in advance will normally be better than trying to improvise on the spur of the moment. Of course, in some circumstances you will have no option but to improvise. Even so, the more scenarios you consider and (ideally) practice in advance, the more quickly and more easily things will go if catastrophe strikes.

In other words, it is always a good idea to hold a full operational emergency drill with your entire team. You can easily do this in an office with a table-top exercise, by bringing together the relevant team members in your conference room (which becomes the crisis centre) and confronting them with a specific scenario. Alternatively, you can also do a large-scale exercise on-site, complete with stand-ins to play the role of the public. In this way, everyone learns about their individual role, potential communication problems come to the surface and responsibilities become clearer. I sincerely hope that no one reading this book is ever confronted with a genuine emergency or disaster, but if it does happen a practiced team will be able to deal better with the difficult circumstances than an unpracticed one. Use scenarios for your drills

that are realistic, but not necessarily obvious. What, for example, will you do if there is an attack on a metro station close to your venue? Do you evacuate your event? Or go into lock-down? What do you tell people? What information do you need to make decisions? Who can provide this information as quickly as possible? Who communicates with the emergency services? What do you do in the meantime? Let the band carry on playing? Try to occupy people in some other way? How do you communicate with your stewards and hostesses if your radio communication is lost? And what do you do if a bomb warning is suddenly received? Try to think out of the box. Better now than if the worst ever happens.

Also make sure that you only use experienced personnel in your crisis centre. For example, the controller of your radio communication will receive huge amounts of information to process: he/she must be able to keep a cool head, sort the relevant material from the irrelevant, and on this basis take necessary decisions. Many event organisers feel obliged to take control of emergency situations themselves, but forget to appoint back-up staff if things get seriously out of hand. If the regional disaster plan is activated and the emergency services are mobilised, it will be necessary for the organiser to consult with local or regional authorities. This may require him/her to leave the event site, but somebody must be left in charge, so that necessary action in response to the changing situation can still be taken.

▶ www.eventplanner.net/book/tv-disasters

CROWD AND TRAFFIC MANAGEMENT

Large (public) events not only attract impressive numbers of visitors to the event venue, but also to its immediate surroundings. Taking the necessary measures to deal safely with this mass of people is known as crowd management. If you need to actively intervene in or around the venue, because the situation is becoming unpleasant, uncomfortable or even dangerous, this is known as crowd control.

Investigate well in advance where bottlenecks are likely to occur. Think carefully about the adequacy of the different entrances and exits. Try to assess all the risks and develop appropriate solutions. Take proper account of potential overcrowding in limited spaces such as staircases, narrow streets, train platforms, open spaces (where people are likely to congregate).

 Large flows of visitors can be channelled into pre-determined routes by using crowd-control (Heras) barriers.

There are a number of basic rules for the management of large crowds in relatively confined areas:

- ✔ **Provide the right information**. Do this both visually (digital boards, banners, etc.) and by broadcast announcements. For example, explain why people may have to wait at certain points along the route to the venue.
- ✔ **Design the event area in a simple and logical manner.** If you take proper account of the capacity of access ways, entrances and exits, as well as their relevance to your safety and service requirements, you should be able to create a layout that encourages your visitors to behave in the manner you want.
- ✔ **Avoid large flows of people moving in different directions at the same place and time.** This was the cause of the disaster at the Love Parade in Duisburg in 2010.

- ✓ **Monitor the number of people per m²**. Never more than three per m² over the net surface area! Close to the podium you will sometimes have peaks of five to six people per m². This is okay, providing there is sufficient room to leave the area, should the need arise.
- ✓ **Avoid aggressive behaviour** by reacting in an authoritarian manner too quickly or unnecessarily; hostesses are more successful in managing streams of people than armed guards!
- ✓ If possible, programme your event so that its **different elements do not all start or finish at the same time**. By dividing up the flow of people in this way, you can avoid bottlenecks and peak moments of overcrowding. It also helps to relieve congestion in car parks, at entrances/exits and on access roads.
- ✓ **Create buffer zones** for any bottlenecks that cannot be eliminated, so that there is space to accommodate temporary overcrowding at these sensitive areas.
- ✓ Install **cameras** at all the crucial points relating to your venue (both inside and outside) and set up a command post (CP) where experts can keep in touch with traffic controllers, crowd managers and the police.
- ✓ **Employ experienced personnel** for your crowd management activities, not only in the central command post, but also on the ground.

> 📌 Think carefully about the layout and design of your event space. You will probably have been at events where you finally get inside but are immediately confronted with long rows waiting to buy drink tokens or toilet facilities that obstruct the smooth inflow of visitors. This kind of major design fault must be avoided at all costs.

> 📌 Always arrange for a sufficient number of evacuation routes and emergency exits, should things go wrong. In this respect, clear direction boards/instructions are essential. One option is to make use of an automatic system that can activate all the screens at your event (on the podium, in the bars, and so on) at the touch of a single button to provide your guests with relevant information and details of the emergency scenarios that you have worked out in advance.

In this context, the British professor Dr. Keith Still talks about the DIM-ICE model. DIM stands for design, information and management. We have already covered matters relating to design and information earlier in the book.

Management relates to all the efforts you make and all the activities you carry out on the day of the event itself. For example, it is important that everyone at the event venue knows exactly what is expected of him or her. The second part of the model is ICE, which stands for ingress, circulation and egress. Your guests need different information when they are entering your event (ingress) than when they are leaving it (egress). For each of the DIM phases, an event organiser needs to draw up appropriate ICE scenarios.

Imagine, for example, that you are expecting 20,000 visitors to your event. 9,000 are already inside, while the remaining 11,000 are still awaiting entrance control. What will you do if a scenario suddenly develops that makes it necessary to evacuate the venue site? The people still outside will be blocking the escape routes for the people already inside. How can you disperse the 11,000, so that the 9,000 can be led to safety? These are the kinds of things that you need to consider in advance. As far as this example is concerned, this is one of the reasons why you often see loudspeakers and information boards on the outside of event venues, so that new arrivals can also be properly informed.

If you think that your event is likely to attract very large numbers of people, it is advisable to engage the services of an experienced bureau that can make computer simulations of the different scenarios in advance. These simulations will allow you to check matters like what would happen if one of your emergency escape routes is blocked. Crowd management is not something that an inexperienced event planner should attempt to organise alone. Too many lives are potentially at stake.

 Make the necessary arrangements for crowd management and crowd control with the emergency services well in advance of your event, so that private partners and relevant local authorities know exactly who does what. This will save precious time if something goes seriously wrong.

www.eventplanner.net/book/tv-crowd

 www.eventplanner.net/book/tv-crowdpsychologie

Traffic flows

The arrival of so many visitors at the same time and in the same place can result in traffic chaos on the approach roads leading to your event. This is not pleasant for the visitors (who can sometimes sit for hours in a traffic jam) or for the people who live in the vicinity. A good mobility and traffic circulation plan is therefore essential. Large events frequently ask experienced bureaus to draw up these plans, for which there are a number of basic principles:

- ✔ Encourage the use of public transport. This not only reduces traffic jams, but also alleviates (in part, at least) parking problems. For major, large-scale events (such as pop festivals) ensure that there are dedicated access routes for the exclusive use of public transport and the emergency services, so that these crucial facilities can never get stuck in traffic.

> Add the widgets of the rail and bus services to your website. This will allow your visitors to discover at the click of a mouse which buses and trains can take them to your event.

- ✔ Do an advance test run along all the access roads at a busy time of day. What might possibly go wrong? Where do you need to position traffic lights so that the flow of traffic can be optimised? Discuss these measures with the local **traffic police.** What can they do to help and at what points can they control traffic during peak moments?

- ✔ **Good direction signs are a must**, but digital signposting is even better. This can be controlled at a distance in response to changing circumstances and can be used, for example, to announce unexpected delays or suggest alternative last-minute routes.

- ✔ As far as possible, adjust your **programme** to take account of potential traffic difficulties. For example, you can open the camping next to your venue the day before the event actually starts, so that the first peak period can be spread over two days. At congresses you can achieve a similar effect by starting with a networking breakfast, which will encourage delegates to arrive more gradually than if the keynote speaker is immediately programmed for 9 o'clock in the morning. Likewise at the end of your event: if your star-performer/speaker is programmed last, everyone will want to stay right to the end; but if you programme a less well-known performer/speaker as the final act, people will leave more gradually.

✓ **Give proper advance information** about the accessibility of the event venue. Only 25-30% of your visitors will check this information for themselves via your website. You will need to communicate more actively with the other 70-75%, if you wish to prevent them from simply jumping into their cars and trusting to their GPS!

% www.eventplanner.net/book/crowdmanagement

FIRE SECURITY

In most professional venues fire security will already be in order: evacuation plan, fire extinguishers, fire alarms, etc. Nevertheless, it always pays to check on these matters. And remember: if you change anything in the layout of the venue, you may need to amend the normal evacuation routes! Fire extinguishers and fire detectors may no longer be as easy to reach or activate as in their original locations, if your decoration or stage is now in the way.

 Always keep a number of illuminated emergency exit signs in reserve. Is part of your decor standing in front of one of the permanent signs? If so, hang one of your reserve signs in an alternative visible position.

Decorative pieces always require extra attention. Textiles and synthetics (e.g., curtains, Christmas trees) should be specially impregnated with a fire-resistant spray. Check the ground plan and the proposed decoration thoroughly with both the fire service and your decorator. In this way, you will be able to devise a solution that is acceptable to everyone from a fire safety point of view. In many cases, a fire officer will come to inspect the final layout of the venue shortly before your event.

Make a plan of the location and mark the position of the fire extinguishers and the fire alarms. The **evacuation plan** and its related procedures should be written into your general action plan. Remember to pass on this important information to your suppliers, caterers, etc. Give them a clearly marked plan with all relevant details. Also ensure that there is adequate signalisation to inform your guests of what they need to do in the event of fire. Your staff should also be briefed about what they are expected to do. Make sure that they know where all the firefighting equipment is kept and how to use it.

FIRST AID AND DOCTORS

For events with only a limited number of guests and relatively few risks, it is usually sufficient if the organiser has the telephone numbers of the nearest first aid post, doctor or hospital.

Larger events or events with a higher risk of injury (such as adventure programmes for teambuilding and sport events) require a greater degree of vigilance on the part of the organisers. This is equally true of relatively small events in locations where the temperature can rise quickly and unexpectedly, so that there is a potential risk of guests becoming unwell or even fainting. Events where alcohol is served will also require special precautions. In all these latter instances, it is advisable to set up a first aid post on site. There are various suppliers who can do this for you. Some even provide their own ambulances and emergency doctors. Others limit themselves to nursing staff.

> When the temperature inside or outside the venue is extremely high, provide free bottles of water for all your guests.

 www.eventplanner.net/book/firstaid

Also make sure that a number of your team members have followed a recognised first aid course and know how to use an AED or defibrillator.

SAFETY FIRST

As organiser, you are responsible for the safety of your guests and your crew. This is a responsibility that you must take seriously. It is impossible to fully exclude the possibility of accidents, but it your duty to do everything in your power to prevent them. Most accidents occur as a result of human error, often caused by a lack of knowledge or a failure to follow safety instructions. If anything, the pressure associated with the event sector increases the risk: your stage must and will be ready before the show begins.

That being said, there are still many things that you can do as organiser to improve the level of safety at your event, many of which can be actioned long before the day of the opening. Conduct a risk analysis of potentially dangerous situations, such as the construction and dismantling of the podium, the arrival and departure of suppliers' lorries, the use of fork lift trucks and elevated work platforms, and so on. In many countries an event is regarded as a mobile building site and needs to comply with the same health and safety regulations. This means, amongst other things, providing your people with the necessary personal protective equipment and ensuring that they use it. This PPE includes things like harnesses for those working at height, ear protectors, safety helmets, goggles, boots and gloves. Install fire extinguishers and evacuation route signage, even during the construction phase. As the organiser, you are responsible for the supervision of all safety matters. Alternatively, you can delegate this to a specialist safety coordinator.

Proper safety training is essential, not only for working safely at height, but also for matters like first aid and fire safety. If you work with an external company for this training, ask to see the certificates of competence for their trainers in the relevant disciplines.

Provide clear signs for potentially dangerous situations, such as uneven surfaces or the risk of falling tools, and ensure that they are properly cordoned off. Also make sure there is sufficient lighting where people are working and keep your work areas tidy, with no unnecessary equipment and materials left lying around. The use of alcohol or drugs by your personnel must be strictly forbidden. Respect the agreed hours of work and break times: overtired workers are at greater risk of causing an accident.

Special attention needs to be devoted to safety during the assembly and dismantling of scaffolding, truss constructions and rigging constructions. Load bearing capacity (and wind load for external structures) must always be calculated and must leave a wide margin of safety. Spotlights and speakers that are hung from walls or ceilings must be fitted with an extra safety loop or strap.

If your event makes use of tents, tribunes or special attractions, always check that the required safety permits are fully in order and that the periodic checks required by law have been carried out. If you wish to be even more certain, you can appoint an independent health and safety adviser, who will re-examine all podia, installations, etc. In many cases, the event insurers will insist on this kind of additional monitoring.

In particular, safety must be paramount during the construction and dismantling of your event site. Once the event has taken place, contractors are usually anxious to get everything done as quickly as possible (so that they can move on to the next venue), but this is often when accidents occur. Having a safety adviser for the entire event, including construction and dismantling, is by no means an unnecessary luxury.

If, unfortunately, something does go wrong – and I hope sincerely that no one gets hurt – analyse what happened and how safety can be improved for your next event. Keep a logbook of all accidents and near misses.

▶ www.eventplanner.net/book/tv-eventsecurity

WEATHER MONITORING

Following the tragedy at the Pukkelpop festival in Belgium in 2011, when a sudden storm caused the collapse of tents and masts, resulting in five fatalities and many injuries, everyone in the event business will now be well aware of the need to monitor weather developments if you are organising an outside activity. This means more than just keeping an eye on one of the various rain-radar sites now available on the internet. The only way to be 100% certain that you have the right information is to employ the services of a professional meteorological bureau, which can monitor the weather for the specific location where your event is taking place.

HOSTS AND HOSTESSES

Sometimes you may find that you simply do not have enough personnel of your own to give your guests the attention they deserve. In this case, it is probably a good idea to hire a number of hosts and hostesses to lend a helping hand. This not only creates a good (and professional) impression, but frees your own people to handle other more crucial matters. You can use this hired help to assist in a variety of different tasks, the most common of which include:

Select your hosts and hostesses with care: they are the visiting card of your company.

- ✔ **Welcoming guests**, ticking them off the guest list, registering visitors, distributing name badges, etc.
- ✔ **Providing information and guidance** to guests, issuing programme books, etc.
- ✔ **Distributing** promotional material or gifts.
- ✔ Manning **the cloakroom**.

You need to **select** your hosts and hostesses with great care. They are the visiting card of your company and will frequently come into contact with your guests. Important factors in your choice include their representativeness, experience, friendliness, linguistic skills and (above all) their ability to work independently. Also ask if they have (or are prepared to wear) uniforms. Give the uniforms a personal touch by adding a scarf or tie in your company colours.

> When you are organising an event, always try and put yourself in the position of your guests. Treat them as you would want to be treated yourself.

Hosts and hostesses can only make a professional impression when they are in possession of all the information they need. Give them a thorough briefing which covers all relevant matters in detail, so that they can correctly inform your guests and help them to solve any problems which may arise.

The following is a list of things that your hosts and hostesses need to know/have as a minimum:

- ✔ The objective of your event.
- ✔ Information about your company and/or product.
- ✔ The tasks that they must perform. What do you expect of them? Who can they turn to in the event of problems?
- ✔ The guest list and name badges, plus an explanation of the registration system or the ticket scanning app (if any).

- ✓ Instructions for the welcoming of the guests, such as style of address (sir/madam or Mr./Mrs.) and use of language (formal or informal). How do you want your VIP's to be treated?
- ✓ A ground plan of the venue (location of the toilets, different rooms, emergency exits, etc.).
- ✓ The programme of your event: when are the different elements/performances taking place, and where?
- ✓ Where and when they can take a break and get something to eat/drink.
- ✓ What they should do in the event of an emergency. Do you expect your hosts and hostesses to keep people informed? Should they guide your guests to the nearest emergency exits? If so, they will need to know where to get the information they must pass on and also know the location of all the exits.

> 📌 Remember to give the name of a contact person from whom the hosts and hostesses can obtain more detailed information about the event, company, products, etc.

> 📌 If you are working with more than eight hostesses, it is a good idea to appoint a team leader. Book the hostesses to arrive 30 minutes before the event starts.

> 📌 Agree what the hosts and hostesses should do with the guests who arrive late. Invitees who storm out of breath into your event room in the middle of a keynote speech can disturb the other participants. For this reason, it is sometimes better to only let your guests into the main event area during the first break. You can always arrange to set up a plasma screen in a room nearby, so that they can still follow the event 'live'.

> 📌 When guests from different companies have been invited, it is useful to have someone from each company at the reception desk, not only to welcome the guests, but also to help out with any problems (forgotten invitations, mistaken identities, etc.). It is not always possible to leave this to the 'ordinary' hostesses.

Make sure that your hosts and hostesses have all the material/equipment they need. A reception desk will need standard office materials (pens, scissors, staplers, etc.), as well as a printed list with useful telephone numbers (doctor, taxi, hotel).

 Arrange for a number of umbrellas at the entrance/reception area, so that your hosts and hostesses can keep your arriving guests dry in the event of rain.

 During winter periods or when rain is expected, put additional hostesses in the cloakroom. In summer this will not usually be necessary, since fewer guests will bring a coat with them.

Registration

Handing out badges at the event reception desk is always something of a logistical challenge. For this reason, it is important to ensure that you have sufficient hostesses, a sufficiently large desk and an efficient registration system. The number of hostesses you will need is dependent on the number of guests and the time that you have foreseen for their arrival and registration (usually between 30 minutes and one hour). There is a huge difference between processing 200 guest in 30 minutes or in two hours! You can save valuable time by working with a scanner system, so that your hostesses don't need to write every name on every badge.

When you are working with badges, you will normally need two hostesses for every 150 guests. Add an additional hostess for every additional 75 guests. If you are working with a scanner system, one hostess per 150 guests will usually be enough. If you have invited more than 300 guests, it is advisable to set up a separate information desk in the reception area.

 Arrange the badges in alphabetical order before the event, so that they are quick and easy to find. Are you expecting more than 500 guests? If so, it is a good idea to divide your reception desk into alphabetical sections: for example, one desk for family names beginning with the letters A-F, another for G-L, and so on.

📌 Always tick off the names of the guests who have arrived on your guest list. This is useful after the event, when you want to confirm how many people were present or if you want to send 'thank you' letters. At some events, it may also be necessary from a security point of view.

📌 To eliminate logistical bottlenecks in the reception area, you may consider sending the badges to your guests by post before the event starts. The disadvantage of this method is that they may forget to bring them, or even pass them on to someone else who you have not invited. Printing your badges 'live' is an alternative, as long as you have reliable equipment and a back-up printer.

🔗 www.eventplanner.net/book/hostesses

 🔗 www.eventplanner.net/book/promoteams

🔗 www.eventplanner.net/book/visitorregistration

Permits and insurance

Permits and insurance are, in the first instance, of importance to you as an organiser. If you are in order with all your paperwork, this can save you an awful lot of headaches and protect you from a possible financial hangover. Your guests will not initially be concerned with these matters – until something goes wrong and there are consequences that need to be borne or compensation that needs to be paid. So make sure that you don't overlook this important aspect of your event preparation – and start in plenty of time.

PERMITS

When you are organising an event, you will probably need to apply for various permits and permissions. The following list gives an idea of the kinds of permits you are most likely to require. The number and type of permits can vary widely from region to region, and for this reason I do not propose to go into detail. Ask for these details at the town hall which is responsible for the town/city where your event is taking place. In fact, it is always a good idea to let the town hall know what you are planning, even if there is no obligation to do so (although there often is).

> 📌 Always keep copies of all permits on site at your event venue, in case you need to produce them for inspection/consultation.

> 📌 Be extra careful if you are organising an event abroad. For some countries, you (and your guests) may need to apply for visas. Your team members might also need a work permit. This may even apply to your speakers and performers. In some places you might even be obliged to work with a local crew for site construction and dismantling. Also check out the VAT regulations and ask whether or not you need to pay (temporary) import duties on the equipment and materials you need to bring into the country.

Your suppliers and service providers must also ensure that they have all the permits necessary to allow them to carry out their professional activities. This is particularly important, for example, for catering companies and firework specialists. Always ask to see these permits.

Event permits

Are you organising an event in a publicly accessible place? If so, it is possible that you might need an event permit from the local authority. For smaller events it is sometimes sufficient simply to notify the local authority of your intention. If the event is taking place on or near water, you many need to refer the matter to a higher (provincial or regional) authority or the relevant department in charge of the water in question.

The permit holder (usually the event organisation) is responsible for the order and safety of all personnel and visitors at the event site. The permit will specify what actions the organiser needs to take to ensure public order, health and (fire) safety during the event and will also detail how any incidents must be dealt with. Drawing up a safety plan, action plan and/or risk analysis can sometimes be a compulsory part of this procedure.

Copyright, royalties and performance rights

When there is music at your event, even if it is only background music, you will need to pay royalties to the composer and performance rights to the performers/producers.

Excess noise

Does music play an important role in your event or are your guests likely to make a lot of noise themselves? If so, you may need a permit to exceed existing noise limits. This limit – expressed as a maximum number of decibels – is usually part of the environment permit that you will almost certainly need. In particular, noise levels in residential areas and on Sundays are subject to strict monitoring and control. For this reason, some event venues are equipped with a 'sound restrictor'.

In some cases you may not need to apply for an environment permit. Ask the relevant local authority for full details about possible exemptions. In recent years, however, the regulations relating to noise emissions have become stricter, so that it is advisable to measure the likely noise volume of your event in advance (for larger events, such as fairs and festivals, this is compulsory). In some countries the issuing of ear protectors to audiences is also obligatory, if the decibel level exceeds the permitted norm.

Erection of tents, podia, scaffolding and tribunes

You must ask the permission of the local authority when you want to erect a tent, podium, scaffolding or tribune (for public seating). The fire brigade will need to inspect both the location and the structure and declare them to be safe. To apply for this permit, you will need the following documents/information: a ground plan (marked with emergency exits and evacuation routes), the dimensions, the layout, the materials used, the number of guests, etc.

> 📌 Always apply for your permits in good time. It can often take weeks, even months, before they are finally granted.

> 📌 For large events, it is wise to involve the health and safety department of the local authorities at an early stage. If they help you to draw up your plans and applications, there is a much greater likelihood that they will be approved at an official level.

> 📌 If you place large attractions at your event, bear in mind that additional safety checks and approvals may be necessary.

Hours of closing

Many locations operate strict hours of opening/closing, which they are loathe to exceed. Legislation states that local inhabitants may not be inconvenienced by your event or your guests after 10 o'clock in the evening. Do you want an exception to be made to this general rule? If so, you will need to ask the permission of the local authority.

Serving of alcohol

When you want to serve alcoholic drinks at your event, you will need two separate permits: a licence to serve beer and other (alcoholic) beverages and a license to serve spirits (strong drink). In many cases, your venue will already possess these permits. If this is not the case, or if you are creating your own venue, you will need to apply to the local authority. In some regions the need for a permit to serve beer and spirits has been abolished for one-off events, although approval from the local municipality is still necessary. You should always contact this municipality for all relevant information.

Food

There are very strict regulations relating to the preparation and serving of food. Always check that your caterers or the proprietors of food stalls (chips, hotdogs, etc.) are in possession of all the permits they require.

Fireworks

If you are planning to use fireworks in a professional event context, you will need to have an operator's license from the local or provincial authority. If you engage the services of a pyrotechnics company, you can usually ask them to obtain the necessary license for you. This will usually be quicker than applying yourself. Of course, the company must also be in possession of all necessary permits and permissions to cover its own activities.

Drones

Do you want to fly drones over your event? Perhaps for some great aerial photos or even a spectacular drone show? In most regions you will need a special permit to make this possible, especially if the drones will be flying over your public. Also bear in mind that the use of drones in some areas, such as close to airports, is strictly forbidden.

INSURANCE

The total costs of an event can quickly mount up. As an event organiser, you could be facing financial disaster if your event is cancelled at the last minute due to external factors beyond your control or if you are the victim of fire, theft or vandalism. Fortunately, there are numerous ways in which you can insure your event against these possibilities. Once again, however, there are huge differences between different countries, so make sure you get the right information before you act!

 Ask to see the insurance policies of your suppliers. Does the events agency have sufficient insurance cover? How are the different liabilities distributed?

📌 Contact a specialist insurance agent. He will help you to choose the best policies at the best prices to cover the types of risk associated with your particular event.

📌 Some insurance policies can be very expensive. Before you sign anything, make sure that you really need the policy and consider whether it might be more advantageous to actually cover this risk yourself.

📌 Are you organising a paying event or an event for a third party? If so, you may be able to cover/eliminate some risk by the careful wording of your general conditions of sale. Seek proper legal advice on this matter.

Civil liability

As event organiser, you are liable for the damage incurred by third parties as a result of your event. You are also liable for any damage resulting from your own negligence. You are further liable for the actions of the people in your employ (either directly or indirectly) and for the actions of any volunteers you may use.

There are three conditions for establishing your liability:
1. an error must have been made by the organiser or someone acting for him;
2. there must be damage;
3. there must be a causal connection between the error and the damage.

Specific policies exist which cover your third party liabilities as an event organiser for both physical and material damage. It is important to note, however, that 'contractual' liability is not covered by this policy. Contractual liability is the liability resulting from the non-implementation or the incorrect implementation of a contract, undertaking or agreement, whether written or verbal.

EXAMPLE
In your capacity as an event organiser, you hire the use of a sound system for your event. During the removal of the system after the event, an expensive piece of equipment is dropped and seriously damaged. The owner of the system holds you liable for this damage. However, damage of this kind is not covered by your 'third party event organiser'

> policy, since the use of the equipment in question forms part of the contractual agreement for its hire. To cover this type of situation, you need a further insurance policy for 'material damage' (see below).
>
> However, if the equipment in question had fallen on one of your guests, your 'third-party' policy would cover the physical injury suffered by this guest.

The civil liability of professional event organisers is usually covered by an 'operational activities' policy. People who organise events sporadically or on a 'one-off' basis are advised to check the extent to which their existing civil liabilities policy may cover any of the risks they run. If this is not the case, they are strongly recommended to take out 'event organiser' insurance. The payment of damages – for example, for someone who incurs physical injury with permanent invalidity as a result – can sometimes run into hundreds of thousands of dollars.

As an addition to your 'event organiser' policy, you can also opt to pay an extra premium which will cover legal advice and legal costs (for example, lawyers' fees and court costs for any damage claims which may need to be contested).

> In addition to checking whether or not you have cover for specific liabilities, also check for what amounts you are covered for each individual damage claim and also the maximum amounts payable by the insurance company for each insured period. Usually, there is also a certain amount per claim (the franchise) that you will need to pay yourself. Check this amount as well.

Material damage

For most events, whether big or small, you will usually engage the services of third parties to provide goods, materials and/or equipment. This might include tents, audio-visual equipment, stages, your event location, etc. As the hiring party (lessee) of this 'property', you have an obligation to return it to the owner (lessor) in the same good condition after use. Except in cases of force majeure, this means that you will have to pay for any damage or loss. And no matter how careful you are, damage and loss can always occur (theft, accident, storm damage, etc.). You can cover this type of risk by taking out additional insurance against 'material damage'. Always ensure that the amount for which you are covered reflects the real value of the material concerned and not simply the amount that you paid to rent it. Ask the lessor for an estimate of this value.

> 📌 'Naked theft' is not covered. This is theft or loss where there are no signs of a break-in to the secured area where the material was kept or no evidence of physical attack involving (security) personnel.

> 📌 The 'material damage' policy only covers goods and materials that are directly used as part of your event and not the subsidiary goods and materials that may be used to transport, process or prepare these goods and materials for use. In other words, items such as fork-lift trucks, tool-boxes, etc. are not insured.

Cancellation

A cancellation insurance can be your salvation when you need to interrupt, postpone or annul your event. The amount of compensation you receive will be dependent on the amount of premium you have paid and the amount of cover you have agreed with your insurance agent. You can take out insurance to cover both the costs you incur as a result of the cancellation and the resulting loss of profits.

Under the event organisers' motto of *'the show must go on'*, a total cancellation is probably the very last action that you will want to take. This is also the way the insurance companies think. In addition to the financial implications of scrapping your event, the negative effect on the image of your company can be far-reaching.

> 📌 Make sure you arrange your cancellation insurance in good time. It is advisable to do this as soon as you have signed agreements for your venue and your performers. From this point onwards, you are responsible for a number of costs which can add up to quite a tidy sum. If you only conclude your insurance at a later stage, you may find that these costs may not be covered by the policy. Similarly, unforeseen situations may develop in the intervening period for which it may no longer be possible to obtain insurance, such as the corona virus, a new outbreak of Mexican flu or a new cloud of volcanic ash from Iceland.

You can arrange cancellation insurance to cover a wide variety of possible causes which may prevent your event from taking place in whole or in part. Here are some of the possibilities:

✓ **Weather**
This cover is only relevant for events taking place out of doors and compensates you for any costs incurred as a result of the cancellation of your event as a consequence of 'unforeseeable climatological circumstances'. The precise definition of what this means may vary from insurer to insurer, but will almost certainly cover:
- heavy rain
- storm (thunder and lightning)
- hail and snow
- high winds
- …

Many insurers will only pay out on this policy in the event that these extreme conditions (could) represent a threat to the public. A shower or two of rain will not normally be accepted as a valid reason for postponing or annulling your event.

The insurer will usually demand that your stage/podium is covered and that materials are waterproof or at least protected from the elements.

> Take account of the fact that the weather conditions relating to any cancellation claim must be capable of objective assessment. In most cases, this will be meteorological data provided by the nearest official weather station. This may, however, be a problem if the distance between this station and your event venue is relatively large. In these circumstances, your event might be washed out as a result of a sudden cloud burst, while it has remained bright and sunny above the weather station.

✓ **Unavailability of important persons or artists**
The non-appearance of artists may force you to postpone your event, or even cancel it indefinitely. This 'non-appearance' cover pays compensation for any costs incurred and any income lost as a result of the failure of an artist to turn up to your event as agreed, providing that this failure is not the result of your own actions or any other actions within your control.

> **EXAMPLE**
> In 2009 Michael Jackson died suddenly, three weeks before the start of a tour involving some 50 concerts in the United Kingdom. The loss to the tour organisers amounted to an estimated 350 million dollars.

Death is obviously an extreme reason for the non-appearance of an artist, but other less dramatic reasons will usually be accepted as valid, such as sickness, strikes, death of a close friend or relative, etc. You can also take out cover for the following 'indispensable' persons:
- keynote speakers at congresses;
- CEOs at company celebrations;
- head organisers of events;
- main product developers at product launches;
- the king or queen at important national events;
- ...

The premium payable for this cover is dependent on the status of the person concerned and his/her past history of non-appearance (medical problems, notoriously unreliable, etc.).

✓ Non-appearance of public for reasons of force majeure
This cover compensates organisers for any net loss incurred when a significant part of the public is unable to reach the event for a reason specified in the policy. Policies of this kind are usually advisable for events with a large number of participants, such as festivals, concerts and congresses. The threshold of non-appearance – usually expressed as a percentage of the total expected number of participants – must be agreed event by event with the insurance company.

✓ Terrorism
It is possible to include a clause in your cancellation insurance which relates to cancellation as a result of an act of terrorism or as a result of a realistic terrorist threat. This clause will usually be restricted both in terms of time before/after and distance to/from your event. The level of premium payable will be dependent on the venue, the identity of the organisers, the objectives and the timing of the event.

✓ Routine cancellation
A wide variety of unforeseen circumstances may make it necessary to cancel your event. These are not covered by the types of policy already mentioned above, but specific cover can be arranged with most insurance companies. Example of these circumstances include:

- unavailability of the venue as a result of fire, storm, water damage, etc.
- inability to reach the venue as a result of strikes involving airlines, ferries, public transport, etc.
- electrical failure (power supply)
- national mourning
- natural disasters
- retraction of previously granted permits
- epidemics
- …

Accidents involving physical injury

Accidents involving physical injury can cost a small fortune (medical bills, hospital fees, loss of income, funeral costs, etc.).

If, as an organiser, you make use of paid employees, you are legally obliged to take out minimum accident-at-work insurance cover. However, the situation is less clear-cut with regard to the use of volunteers. They often face the same hazards as paid staff but run the risk of having to meet all the costs themselves in the event that something should go wrong, unless the accident was caused by an identifiable third party who is covered by the event's civil liability insurance.

To avoid this kind of situation, it is best to take out 'accident and physical injury' insurance to cover all your volunteers. You will usually be able to agree the maximum amounts of cover with your insurance agent, and this will generally include:

- **Medical costs**: repayment of doctors' fees, hospital charges and the cost of medicines, although there will usually be an initial sum (franchise) payable by the insured party.
- **Temporary invalidity (inability to work)**: the insured party will be paid a daily allowance based on the level of temporary economic invalidity (expressed as a percentage), for the full duration of their incapacity to work.
- **Permanent invalidity (inability to work)**: the insured party will receive a lump sum dependent upon the level of permanent invalidity, expressed as a percentage.
- **Death**: a fixed lump sum (previously agreed) will be paid to the next-of-kin of the deceased.

This cover can be extended, so that it not only includes your volunteers, but also the people actually participating in the event. The relevant premiums are calculated per person per day, and are usually quite low.

Money

Some events generate large amounts of cash money (admission fees, bars, snack stands, etc.), which need to be held temporarily at the event venue. You can take out insurance to provide cover against the possible theft of this money or for the passing of counterfeit banknotes at one of your cash points. Having said this, insurance of this kind tends to be the exception rather than the rule and many insurers are reluctant to provide this cover for events.

Transport

If you have your own fleet of vehicles, you may decide to use this fleet to transport all the materials and equipment for your event. But be careful: your standard company vehicle insurance will often only cover journeys to and from your suppliers, but not to your event venue. For this, you may require additional insurance for the transportation of goods.

It is worth checking to see if your insurance against material damage (as mentioned above and assuming you have it) also covers the transport for which the organiser is liable. If so, separate insurance for the transportation of goods in your own vehicles may not be necessary. But remember that the reverse is also true: insurance for the transport of goods will not necessarily cover damage incurred during stays at the event venue.

Sustainable events

The transition to sustainable and socially responsible events is now in full swing. Large companies need to comply with sustainable development goals (SDGs) and this obligation is also passed on to the event bureaus they employ. This trend is here to stay, because participants and clients now also expect to take part in sustainable events. Event organisers who fail to work sustainably will find themselves increasingly excluded from the market.

Nevertheless, it is a concept that still frightens off many organisers. This is often because people widely assume that sustainability is significantly more expensive. But this is far from true. If you approach matters sensibly, 'green' thinking can actually save you money. And who is not interested in saving money?

Forget everything you have previously (and incorrectly) been told and start looking at your events in a new light. You will soon see that there are numerous possibilities to reduce both the ecological footprint of your activities and your costs. For example, what about the huge banners that you use to announce events that take place year after year. In addition to the name of the event, it is common practice to add the year in question: 'Trade Fair 2014', for example. This means that a new banner has to be made every 12 months. But do you really think that your visitors don't know what year it is? By omitting the year figures, you can use the same banner for several successive years: good for the environment and good for your wallet! Large events spend tens of thousands of dollars on bannering, flags and signs – so just think of the money you can save if you can cut a large part of this expenditure out of your budget each year.

And you can take this thinking several stages further. What about a complete event set-up (location, tent, light, sound, etc.) that you can reuse for a variety of different events? This is another new trend in event land: several different companies making use of the same infrastructure (often arranged through the same event bureau). Construction and removal costs are one of the biggest budgetary posts for any event. If these costs can be shared between several events, the savings can be enormous. At the same time, you reduce the need for transport, which is good for the environment.

Sustainable organising also means inclusive organising. Inclusive not only in terms of your target group and personnel, but also in terms of the range of speakers you engage and the topics they discuss. Make sure that you do not have exclusively male speakers and also allow sustainability issues into your programme.

SUSTAINABLE SUPPLIERS

The first step that you can easily take towards organising a sustainable event is to select a venue and suppliers that are already known for their efforts to work sustainably. With this in mind, at eventplanner.net we have launched an eventplanner.eco label that will help you to choose the right partners.

www.eventplanner.net/book/eco

WASTE

The first objective of the waste management policy for your event should be to create no waste at all (zero waste). Perhaps this is a utopian ideal, but nowadays there are numerous ways to reduce the size of your waste mountain. For example, you can make use of reusable cups, plates and glasses instead of disposable ones. You don't even have to pay for them yourself: if you give a reduced drinks price to people who 'buy' such a glass, the news will soon spread like wildfire! And if you print the glasses with the logo of your event, there is a good chance that your guests will want to take them home as a souvenir.

Another obvious way to tackle the waste problem is to take measures to counteract the 'no-show' phenomenon. If you expect 1,000 guests for a seated diner but 20% fail to turn up, you will have to throw the remaining 200 meals in the dustbin. This is not only a waste of money, but also a waste of valuable food at a time when many people are still going hungry. So why not re-read the paragraph in chapter 7 that tells you how to reduce 'no-shows' to a minimum.

Also choose reusable decorative elements and avoid throw-away items like balloons. Green plants are a fun alternative.

And if there is no alternative to the creation of a certain amount of waste, then make sure that this waste does not contain plastic or other materials that are not easily bio-degradable. Fortunately, many soft drinks suppliers now supply their products in recyclable and ecologically-friendly PET bottles. This applies equally to glasses, plates, cups and even consumption tokens. Eliminate plastic completely from your planning. For example, why not use a digital programme book in the form of an app or digital invitations instead of piles of paper? You still prefer paper? Use recycled paper and point this out, so that people know that you are organising your event sustainably.

The handing-out of gadgets (swag), many of which contain plastic, is increasingly being scrapped at events or at least replaced with more sustainable alternatives. Think carefully before you give things away: are you sure that they will not be put straight into the bin by your guests? This is not only bad for the environment, but also a waste of your money.

Make sure that you have enough rubbish bins at your venue, so that you can restrict the amounts of unnecessary litter at your festival site or in your event building to an absolute minimum. If you want to take matters another step further, you can even sort the rubbish you collect. Better still, get your guests to do it, by providing different bins for different types of waste. But don't be under any illusions: even if you have a series of large, well-indicated, coloured bins, you will still be unlikely to persuade everyone to throw their rubbish in the right ones. At large events in particular, you can increase your chances of success by using an animation team to increase public awareness of the need for responsible waste disposal. Even then, it may take several editions before this policy begins to bear fruit.

TECHNOLOGY AND EQUIPMENT

In recent years there have also been significant sustainability improvements in the technical field. Energy-guzzling podium spotlights can now be replaced by more economical LED lights. These not only use considerably less electricity, but also last much longer. And perhaps for your next event you can buy in green energy, instead of relying exclusively on dirty and polluting diesel generators. Setting up solar panels for temporary events is another viable option.

TRANSPORT AND TRAVEL

Did you know that aeroplanes are one of the biggest polluters associated with international congresses? Flying in guests from all over the world leads to huge additional emissions of CO_2. Is it really necessary that everyone is physically present at the event venue? In some cases, the answer to this question will be 'yes'. But sometimes there may be other alternatives. People who can follow your event via the internet not only save a great deal of time and money, but also make a contribution towards reducing the amount of harmful greenhouse gases in our atmosphere. It is not possible to reduce your CO_2 emissions in this way? Find some other way to make compensatory reductions.

Are you using shuttle buses? Choose electric ones. You can also cut down the amount of logistical movement to and from your event by working with local suppliers.

CATERING

There are also numerous possibilities for making the catering at your event 'greener', a subject that I discussed in more depth in chapter 10. For example, you could opt for organic and local produce or make vegetarian dishes the standard menu choice, with meat being the exception rather than the rule.

Production

Showtime! After months of preparation, the big day has finally arrived. You can at last start with the setting-up of your event. In theory, this is the point at which you can sit back and relax: you have already done all your hard work in the previous period, haven't you? Sadly, the reality is very different. No matter how well you have organised things so far and briefed people thoroughly, unforeseen challenges will inevitably occur in the weeks ahead. Perhaps you will discover things that can be done better than you originally thought. Or circumstances that have changed, necessitating a new approach to some elements of your event. Fortunately, your good planning will allow you to respond to these matters flexibly, so that last-minute changes or improvements, although sometimes irritating, do not throw you into a panic.

The most important thing is to ensure that you make clear arrangements in advance about who is responsible for the different aspects of the event. For small events this might be just one person. For larger events, the different tasks will need to be shared: someone for the catering, someone for technical matters, someone for decoration, and so on. If you are working with an event bureau, they will arrange this for you. A separate technical producer will usually be appointed to take care of all your event technology. In each case, the person designated for a particular aspect must be the only person authorised to make changes that deviate from the original plan. In this way, you will be able to keep a good overview of the situation as a whole and prevent different event managers from contradicting each other, which can only lead to confusion among your crew and the loss of precious time.

Meet each supplier when he arrives on site, show him where to go and introduce him to the person responsible for the aspect of the event on which they will be working together. Many suppliers will already know each other from other events . Even so, it is worth spending time to introduce them to each other formally. They will need to collaborate in pressure situations, so that it is better to ensure that everyone knows everyone else and who they need to approach in the event of problems.

Monitor your call sheet or action plan and tick off each point as soon as it has been completed. You can do this easily in the eventplanner.net software via the app, so that your entire team can see what has already been done and what still needs to happen. Always keep a paper copy of your call sheet as a back-up, in case the internet connection fails.

Is a supplier late? Wait fifteen minutes, but no longer. Then call him immediately. In that way, you will know exactly what is going on – for example, a lorry is stuck in traffic – and can anticipate accordingly. Whenever possible, always try to stick to your plan. It is tempting to allow a caterer who arrives early to start with his set-up immediately, but this might mean that he gets in the way of your decorator or technical people, creating potentially unsafe situations and causing delays.

If your site construction lasts for more than one day, hold a short briefing session with all your crew members each morning. If your event is large, limit this meeting to all team leaders, who can then hold short stand-ups with their own team members. This will give everyone a sense of involvement and keep all noses pointing in the same direction. At many events you will need to work with temporary personnel, so it is doubly important to keep them motivated in this manner. On the day of the event, do the same with hosts/hostesses, waiters/waitresses and security staff. A short pep talk from you as organiser can work wonders. Emphasise that everyone is an important part of the same large team and that the event will only be a success if everyone works together. If, for example, a hostess sees an empty glass, she can take it back to the bar without waiting for a waiter, who may be busy with something else. Repeat briefly the names of the people who are responsible for the different aspects of the event. Once the event starts, your crew are your eyes and ears. If someone sees something wrong, it needs to be reported immediately to the team leader, so that he/she can take necessary action before the situation gets out of hand. This final briefing is also a good moment to run through the safety procedures one last time.

As mentioned earlier, make sure that you provide your crew with healthy and nourishing food and drinks. In the morning and on cold winter days a heart-warming cup of coffee or tea will be much appreciated. During hot summer days cool water is a must. Or why not treat your crew to an ice-cream?

Safety always comes first, at all times and in all places. Check before, during and after the event that the necessary safety precautions are being followed to the letter. You need to be strict in these matters, since the safety of everyone, both crew and guests, is at stake.

As organiser, you are the captain of your event ship. And a captain is always the last person to leave his vessel. I often see event organisers who leave together with their guests, even though the dismantling of the site still needs to be carried out. Your responsibility only ends when the last supplier has left the site – and not the last guest! Of course, you have had a busy and tiring day and perhaps you do not feel fresh enough to carry on into the night. In that case, appoint someone else to supervise the dismantling in your place, so that it can be completed quickly and safely.

PRODUCTION OFFICE

You probably won't need one if you are organising a wedding, but as soon as you take on anything bigger it is advisable to set up a production office. With this in mind, you need to pick out a suitable room during your initial inspection of the event venue. Alternatively, you can bring in portable cabins. Wherever it is located, your production office is the nerve centre of your event.

For very large events and festivals, in addition to your production office you will also need a command centre, where all the different disciplines can intervene to take remedial action when things threaten to go wrong (also see chapter 15). This is the place where the images from all the on-site cameras are displayed on banks of screens, so that you can see what is happening at all times. Radio and other communication channels are also centralised here. Make sure that your production office is fully equipped. Here is a checklist of things that you should not forget:

- ✔ **Office material**. Biros, marker pens, scissors, utility knife (cutter), perforator, post-it notes, elastic bands, staples, paper clips, drawing pins, selloptape, paper, laminator, etc.
- ✔ **Printer** or **photocopier.** If you are organising an event in a congress centre, you will almost certainly need to make copies, but probably not if you are organising a music festival. Remember to take spare ink cartridges with you.
- ✔ **First aid kit.** Add sun cream if your crew are likely to be working outdoors for long periods in hot weather.
- ✔ **Sewing kit.** Handy if someone tears their trousers or loses a button. Add some safety pins, which always come in useful.
- ✔ **Lighter** or **matches**
- ✔ **Toothpicks**
- ✔ **Wet wipes**
- ✔ **Deodorant**. Best use a unisex brand.
- ✔ **Gaffa tape**. You can use it to stick almost everything! Buy better quality tape and ignore cheap alternatives. Good tape is easy to tear, adheres well and is super-strong, yet easy to remove without leaving a trace. This is important: some venues deduct a sum from your security deposit if you

leave behind residues of adhesive on their walls and windows. And this will cost you more than a roll of decent tape!
- ✓ **Tyraps** or **cable ties.** No event can do without them!
- ✓ **String, wire** and **fishing line.**
- ✓ **Double-sided sticky tape**.
- ✓ **Empty USB sticks.** In case you need to transfer a presentation at the last minute.
- ✓ **Battery chargers** and **adapters**.
- ✓ **Batteries.** In all shapes and sizes.
- ✓ **Cables.** Power cables, power strips, ethernet cables, etc. You can never have too many cables. Also remember travel adapter plugs for your international guests, so that they can use and recharge their electrical devices.
- ✓ **Rubbish sacks.**
- ✓ **Tool kit.** Screwdrivers, pliers, hammer, allen keys, pen knife. Hopefully you won't need them, but you never know...
- ✓ ...

KEEP CALM!

One thing is certain. At some point, something will always go wrong during an event. When it happens, what do you do? First and foremost, take a couple of deep breaths to calm yourself – and don't panic! Why is this so important? Look at it from your visitors' point of view: 'We have paid good money to come to an event and enjoy our evening, but what do we find when we arrive? An event manager running around like a headless chicken and cursing like a trooper, while his poor staff look on in confusion and haven't got a clue what they are supposed to do!'

It goes without saying that this would detract from the overall pleasure of your guests. Stressed event managers and personnel have a negative impact on your event experience. What's more, panicking solves nothing! So no matter what goes wrong during your event, always remember the following rules:

- ✓ **Hide your panic**
  Even if you think that your event is on the point of disintegrating, you should never let your guests notice that something is wrong. Being a professional does not mean that you can predict every problem and find a solution for all of them. Being a professional means that you accept that you cannot control everything, but that you have the self-confidence to believe that you can rise to the occasion and meet the challenge posed by any problems. Remember this whenever 'a catastrophe' occurs. Hide your despair from the public and solve the problem with a clear mind.

✔ **Don't forget to smile**
Sometimes visitors will trouble you with relatively unimportant matters while you are busy trying to deal with more urgent issues, such as cancellations, delays or technical problems. Always remain friendly. Smile and listen to what they have to say. Then pass them on to one of your team members to give them the help they need.

✔ **Never get angry**
What is the worst thing that can happen during an event? That your technology lets you down at a crucial moment? No. The worst thing that can happen is that people see you, as the event organiser, losing your temper with your personnel or (even worse!) your guests. Even if someone is being extremely irritating, never respond with hostility or aggression – even if they deserve it.

✔ **Stay calm**
Visitors do not like to see an event manager looking as though he is in the middle of a crisis. It is your job to give the impression that everything is running smoothly. Don't worry: this is something that comes with experience. In the meantime, try to maintain a poker face whilst in the presence of your guests, even if you feel like the world is crumbling around you.

Cyber security and privacy

In an age when digital technology has become an integral part of organising events, cyber security and privacy continue to become increasingly important. Sadly, this importance is still underestimated by many event organisers. For this reason, I intend to devote an entire chapter to the subject.

As an organiser, you are responsible for protecting all the personal and sensitive data of both your personnel and your event participants. In addition, you also need to protect your own interests, such as safe ticketing, safe payment facilities, a reliable network and (of course) your own reputation.

WHY IS PRIVACY SO IMPORTANT?

More and more countries are introducing strict privacy regulations, while the European Union's General Data Protection Regulation (GDPR) has set the standard for the European continent as a whole. Although there is often much grumbling about the implementation of these regulations, it is nevertheless surprising that many companies and organisers still refuse to make the safe and correct processing of personal details a priority. When you are dealing with events, you inevitably collect and collate large amounts of this kind of data, often including sensitive information such as medical details (allergies, food preferences, etc.). This data must be treated with great care.

Privacy legislation

In this chapter, I will focus primarily on the General Data Protection Regulation (GDPR), because most other privacy legislation worldwide is based to a large extent on the same premises and standards.

However, it is not my intention to offer legal advice. I simply wish to sketch a framework within which event organisers can operate. Always consult an expert for proper legal guidance and always check the relevant local guidelines relating to implementation.

The basis of privacy legislation is the assumption that the individual must have control over how his personal details are collected, used and shared. As a result, the legislation contains a number of different components:

- **Rights of the individual**: People have various rights relating to their personal details, such as the right to access, rectification, object, withdraw consent and portability. As event organiser, make sure that your participants and personnel have access to these options; for example, via your website or app.
- **Consent**: Organisations must seek the explicit approval of individuals before collecting and processing their personal data. Moreover, the organisation must be able to prove that they have received this permission.
- **Data Protection Officer (DPO)**: Large organisations and companies that process large amounts of sensitive data must appoint a Data Protection Officer.
- **Data security**: Organisations must take the necessary technical and organisational measures to guarantee the security of personal details. We will look at this further in the section on cyber security, because this is where things often go wrong.
- **Obligation to report data leaks**: Any leakage of data must be reported within the legally stipulated time frame to the Data Protection Supervisor and, if necessary, to the individuals concerned. Take account of this requirement in your planning.

In addition, it is not permitted to keep people's personal data for longer than is strictly necessary for the purposes for which it was collected. This means that if you are organising a one-off event, you are expected after a certain period (to be determined on the basis of justifiable arguments) to remove or anonymise all the personal data you have processed. Anonymise means that you must replace all actual personal details with fictitious data. In this respect, bear in mind that IP addresses can also be regarded as personal details.

Breaches of the privacy legislation can result in the imposition of heavy fines, especially when organisations have dealt carelessly with personal data or when they have flagrantly ignored the regulations. In other words, it pays to invest both time and money to make sure that you do what the legislation expects you to do. On the plus side, this is not really all that difficult and it also yields a number of positive benefits. For this reason, you should not see privacy and cyber security as a burden, but as an opportunity to shine and set yourself apart from the competition.

To comply with the privacy legislation, there are a number of important matters you need to arrange. To begin with, you must draw up a clear privacy statement that is easily accessible. This statement stipulates what personal data you collect, for what purpose and for how long, as well as setting out the rights of individuals and how they can make a complaint to the relevant authorities. A specialised lawyer or jurist can help you to prepare such a document. Your cookie statement and the correct functioning of your cookie banner (especially the option to reject non-essential cookies), together with the keeping of registers like the data processing register, incident register and processor register, are other important steps. Finally – and this is something that is often overlooked – you are obliged to make all your sub-contractors and suppliers, who also process personal data relating to your event, sign a data processing agreement. This document specifies how they must deal with the data and what they must do in the event of a data leak. Such a DPA protects your own interests, so make sure that you have one. If you are an event bureau, you also need a DPA between your bureau and the client.

Are you organising an event for your own company? If so, contact your DPO. Many of the things you need to do will already have been done in the past and he can show you how.

It is not possible to cover all aspects of the GDPR in this book. There are plenty of other publications covering the subject in more detail. However, I hope that this brief introduction will help you to understand the importance of privacy legislation and encourage you to include it in the action plan for your event.

WHAT IS CYBER SECURITY?

Cyber security refers to the measures that you need to take to protect your computer systems, networks and data from digital attack, damage, loss and unauthorised access. In other words, it is not just about protecting the personal details we discussed in the previous section, but relates to all the data and systems that you manage. In terms of your event, this applies equally to your event network, payment facilities, ticketing, website, apps, and so on.

In recent times, you hear something in the news almost every day about hacking, ransomware and other digital threats. Sadly, the event industry is not immune from these increasing threats. In fact, the industry is an attractive target for this kind of criminality. The large amounts of data that event organisers collect and the relatively poor protection of their systems mean that the event world is particularly vulnerable.

In addition to the threats, there are also judicial obligations that you need to take into account. For example, in Europe there is the NIS2 guideline, a cyber security directive that is applicable to critical sectors. Understandably, you might think that events are not 'critical' and that consequently this legislation does not apply to you, but you need to bear in mind that companies that are subject to NIS2 expect their suppliers – which might be you – to comply with the same standards, creating a kind of domino effect.

It is remarkable that 98% of event planners say that they regard cyber attack as a serious threat, but only 48% have taken measures to counteract this risk. The worldwide cost of cyber criminality to the event industry in 2017 was estimated at 600 billion dollars, an amount that has no doubt increased significantly since then, given the growing prevalence of cyber crime. In 2019, the cost of each individual incident averaged 200,000 dollars. Even more disturbing is the fact that in 2024, some 32% of event companies were affected by data leaks, 90% of which were the result of human error. These figures emphasise the urgent necessity for introducing robust cyber security measures throughout the event industry.

Cyber threats

In brief, the most common cyber threats are as follows:

- **Phishing**
  Phishing attacks are attempts by fraudsters to portray themselves as reputable organisations for the purpose of misleading people into revealing sensitive information. This is often done by using fake e-mails, messages or websites that are designed to steal the target's personal data. Always verify the source of communications you receive online before sharing personal details. In a typical phishing scenario, the attacker will send an e-mail that seems to come from a reliable supplier, like a bank, with a request for password updates, so that you provide them with your log-in details.

- **Deepfakes**
  Deepfake technology can be used to create convincing false videos that have stolen millions of dollars from companies in recent years One well-known case involved a British engineering bureau that lost 25 million dollars as a result of a deepfake attack. The attackers made an AI video of the bureau's CFO in which 'he' asked for an urgent money transfer to be made.

- **Ransomware**
  Ransomware encrypts the files of the victim and blocks access to all their devices. The attackers then demand the payment of money – a ransom –

before they will repair the targeted systems. Regular back-ups and robust security defences are essential for reducing the risk of this threat.

✓ **Malware**
One of the biggest hacks in history took place in 2018, with an international hotel chain as the victim. The data of some 500 million guests were made public, including passport information, credit card details, arrival and departure dates, and other personal details. The attack made use of e-mail spoofing and malware to target vulnerabilities in the outdated IT system of the chain, which had to pay serious fines for failing to comply with the GDPR.

✓ **Hacking**
Hacking incidents, such as the data leak at one of the world's largest ticketing agencies, have led to the compromising of huge amounts of data. In the agency's case, 1.3 terabytes of information relating to 560 million users was accessed via vulnerabilities in the systems of sub-contractors.

✓ **Data breaches**
Data breaches or leaks occur when unauthorised persons gain access to confidential information, often as a result of cyber attacks, weak security or human error. These breaches can lead to identity fraud, financial loss and serious reputational damage.

✓ **DDoS attacks**
Distributed Denial of Service (DDoS) attacks disrupt normal internet traffic by overwhelming a server with a flood of data, so that digital bottlenecks are created. This can lead to long downtimes and serious financial loss for the companies affected. Event planners, who are dependent on online registration and ticketing systems, are especially vulnerable for attacks of this kind.

✓ **Insider threats**
Insider threats come from within an organisation itself, often in the form of malicious intent or negligence. For example, a dissatisfied employee might deliberately sabotage the logistics of an event or a careless employee might accidentally reveal sensitive information by falling into a phishing trap.

HOW TO DEAL WITH CYBER SECURITY RISKS
What is the best way to deal with cyber security risks? The following list of best practice will give you tools to significantly reduce your vulnerability to cyber incidents. Bear in mind, however, that this list is not exhaustive and that the ingenuity of cyber attacks is evolving all the time.

✓ **Regular software updates and patching**
Ensure that all your software and devices are regularly updated. Cyber criminals often make use of known vulnerabilities in outdated software.

✓ **Strong passwords and two-factor authentication**
Follow best practices for password management and make use of two-factor authentication. Strong passwords must be unique and complex, with a combination of letters, numbers and symbols. Use a password manager like 1Password to ensure unique passwords for every service and shift. Two-factor authentication adds an additional layer of security, making it more difficult for intruders to gain unauthorised access to your systems.

✓ **Endpoint security**
Install comprehensive endpoint security software. Endpoints include all the devices you use, such as laptops, telephones and tablets. Endpoint security therefore goes much further than standard anti-virus software. For example, it makes it possible to wipe your laptop clean at distance, should it ever be stolen. It can also monitor the presence of encryption and other threats. Solutions like Sophos Endpoint Protection offer a holistic approach to endpoint security, which is essential for devices used by event personnel and volunteers.

✓ **Training of staff**
Arrange regular training sessions and awareness programmes about cyber security. Educating your personnel about phishing, social engineering and other common cyber threats can significantly reduce the risk that human error will result in breaches of security. In particular, interactive training sessions and simulated phishing exercises can be highly effective.

✓ **Regular back-ups and safe data storage**
Make regular back-ups of your data and ensure that it is safely stored. Back-ups should be taken several times a day and the data housed in safe and encrypted locations. Regular testing of your back-up strategies and recovery procedures make it possible to restore your data quickly in the event of a ransomware attack or some other form of data loss.

✓ **On and off-boarding procedures**
Use checklists to manage access control when members of staff join or leave. In the event branch there are frequent changes of personnel and people are often employed for only a short period before the event. The principle of 'least privilege' should be applied. This means that personnel are only given access to the data that is essential for doing their job. Regular auditing of access rights can help to identify and cancel rights that are no longer necessary.

- **Secure networks**
  Use VPNs and firewalls, especially at event venues. VPNs encrypt your internet traffic and protect data from interception on public or unsafe networks. Firewalls can block unauthorised attempts to access your systems, which adds an extra layer of security.

- **Safe channels of communication**
  Always use encrypted channels for sensitive communication. Tools such as encrypted e-mail services and secure messaging apps ensure that your confidential information is adequately protected. During events, setting up a private network can eliminate communication problems for your organisational team and improve your overall security.

- **Screening your suppliers**
  Make sure that your suppliers also comply with current cyber security norms. This means checking that they have the necessary certificates, such as ISO 27001 or SOC2. Suppliers who need to process large amounts of personal data, such as those responsible for your ticketing and payment facilities, must be able to show that they have installed robust cyber security measures and, for preference, must again possess the necessary certificates.

- **Screening individuals**
  Screen individuals who have access to sensitive information relating to your event. Background checks and constant monitoring, within the legal guidelines, can help to identify and eliminate potential internal threats.

- **Security tests and audits**
  Conduct regular security tests and audits. Penetration tests, social engineering tests and cyber security audits can expose vulnerabilities and identify points for improvement. Larger organisations can also consider the use of bug-bounty programmes to involve the wider cyber security community in the tracing of potential problems and threats.

- **Insurance**
  Cyber insurance offers crucial protection against the financial consequences of cyber incidents. Cyber insurance policies generally cover liability in the event of data breaches, financial loss resulting from business disruption and costs for research and crisis management. In addition, good crime insurance also provides cover for ransom payments in the event of ransomware attacks. Access to a hot-line manned by the insurer's cyber security experts gives you access to direct support during an incident.

INCIDENT RESPONSE PLANNING

No system is 100% secure. Even the best protected museums in the world can still fall victim to theft – and the same is true of computer systems. In spite of all the precautions you take to protect your data, leaving open digital 'doors' can attract the attention of cyber criminals and result in massive fines for failure to comply with the GDPR legislation. For this reason, it is crucial to prepare a comprehensive response plan, so that you can quickly limit and repair the damage when something goes wrong.

This plan must set out clearly the roles, communication strategies and recovery procedures that should be implemented in the event of a cyber attack. It must describe in detail the steps to be taken, so that your response can be prompt and efficient. In some ways, it is similar to drawing up an action plan for an event.

Important elements in an incident response plan include:

- **Incident response team**: Appoint a team that is responsible for managing cyber incidents. This team should include members from your IT, legal and communication departments, supplemented with a number of key managers.
- **Communication plan**: Develop a plan for both internal and external communication during the incident. This will involve informing the affected parties and, if necessary the relevant regulatory authorities.
- **Recovery procedures**: Detail the procedures that need to be followed to ensure the quickest possible recovery of systems and data. Test these procedures regularly to ensure that they are still fast, efficient and fit for purpose.

HOW CAN EVENT SOFTWARE HELP?

Special event software, like our own eventplanner.net software, can significantly improve the cyber security of your event. Many event planners still make use of Excel spreadsheets, which can be useful but increase the likelihood of human error, often resulting from inadequate rights management or the overlooking of roaming folders. This makes compliance with the GDPR norms that much more difficult. In contrast, good event software offers functions like:

- **Safe 2FA password protection**: This ensures that only authorised people have access to sensitive information. Two-factor authorisation adds an extra layer of security, so that cyber criminals find it harder to compromise your account.

- **Correct rights management**: This manages your user rights effectively, so that your personnel are only given access to the data they need to do their job. This reduces the risk of unauthorised access and data leakage.
- **Compliance with privacy legislation**: This helps to ensure the proper management of authorisations and the anonymising of personal details after your event.
- **Collaboration functions**: These facilitate safe collaboration and data management. Good event software can support large teams and multiple events, ensuring that data can be safely and efficiently shared.
- **Human error reduction**: This involves the automation of key processes, such as data input, to minimise the risk of human error that can lead to security breaches.

In addition to improved cyber security, event software also offers a number of other important benefits. Scalability is one such benefit, which allows you to efficiently manage events of any size, from small meetings to major conferences, but without compromising performance or data integrity. Event software also saves you time through the automation of various tasks, such as registration, ticketing and data management. This reduces your overall administrative burden and frees up personnel to concentrate on providing your guests with a unique experience. Our own eventsoftware.net software is also ISO 27001 certified, but on our website you can also find other alternatives.

www.eventplanner.net/book/eventsoftware

Evaluation and wind-up

Your big day has finally come and gone. The last guests have left and you have turned the key for the last time in the door of your venue. But for you as event organiser, things are far from finished. There are still plenty of things that need to be arranged before you can finally say that your event is 'over'.

WIND-UP

There are still a number of internal administrative and financial matters that need to be finalised. The level of complexity of your wind-up procedures will depend on several different factors, including the agreements you have made with your suppliers and service providers. The financial side of things can most efficiently be arranged if suppliers submit their invoices promptly and with a clear description of the items for which they are charging, so that these can easily be allocated to your different budgetary posts. Make transparent arrangements with your suppliers on these matters.

Check each invoice carefully and make a **re-calculation** of your overall budget, post by post. Was your estimate for 'refreshments' adequate? Were there any items of unforeseen expenditure? Add up the totals of your actual expenditure and compare this with your original budgetary provisions. This will allow you to compile an accurate financial report for your event.

Matters of dispute can only slow down your wind-up procedures. As has already been stated, try to avoid this by making good and clear arrangements with all your suppliers. If something does go wrong, take the necessary steps to get it sorted out as quickly as possible.

Complaints? When a supplier fails to comply with the agreements you made with him or if there are aspects of his service about which you were not satisfied, you will need to draw up a letter of complaint or default. Send your letter by registered post to avoid any possibility of legal wrangling later on. Ask for an evaluation meeting with the supplier in question and try to reach a mutually acceptable agreement for a discount or some other form of compensation.

Deal promptly with all incoming claims for damage compensation and finalise all insurance matters as quickly as possible. Make sure that all items of lost property are returned to their owners (where known) with a minimum of delay.

Update your action plan for a last time. It will serve as a good starting point and guide for the organisation of your next event. Find time to draw up a final press release and a report for your in-house magazine or professional journal.

Don't forget your own after-sales service. Send a letter of thanks to your guests, speakers, performers, suppliers, partners, volunteers, etc. You can link this to the distribution of presentational hand-outs, photographs, video material, etc.

 The winding-up of your event will not take as long as its preparation, but you still need to allow a reasonable period of time in your diary. For this reason, it is important to ensure that your events do not follow each other too closely.

EVALUATION

A good and thorough evaluation will demand a final effort from your organisational team. No matter how small your event, it is important to conduct an in-depth evaluation. This is the only way to check whether you have reached your set objectives in a manner which offers good value for money. It would be a great shame to let all your detailed preparation and implementation work go to waste by failing to carry out a proper evaluation. A good ex-post assessment allows you to identify not only your most successful points, but also points where there is still room for improvement in future events. This can only work to your advantage.

 Make a written report of your event evaluation. Add an *executive summary* for senior management.

> Check with your suppliers to see if they have any tips for improving your next event. They are involved with a wide range of events on a daily basis and therefore have a broad frame of reference to provide you with valuable feedback.

Remember to ask the opinions of your invitees. You should not think that your guests will regard this request as burdensome. On the contrary, most of them will feel flattered to be asked. By showing that you are interested in what they think, this will also contribute towards their positive experience not only of your event, but also of your company, product and/or service in general. Make sure, however, that your evaluation forms are short and to the point, so that they do not take too much time to complete. In addition, measure the KPIs that you agreed before the event to evaluate its success. It is nice to know from your guests that the appetisers were tasty, but what really counts is whether or not the event had the impact that you had hoped for. This, after all, is the reason why you organised the event in the first place!

The manner and the level of detail of your evaluation will be determined by a number of different factors:

- **Series**
  Was this a 'one-off' event or will events of a similar nature be organised in the future? A repeat event requires a more detailed evaluation, so that you can learn from the mistakes of the past.

- **Type**
  An informal meeting does not require the same level of evaluation as a congress. In the former case, an evaluation form is probably not needed; in the latter case, it almost certainly is.

- **Paying or non-paying event**
  Guests who pay to take part in an event have a higher level of expectation than guests at 'free' events. The former demand (not unreasonably) good value for money. For this reason, it is usually advisable to send an evaluation letter/form to guests at paying events.

There are several different ways to ask your guests' opinions about your event. A written evaluation (online or on paper) is one option. Or you may prefer to send them an e-mail answer form during the course of the following week. In general, however, the longer you wait before requesting feedback, the lower the response is likely to be. If you want to know which parts of your event were most memorable, you need to act within days or weeks – not months.

USEFUL TIPS FOR DRAWING UP A SURVEY/QUESTIONNAIRE:

✓ **Ask for feedback quickly**
Don't wait too long. The ideal moment is the day after the event. Under a heading like 'What did you think of yesterday?', you can send a short e-mail asking for comments and criticisms. If you prefer, you can even ask for feedback on the day of the event itself. In this case, it is better to use the classic 'fill-in' card. Alternatively, your hostesses can canvas opinions amongst the participants with an iPad or you can even project QR codes that link through to a satisfaction questionnaire.

✓ **A (small) incentive works wonders**
To increase the level of response, it is worth offering a small incentive to your feedback-givers: a reduction on your next event, access to the digital presentations of the last event, the chance to win a fun prize, etc.

✓ **Spread the word**
Announce your intention to make an evaluation during the event itself. Inform the participants that you will be sending them a questionnaire tomorrow and encourage them to complete it.

✓ **Keep the questionnaire clear and concise**
Ask your participants to give scores for specific aspects such as location, price, timing, speakers, etc., but also ask for an overall score. For the elements that score badly, send a follow-up mail asking the participants to clarify the reasons for their low score.

✓ **Don't ask for information you already have**
You already know your guests: their names, background, language, etc. So don't ask them to repeat this information in your evaluation questionnaire: they will find this both irritating and unprofessional. It is also totally unnecessary: when analysing the results you can easily extract these details from your contact database.

✓ **Give room for open feedback**
End your questionnaire with an (optional) open question in which you ask your guests if they have any other tips, comments or suggestions. You can use these learnings constructively when preparing your next event.

> ✔ **More than one survey**
> It is not a bad idea to also send a short questionnaire to your 'no-shows'. Why did they fail to turn up? And if there were stand holders at your event, try to find out if they were satisfied or not. Did the event live up to their expectations in terms of public interest, return, etc?

A verbal evaluation is another option. This implies that you simply canvas the opinions of your guests while the event is still taking place. If conducted well, this type of informal conversation can often be most revealing. Telephone interviews after the event are another possibility. With this option, it is important to ask direct and well-targeted questions about specific aspects of the event, such as the programme, the location, etc.

> 📌 You can either survey all your guests or just a representative sample (providing that the sample is indeed 'representative'). This applies for both written and verbal evaluations.

> 📌 For verbal evaluations, your own account managers are often the best people to act as 'interviewers'. They have already built up good relations with your suppliers/customers/guests and are therefore more likely to elicit an 'honest' reaction, since the atmosphere surrounding the conversation will automatically be more informal. For written evaluations, they also have a perfect excuse to contact the 'interviewees'.

If you want to collate the results of a verbal evaluation, it is important to ensure that all your interviewers ask the same questions. Bear in mind that an interview conducted by one of your own members of staff will always be interpreted more favourably than an interview conducted by a neutral third party.

The following methods of assessing the results of your evaluation do not constitute 'hard proof' but nonetheless offer some indication about the success or failure of your event.

- ✔ Do you have the feeling that the results matched the objectives which you had previously set for the event?
- ✔ Did the actual number of participants live up to your expectations?
- ✔ Were the first reactions of your guests generally positive or negative?

- ✔ Was the atmosphere good?
- ✔ Is your own 'gut feeling' about the event positive or negative?
- ✔ Did the organisation run smoothly?
- ✔ Did your event attract media attention?
- ✔ What kind of feedback has been posted on X, Facebook, etc.?

If you want more detailed insights with regard to your return on investment (ROI) and the overall efficiency of your organisation, you will need to dig deeper. This means conducting a detailed evaluation of each separate phase of the project: namely, the preparations, the implementation and the wind-up.

Preparations

During the preparation phase, you and your team carried out a huge amount of planning work in a process which required intense collaboration. Evaluate the performance of the team and the efficiency of the planning.

TEAM
- ✔ Did the internal communication between the different team members work well?
- ✔ How effective was communication with suppliers and service providers? Was there enough consultation and feedback? Were there any misunderstandings?
- ✔ Was the composition of your team ideal? What skills were lacking? Is it possible to train someone in these skills or do you need to turn to an external service in future?
- ✔ Was the workload for each team member reasonable? Was the distribution of tasks fair and equitable? Can some tasks be carried out more efficiently in future?

PLANNING
- ✔ Was the agreed planning realistic? Which elements caused problems?
- ✔ Were the action plan and its various updates sufficiently detailed?

Event

Evaluate each individual element of the event, one by one. Some of these elements will only be capable of internal evaluation, whereas others can be evaluated on the basis of both internal and external input. For example, you can ask everyone (both staff and guests) what they thought about the general quality of the speakers. In contrast, only you will be able to decide whether or not the speaker successfully complied with your specific wishes, as agreed in advance.

> 📌 Your programme of activities can act as a good general guideline of the things you need to assess, but will not be sufficient to cover everything. If you rely exclusively on the programmed elements, you may overlook the performance of the caterers, lighting, hostesses, etc. Remember also to consult your budget during the evaluation process. Many of the points you need to examine will be specified in the individual budgetary posts.

Reassessing your previously set objectives is perhaps the most crucial element of the evaluation process. This not only offers the clearest picture of the level of your event's success but also helps to set patterns of expectation for the future.

- ✓ Did you achieve your (SMART) objectives? If you formulated these objectives in a clear and impartial manner, you should now have a measuring tool to assess the success and the return on investment of your event.

- ✓ How high were the levels of attendance at your event? Did you estimate the likely number of participants and the no-show percentage accurately? What do the figures tell you about the relative attendance rates of your different target groups?

Wind-up

Don't forget to evaluate your wind-up procedures. Financial matters need to be assessed internally. The after-care of your target groups is best discussed externally. Has everyone received a thank-you letter and/or gift? What did they think of the photographs and video material that were made during the event?

A thank-you mail

Send a thank-you mail to your suppliers. Many of them have worked hard in challenging circumstances to make your event a success. Showing that you appreciate their efforts does you credit as an organiser. What will please your suppliers and venue even more is to give them a positive review on their eventplanner.net business page. In this way, you will not only help them, but also other organisers who want to make the best choices for their event.

Wedding *planner*

In essence, there is little difference between organising an event and planning weddings and celebrations. The underlying mechanisms are almost the same. Many of the elements involved in organising a wedding reception have already been dealt with earlier in the book. However, there are a number of specific elements that only apply to weddings and it is these that we will look at in this chapter.

Whether you are organising your own 'best day ever' or are acting as a wedding planner for the happy couple, these extra tips will help to make the event an unforgettable one.

 www.eventplanner.net/book/wedding

WEDDING PLANNER OR MASTER OF CEREMONIES?

Think carefully about whether or not you wish to make use of a wedding planner to help you with your organisation. A wedding planner can remove a lot of the stress from your shoulders and will ensure that everything runs smoothly on the big day. If you want to organise your own wedding reception, I would recommend that at the very least you should work with a master of ceremonies. This person will coordinate all activities on the day itself, allowing the bridal pair to enjoy their special moment to the full.

> 📌 What if your wedding planner or master of ceremonies falls ill? Can he/she guarantee a back-up? You should ask this same question to your DJ, band and other crucial suppliers.

 www.eventplanner.net/book/weddingplanners

349

It often happens that the parents of the bridal couple help to pay the costs of the marriage ceremony and subsequent reception. But even if they don't, there is a good chance that they will want to have their say about the day's organisation. Parents often want to invite their own friends or have ideas about how the reception can best be arranged. A professional wedding planner knows how to deal with this. If you are organising your own celebrations, make sure that they remain your celebrations and not your parents'. After all, you only get married once (hopefully).

MARRIAGE PROPOSAL

The proposal marks the start of every marriage journey. The moment when your partner asks you to marry him/her can be arranged in many different ways. Think carefully about what best suits you as a couple and make sure that the setting is a memorable one. Some will want the moment to be intimate. Others will prefer some kind of grand gesture. The most important thing is to find something that is authentic and meaningful for both of you. Increasingly, marriage proposals are becoming an event in their own right, for which you can also make use of a wedding planner.

START WITH A MOOD BOARD

When you are planning a wedding reception, it is important to start with a mood board, much more so than for other events. For this you can use the free eventplanner.net software. A mood board is a great way to set out your vision and ideas about the right style, which you can then share with your wedding planner, suppliers and others involved in your big day. What kind of atmosphere do you want to create? Which colours and themes do you want to use? If you and your partner work together on the mood board, you will soon see whether or not you are both thinking along the same lines or if certain choices need to be made.

This is also the phase in which you need to think about the budget you want to spend. Of course, this can change later on in the process, but at this early stage it can help to shape the many decisions you need to take.

www.eventplanner.net/book/weddingsoftware

ACTION PLAN AND PLANNING

It is advisable to start your planning at least 12 months before the proposed date of your wedding. Do not forget to announce the good news of your engagement and perhaps even celebrate it with a party. This is also the moment when you should start searching for a suitable venue. It is important to book this as quickly as possible, bearing in mind that popular locations are often fully booked for 2 to 3 years in advance.

As with other events, you need to draw up a call sheet or action plan for your wedding and reception. Make use of the handy wedding template in our eventplanner.net software. This template also contains a checklist that makes clear which tasks need to be dealt with in the run-up to the marriage. If you are a wedding planner, run through the plan with the bridal couple, so that you can agree with them what decision-making powers you have and what things they want to decide for themselves. Make sure that the action plan has built-in time buffers between the day's different moments. There is always an aunt who turns up late or a ceremonial car that won't start. Also foresee a sufficient number of pauses in the programme for things like photos, freshening up, getting from one place to another, and so on.

🔗 www.eventplanner.net/book/weddingsoftware

INVITATIONS AND RSVP

According to standard wedding etiquette, you first send a 'save the date' and then later a formal invitation. Although paper invitations are still popular, from an organisational point of view it is easier to follow up your invitees' responses using RSVP software, such as our free eventplanner.net tool. You can also combine the digital and paper options: a traditional 'save the date' followed by a digital invitation. As mentioned earlier in the book, do not forget to mention the dress code. A well-organised guest list and efficient RSVP monitoring can save you tons of stress. Drawing up a guest list can be one of the most difficult challenges when organising a wedding. Think carefully about who you want to invite. Do not feel obliged to invite every great-aunt or second cousin twice removed! Invite the people who are important to you and take account of your budget when setting a numbers limit.

You do not need to invite all the guests at your wedding ceremony to the evening dinner and dance. You can invite more distant family members and acquaintances to a separate drinks reception before the meal, but not for the rest of the evening. Agree with your caterer to stop serving about half an hour before the drinks reception is scheduled to end, so that guests who are not staying for the dinner and dance have a suitable moment to say their farewells. Micro-weddings with just 20 to 30 guests are becoming ever more popular. This heightens the intimacy of the occasion and makes possible a more original approach to the day's events.

Also decide whether you want to work with a gift list, money gifts or a combination of both and make this clear on the wedding invitation.

 If you ask for money gifts, add a bank account number into which the gifts can be paid. This avoids having to accept and store large amounts of cash at your wedding venue. Even so, make sure that you have a sufficiently large space at the venue to safely store the gifts and money that many people will still bring on the day itself. Sadly, theft at wedding receptions sometimes happens...

Wedding procession

At a classic wedding, there are often special 'guests' who take part in the wedding procession that follows the bridal couple as they enter the church, registry office or other marriage location. Typical members of the procession are the couple's parents, the best man/woman and the witnesses, the bridesmaids, ushers and pages, with the children first and the adults behind. Members of the procession often wear formal dress throughout the day.

PRINTING

In addition to the invitations, it is important that all other printed matter matches in terms of style, form, colour, etc. Think, for example, of route description cards, programme books, menus, table cards, name cards, thank-you cards, and so on. Often a small token of appreciation for the guest's attendance at the wedding is added to the thank-you cards. This might be something simple like a packet of flower seeds, but it can also be more playful. After one wedding I attended, the next day I was sent a 'survival kit' with some paracetamol tablets to ease the hangover from the night before! That being said, giving away medication at or after an event of any kind is never a good idea.

DREAM VENUE AND CATERING

The venue is an essential part of any successful wedding celebration. Use eventplanner.net to find the perfect venue for you! Or why not consider a 'destination wedding', which involves getting married at some exotic location abroad. This will certainly provide a unique experience, but inevitably means more planning, especially with regard to logistics. For example, who will pay for the extra travel? Not all of your guests will be willing or able to take three or four days leave to travel abroad and/or to pay the high travel and accommodation costs out of their own pocket. Also ask the venue if they arrange for the decoration of the site. At many wedding locations you can choose from different styles of decoration, so that you don't need to worry about this yourself. Other venues will offer you the freedom (within reason!) to decorate their premises the way you see fit. If you go for an outdoor option, always make sure that there is an indoor back-up, just in case the weather is unkind. Are you expecting a lot of children at the wedding? Provide extra space and attractions – perhaps a bouncy castle or a clown? – to keep them entertained.

> 📌 No wedding is complete without a bride's bouquet and floral decoration. Choose a florist who can make fresh bouquets and deliver them to the various wedding locations. Discuss the style of floral displays that will best match what you are wearing and the atmosphere you want to create. Table decoration has been mentioned earlier in the book. Make sure that you do not choose flowers for which some of your guests may be allergic!

> 📌 Is your budget limited? Most weddings take place on Saturday or Sunday, but some venues offer lower rates for weddings on other days of the week. If you plan carefully, you can make smart use of this option. Arrange your wedding reception for the evening of a day just before a public holiday, so that your guests don't have to go to work early the next morning. Venues in cities, especially large cities, are more expensive than those in small towns and the countryside. By looking a little further afield, you can often stay inside your budget. We have noticed that our own B&B Moleneinde 10 in the countryside in Belgium is often booked by couples who live in the region's larger cities. Check to see if the venue has a fixed closing time or special regulations to limit noise nuisance for their neighbours. You can usually find a good solution to deal with this latter problem, but remember that if your music is too quiet the atmosphere at your dance will soon fade away. Also

> ask if the manager or your contact person at the venue will be in attendance on the evening in question. This will give you extra peace of mind.

> At some venues you will not have exclusive use of the location. Is this really something that you want? If you do not regard this as a problem, think carefully about how you will organise your evening, so that your guests don't end up at the wrong party – and vice versa!

Many wedding venues offer their own catering services and organise regular test moments, so that you can try out their various menus and wines before making a decision. Make use of these opportunities. There are also many non-venue related caterers who specialise in wedding dinners, often providing more refinement and luxury, but at a higher price. Whichever option you choose, take account of the allergies and dietary requirements of your guests. Ask them to mention these things in their RSVP. You are not a fan of seated dinners? Then why not go for a food truck or walking dinner. Remember, however, to provide enough chairs for your more elderly guests, who will not be able to stand up for the entire evening. Things do not always have to be traditional. When I was organising my own wedding celebrations, we decided not to have a dinner. Instead, we used the budget to hire a club, where our more than 400 guests enjoyed a memorable evening with dancers, top DJs, performances by well-known artists, oysters, midnight snacks and Magnum ice-creams! People are still talking about it 15 years later. And all for the same budget as a 'classic' approach. Of course, I know that this will not be everyone's cup of tea, but I just want to emphasise that your options for celebrating your wedding are almost limitless. For many couples, the wedding cake is the highlight of their reception. Take time to make the right choice. It often pays to use a specialised pâtissier, rather than relying on your caterer to provide one. After all, everyone has their own strengths and weaknesses, don't they?

There is one golden rule that applies to all venues and all suppliers: always ask about their terms of payment and other conditions. What happens, for example, if you have to cancel your bookings? Perhaps this is not a nice thing to think about, but it does happen and it is important to avoid extra cost and inconvenience if the worst comes to the worst. Make sure that these matters are clearly agreed and understood.

 www.eventplanner.net/book/weddingvenues

GETTING READY FOR THE MOST WONDERFUL DAY OF YOUR LIFE

Will the bride sleep the night before the wedding at her parents' house, so that you only see each other at the ceremony? Or will you start the day together? Make sure that you book a make-up specialist for the bride (and, increasingly, for the groom) in good time and, if necessary, arrange for a last-minute appointment with your hairdresser. Ideally, they should come to the house, hotel or B&B where you are staying. The day ahead is likely to be stressful at times, but a calm preparation can often work wonders for your confidence. Also ask your photographer to start taking photos from this point onwards. Hire a professional photographer and cameraman. If you ask a member of your family to 'take some photos', you will end up regretting it. You do not want your visual memories of your wedding day to be underexposed or out of focus. A professional photographer knows exactly when and where he or she should be to capture every key moment in the day's events.

After the wedding, some professional photographers offer digital photos and/or prints for sale to your guests. Personally, I find it strange that you, as a guest who has made the effort to come to the wedding and has given the bridal couple a nice present, should now be asked to pay for a photo. Make clear arrangements with your photographer about this.

> 📌 Ask your photographer how long it will take before you can receive the photos of your big day. You don't want to be kept waiting for months – although this sometimes happens…

> 📌 Make sure that you have a 'wedding rescue kit' with you throughout the day, containing items like a needle and thread, safety pins, deodorant, paracetamol, and so on. Hopefully, you won't need them, but they are great for helping to deal with small emergencies. It can also be a smart move to keep an umbrella handy.

CEREMONY

The ceremony is at the very heart of your wedding day. Whether you opt for a civil marriage, a religious ceremony or some other form of service, it is important that each and every element is carefully planned.

Every culture has its own traditions and it is not my intention to mention them all here in this book.

 In many countries it is the civil marriage that counts as the legal marriage, while a religious ceremony is purely optional and is not legally recognised. Bear in mind, however, that there is no need to arrange for everything to take place on the same day. For example, if you decide just to do the civil ceremony, it can sometimes be a good idea to hold the wedding reception the next day. Equally, you can do the civil wedding one weekend and the religious wedding the following weekend. I have heard from many couples who tried to do everything in one day that they almost had no time for each other, because of all the different activities that had to be crammed in – which is a pity.

The civil ceremony in the local town hall is usually quite short and based on standard texts. Because this 'official' wedding has to comply with legal requirements, there is little room for making the event more personal. However, there are some wedding officials who are prepared to come to another location than the town hall and who also allow extra speeches from the participants. This is more likely in some countries than others and in certain lands there are also officially recognised wedding locations. In general, traditional religious ceremonies also offer few options for personalisation. If you want a truly unique ceremony – bearing in mind that you must always have a civil ceremony as well – you need to organise it yourself. There are no rules for this kind of private ceremony: a unique setting on a beach, a personal master of ceremonies, texts written specially for the occasion, family reminiscences – almost anything you want. And why not some musicians and a singer? Make sure that everyone can follow the ceremony easily. Choose a location with a good sound system or else hire one. Are you expecting a lot of guests? Set up a screen and camera, so that the people at the back can also see.

 Reserve seats or space at the front for your witnesses, parents and other important family members. A good wedding planner or master of ceremonies will ensure that these people are shown to their places, whereas the rest of the guests will simply be expected to take an empty seat or space, starting at the front. You don't want to see lots of empty seats in your wedding photos!

Traditionally, the father 'gives away' the bride in both a church ceremony and a personal ceremony (but not in a civil ceremony). However, this is by no means obligatory. As the bridal couple, you can choose to walk to the altar together, or arrive separately, or each be escorted by your parents. It's up to you. Think carefully, however, about the music you would like to hear at this and other important moments in the ceremony. Personal wedding vows give the ceremony an extra depth. Write something that comes from the heart and practice it several times in advance.

The vows – the saying 'I do' – and the exchange of rings are highly symbolic moments in the ceremony. Ask a bridesmaid or one of the witnesses to bring the rings. Bridesmaids and ushers can also help with other tasks, such as adjusting the bride's dress, helping with photos and keeping an eye on the time.

RECEPTION AND EVENING DINNER & DANCE

'Wedding reception' is a generic term covering a drinks reception, an evening dinner and a subsequent dance. As mentioned earlier, a drinks reception allows you to invite a larger group of more distant family, friends and acquaintances, who do not then stay for the dinner. Alternatively, you can invite this larger group to the after-dinner dance instead. Whatever choice you make, make sure that the transition between the different elements is a smooth one. You don't want the guests at your drinks reception to still be hanging on while the first course of your evening dinner is already being served, just as you don't want your dinner guests to still be sitting at table when your guests for the evening dance arrive. Set detailed timings in your action plan and make clear who is responsible for ensuring that these timings are adhered to, especially if you do not have a wedding planner or master of ceremonies. Why not add some extra 'fun' elements to your wedding reception, such as a photo booth or a guest book. There are also apps that allow guests to make their own photos, which only become generally available to everyone the next day. Walk-around acts, like oyster men, champagne ladies, actors, etc., can also raise your event to a higher level.

Traditionally, one of the best photo opportunities at a wedding is when the bride throws her bouquet into the crowd of guests. Whoever catches it is supposedly next in line to be married.

Speeches are an important part of wedding celebrations but they need to be kept short (maximum 5 minutes). Speakers need to agree with the bridal couple in advance what they can say and what not; for example, no stories about old boyfriends or girlfriends. Plan the speeches for early in the evening, so that they do not interrupt the atmosphere and flow of the dance party.

Choose a DJ or band that matches your style and preferences. A good DJ will normally ask for a list of your favourite numbers, but will also take account of well-known party hits, so that he/she can get everyone on the dance floor and keep them there. Ask the DJ if he can provide his own sound and lighting installations or whether you or the venue will need to provide them. Ask if he can also provide a wireless microphone for the speeches. The bridal couple's opening dance usually marks the start of the evening's festivities, so choose the number wisely and perhaps even take a few dance lessons to surprise your guests.

Seating plan

Arranging a seating plan for a wedding dinner can sometimes be a tricky challenge, but the following simple guidelines should help you to keep most (if not all) of your guests happy, so that everything runs smoothly:

- **The bridal couple**
  Traditionally, the bridal couple sit at a separate main table, often together with the witnesses and their parents. This table usually occupies a central position, where it can easily be seen by all the other guests.

- **Grandparents**
  The grandparents of the bridal couple are usually placed near to the main table, along with other close members of the family.

- **Family**
  Other family members are usually seated together. Having familiar faces around you makes everyone feel comfortable. Remember, however, to take account of possible family conflicts and make sure that the protagonists are kept apart from each other.

- **Friends**
  Friends of the bridal couple can be seated at different tables, depending on their common interests and relationships. Try to put people who know each other well together: their conviviality will give a boost to the general atmosphere.

- ✓ **Colleagues**
  Colleagues can also be put on tables together, so that they can socialise without feeling uncomfortable amongst your family and friends.

- ✓ **Children**
  If there are children present, you can consider also giving them a separate table, with some table-top activities to keep them occupied. This will allow their parents to better enjoy the festivities.

According to standard wedding etiquette (as far as you wish to follow it), it is usual to seat men and women alternately. Married couples can sit next to or opposite each other, depending on the kind of tables you use (round or rectangular). This applies equally to couples who are living together or have a long-term relationship. At formal weddings, account is often taken of hierarchy. Make sure that everyone knows in advance where they should be sitting. You can do this by putting name cards on each table or by using a clear seating plan positioned at the entrance to the banquet room.

Follow the trends...

The event business is in a constant state of change. New developments and techniques are being introduced all the time, so that tomorrow things will be possible that you can only dream about today. As an event manager, you must monitor these new trends closely. Only then can you continue to provide new, surprising and high-impact experiences for your guests and clients.

The editorial team of eventplanner.net can help you on your way. Thanks to our newsletter, you can receive details about the **newest trends**, **latest news** and **useful tips** in your **mailbox each week**, and all absolutely **free of charge**. All you need to do is subscribe to our newsletter via:

> www.eventplanner.net/book/newsletter

Of course, we will also keep you fully in the picture about what is happening in the event sector around the clock via **Instagram**, **X** and **Facebook**. You can follow us on **instagram.com/eventplanner_net** or **x.com/eventplannernet** and like us on **facebook.com/www.eventplanner.net**.

eventplanner.net event software

With our very own event software you will have all the tools you need to create, plan and implement truly memorable events – and all on a single platform! Mood boards, budgets, call sheets, guest lists, tickets, project management: you name it, our software has got it. While you concentrate on what is most important – developing powerful concepts for high-impact events – we will take care of the more routine matters and ensure that everything runs smoothly. Moreover, we are continuing to invest in our event software, so that in future you will still have access to all the very latest and most innovative tools.

> www.eventplanner.net/book/eventsoftware

Via our eventplanner.academy, you can also follow training that will allow you to understand and use our eventplanner.net software like a true professional. This training is open to individual event planners and event bureaus, and both will receive an official certificate on successful completion of the course. This will look good on your CV and make you a more attractive proposition for potential clients who work with our software and are searching for someone with your event expertise.

www.eventplanner.net/book/academy

eventplanner.PRO

Are you 100% dedicated to your job? Do you want to get the maximum out of your career in the event industry? You do? Then why not become a member of eventplanner.PRO! This exclusive subscription is for true event professionals and offers you access to high-quality content, VIP priority at our network events and – perhaps most important of all –unlimited access to all the functionalities of our event software.

www.eventplanner.net/book/pro

eventplanner.NET-APP

With the handy eventplanner.net app, you always have our powerful event software in your back pocket. It even includes our ticketing scanner, so that your entrance checks run smoothly, while also giving you access to our database with details of all event venues and suppliers, not to mention all the other advice and knowledge that we share on our platform. You haven't downloaded the app yet? Don't delay: do it today!

www.eventplanner.net/book/app

eventplanner.TV AND PODCAST

eventplanner.tv is our online television station and podcast for event organisers and event customers. The station does not offer traditional-style event reports, but concentrates instead on exciting interviews with the key opinion-makers in the events sector, analyses of new trends, etc. In this way, you can discover new event locations, destinations, concepts, technologies and gadgets. eventplanner.tv is informative and shares knowledge – and all in short, clear and easily digestible episodes that you can watch on your computer, iPad, or smartphone… so that you receive maximum information in the shortest possible time.

www.eventplanner.net/book/tv

'GET INSPIRED' EVENTS AND eventplanner.LIVE

eventplanner.net regularly organises network events where you can make new contacts, find new inspiration and share ideas with other event professionals. In a similar vein, eventplanner.live is our annual users conference, where the latest developments on our platform and in our event software are presented. Last but not least, our newsletter will keep you posted about all the latest happenings in the event world.

Reference works and further reading

- Bel, E.J. (2004). *Event-driven marketing.* Kluwer.
- Blok, P. (2010). *Routekaart: Social Media.* Keynote at HSMAI Congress 'Love @ First Site'.
- Godin, S. (2009). *All Marketers are Liars.* Portfolio.
- Godin, S. (2002). *Purple Cow: Transform Your Business by Being Remarkable.* Portfolio.
- Godin, S. (2008). *Tribes: We Need You to Lead Us.* Portfolio.
- Goldratt M, The Goal: *A Process of Ongoing Improvement.* North River Press.
- Highmore Sims, N. (2007). *Workshops. De complete handleiding voor geweldige workshops.* Pearson Education.
- Holiday R. (2014). *Growth Hacker Marketing: A Primer on the Future of PR, Marketing, and Advertising.* Portfolio.
- Janssen, R. & Hamso, E. (2012). *ROI van je Evenement.* Evoluon.
- Judy, A. (2009). *Event Planning: The Ultimate Guide to Successful Meetings, Corporate Events, Fundraising Galas, Conferences, Conventions, Incentives and Other Special Events.* Wiley.
- Kaarsgaren, L. (2003). *Zakelijke evenementen.* Pearson Education Benelux.
- Knapp J. & Zeratsky J. & Kowitz B. (2016). *Sprint: How to Solve Big Problems and Test New Ideas in Just Five Days.* Simon & Schuster.
- Kotler, P. (2004). *Marketingmanagement. De essentie.* Pearson Education.
- Kotler, P. (2006). *Principles of Marketing.* Pearson Education.
- Kuipers, G. (2008). *Basisboek eventmanagement. Van concept naar realisatie.* Coutinho.
- Meerman Scott, D. (2007). *The new rules of marketing & PR.* Wiley.
- Medina, J. (2014) *Brain rules.* Pear Press.
- Newbery, P. & Farnham, K. (2013) *Experience Design: A Framework for Integrating Brand, Experience, and Value.* Wiley.

- Penseel, H. (2006). *Basisboek Entertainmentmarketing. Muziek, film, games, media, sport en evenementen.* Coutinho.
- Rijn. M. van & Damme D. van (2011). *Evenementenlogistiek. De realisatie van evenementconcepten in veilige en servicegerichte omgevingen.* Rijn-Dam.
- Rippen, J. & Bos, M. (2008). *Events & Beleven. Het 5 Wheel Drive-concept.* Boom.
- Schaap, S.D., Rosenthal, U. & Duin M.J. van (2009). *Veilige evenementen.* Boom Juridische uitgevers.
- Sinek, S. (2009). *Start With Why.* Penguin Books.
- Sutherland J. (2015). *Scrum: The Art of Doing Twice the Work in Half the Time.* Random House Business Books.
- Verhaar, J. (2009). *Projectmanagement. Een professionele aanpak van evenementen.* Boom Onderwijs.
- Verheyden, T. & Rumes, T. & Fluit, A. (2014). *How to story.* LannooCampus.

Naturally, as a dedicated reader of trade journals and other related reading matter, in the course of the years I have drawn inspiration from a wide range of publications, blogs and other sources of information in the events industry.

Acknowledgements

The creation and development of *eventplanner* would not have been possible without the generous help and assistance of a number of professional colleagues in the events sector and lecturers in event management. I would like to offer my explicit thanks to all those who made a contribution to all editions of my books, of whatever kind. Brainstorming sessions until the early hours of the morning, tight deadlines, top quality discussions: these were the ingredients without which this book would never have reached the printing presses.

First and foremost, I would like to introduce the people who were kind enough to proofread my drafts. Notwithstanding their own busy schedules, these leading names in the events sector all made time to read the manuscript in full or in part, before offering useful and constructive comments of their own or providing input about their specific area of event expertise. Many of the practical tips in the book are the result of their huge experience in event organisation and management:

- **Alain D'Haese** (G4S Event Solutions)
- **Baja Hoedt** (speaQable)
- **Barry van der Wall** (Van der Maarel Sfeermeesters)
- **Bart Derolez** (KATHO)
- **Bart Pieters** (Antwerps Sportpaleis)
- **Bram Don** (Omnido Evenementenverzekeringen)
- **Cees Van der Maarel** (Van der Maarel Sfeermeesters)
- **Erik Peekel** (Aaaaha! the Actor Factory)
- **Frank Simkens** (to:communication)
- **Frédéric Lycops** (Vander Haeghen & C°)
- **Gerdie Schreuder** (Live Online Events)
- **Gerrit Heijkoop** (HCIBS)
- **Gjilke Keuning** (Master in Event Management)
- **Greet Jansen** (to:communication)
- **Harry de Winter** (Master in Event Management)
- **Herman van den Dungen** (Wi-Fi 4 Rent)
- **Jan-Jaap In der Mauer** (dagvoorzitter.nl)
- **Jo Haegeman** (White Rabbit)

- **Lies Rombouts** (Gigant Stage Builders)
- **Liza Bergman** (Meetingpartners)
- **Ludo Ost** (Veldeman)
- **Martijn van Rijn** (MB Advies & NHTV)
- **Michael van Bree** (Hulskamp)
- **Michel Van Camp** (New Balls Please)
- **Nathalie van Vianen** (tvcn)
- **Remco Teunissen** (RTN Showsupport)
- **Rob Captijn** (Beng!)
- **Ruud Janssen** (MPI & TNOC)
- **Sofie Verhalle** (Talking Heads)
- **Vicky Waldukat** (Novid)
- **Wouter Schamphelaere** (Van der Maarel Sfeermeesters)
- **Wouter Van Beirendonck** (Novid)

It goes without saying that the **editorial team** of **eventplanner.net** cannot be omitted from this list. I would also like to thank **Jan Verhaar** (Mens & Organisatie) for his contribution to the section on project management and **Frederik Imbo** (imboorling.be) for his useful tips on presentation. **Hilde Vanmechelen**, **Niels Janssen, Mitchell Pontzeele** and the entire LannooCampus team deserve a round of applause: without their expertise and friendly advice, this book would never have been possible. Similarly, I would like to thank **Peer De Maeyer** & **Wendy De Haes** for the excellent layout and design of *eventplanner* and **Jan Tils** & **Katrien Brys** for the final editorial revision of the text.

This list of acknowledgements would not be complete without mention of the following people: **Davy Van Bavel** (trabalabra), **Ramon van Dongen** (Van Dongen Events), **Robby Vandenhouwe** (Krasjelrock), **Karen Broeckaert** (Stella Maris Merksem), **Saskia Bodelier** (Verrassend Tilburg), **Kim van der Beek** (Kim regelt dat wel), **Stéphan de Lange** and many, many others, including my studio guests on eventplanner.tv, all of whom inspired me or helped to make this book what it has become.

Last but by no means least, my special thanks go to my husband **Matthieu Allaert** for his endless patience and understanding. Writing a book requires a great deal of time and effort, which takes up numerous evenings and weekends. Without the right person at your side, this would not be possible. Thank you, Matthieu.